Great Commission,
Great Confusion, or
Great Confession?

Great **Commission,**
Great **Confusion,**
OR Great **Confession?**

The Mission of the
Holy Christian Church

LUCAS V. WOODFORD

WIPF & STOCK · Eugene, Oregon

GREAT COMMISSION, GREAT CONFUSION, OR GREAT CONFESSION?
The Mission of the Holy Christian Church

Wipf & Stock
An Imprint of Wipf and Stock Publishers
199 W. 8th Ave., Suite 3
Eugene, OR 97401

www.wipfandstock.com

ISBN 13: 9978-1-61097-877-4

Manufactured in the U.S.A.

To my mom and dad, who so faithfully carried out their vocation as Christian parents; for my darling bride, who is noble and true as a Christian wife and mother; and to my four precious children, who let me rejoice in my vocation of a Christian father: you are all beloved.

Christmas 2011

"For I am not ashamed of the gospel, for it is the power of God for salvation to everyone who believes." (Rom 1:16)

Contents

Foreword

THE EARLY DECADES OF the 21st Century find the Christian Church in a familiar stance: puzzled. The church, it would seem, is forever at a crossroads. The nature of that crossroads varies with each generation, of course, depending on prevailing winds of doctrine. Careful students of church history note that those winds frequently resemble the cultural headwinds; that is, the church is forever tempted to adjust her course to suit the trends of the time.

Lucas Woodford's book brings desperately needed clarity to the contemporary church. He argues that clearer confession leads to clearer mission. It's an emphasis long overdue. In recent decades much ink has been spilled and countless cyber bytes of information have been generated charting a direction for mission, yet confusion abounds everywhere.

From ancient times the church has been pictured as a ship sailing the seas of time en route to eternity. To be sure, there are crosswinds and rough seas to contend with in every era, but few generations have faced the situation we find ourselves in at present: a perfect storm of radical cultural shift and doctrinal indifference. Eagerly tossing overboard what they regard as ballast, captain and crew find themselves increasingly powerless against encroaching secularization all around. It is the theological equivalent of the ethical absurdity described by C.S. Lewis in his *Abolition of Man* nearly seventy years ago:

> In a sort of ghastly simplicity we remove the organ and demand the function. We make men without chests and expect of them virtue and enterprise. We laugh at honour and are shocked to find traitors in our midst. We castrate and bid the geldings be fruitful.

Desperation breeds innovation. When it dawns on churches that they are losing headway in terms of numerical growth, panic ensues. "We've got to do something," they cry. "...here's something; let's do it!" In the name of contextualizing the gospel, it would appear, almost anything goes. Methods from the entertainment and sales industries have been widely adapted, adopted, and imported but to little or no avail. Statistically the church—especially in North America—seems to be in decline.

This trend was anticipated already in 1949 by Chad Walsh in his remarkable book, *Early Christians of the 21st Century*.

> The decline in the total impact of Christianity began at least as early as the eighteenth century. From the deism of the eighteenth century to the agnosticism of the nineteenth century to the confusion and demonic totalitarianism of the twentieth century—one strand in all these developments is the decline of Christianity: its abandonment by most intellectuals and its progressive dilution almost everywhere. Our civilization is far more secular than Christian. And the Christian commentator would add that it bids fair to be short-lived: its dissolution is proceeding swiftly and violently.

Walsh contended that the key to the church's vitality for the looming post Christian era would be the same as in the pre Christian era: doctrinal clarity coupled with corresponding faithful practice.

Woodford's contention is the same. He provides a bird's eye view of contemporary cultural and theological trends. Better than that, he charts a course through the rough seas we face. He writes cogently, compellingly, and personally. He helps modernists come to grips with the postmodern (or post postmodern) world view. He helps evangelists grasp the importance of theological integrity, and he helps theologians see theology's beating heart: the justification of the ungodly in the cross of Jesus Christ, the living Son of God. He explores the essence of the church's liturgy and its impact on contemporary culture. He unpacks the Reformation insight on Christian vocation as it pertains to mission for both clergy and laity ("ministry" and "priesthood" in Lutheran parlance). He sheds light on the "missional" trends of our time and the complexity of the "emergent/emerging" church. He offers a faithful and profound analysis of Christ's mission imperative found in Matthew 28 and explores its use and abuse in recent centuries.

I hope you will be as enthralled as I am with this young pastor's work. His book is chock full of references of interest to the scholar, to be sure. But it's far more than that. You'll find both humor and pathos in these pages. Delightfully candid and theologically substantive, this book is above all pastoral in both essence and impact. You may not always agree, but that's not the goal. Rather, in his book Lucas Woodford seeks to stimulate constructive dialog regarding the church's life and mission for our time. He offers a corrective lens so we can see our way through contemporary cultural and theological confusion to engage an increasingly pagan world with insight, compassion and substance. With clearer vision comes more faithful mission.

Throughout these pages you'll find a plea not to abandon ship or change course. Above all else, you will find encouragement and hope grounded in the chart and compass of the One who promised: "Behold, I am with you always: to the end of the age."

Harold L. Senkbeil, MDiv, STM, DD
St. Timothy, Pastor and Confessor
24 January 2012

Prologue

I BEGAN MINISTRY AS an associate pastor serving a large congregation of 3,300 people. Completing a couple of master's degrees from one of our church's seminaries, it was finally time to get into the parish and serve the Lord's people.

Call day came, the day when pastoral candidates receive their first assignments. My heart was pounding; my wife's was racing. My name was announced. My placement followed: First Immanuel Lutheran Church, Cedarburg, Wisconsin. For the next two-and-a-half years, I would be immersed in the land of "Cheeseheads."

Being a Minnesota boy for the majority of my life, the place where the Vikings and Packers are archenemies, I knew there would be some attempts at proselytizing. Interestingly, one of my Christmas Eve sermons had to compete with the NFL as they had scheduled a game on this day. Of course, it was the Vikings and Packers. The Vikings lost. My hope of making any Vikings converts ended on that day.

Aside from the expected ribbing, ample Cheesehead gifts, and smiling words of consolation, the people were wonderful. My wife and I have many fond memories of our time there. It was a great first call. It was also a great time of learning and ministry experience for me as a pastor.

I was one of three full-time pastors. A handful of part-time retired guys were also thrown in the mix. Having 3,300 souls to care for was no small task, not to mention the congregation's desire to reach out to the lost. The congregation also had a parochial grade school of over 250 students. Thus, besides our regular preaching, pastoral care, shut-ins, hospital visits, marrying and burying, and the crammed-in evangelism visit, there were daily catechesis classes to teach.

The congregation had a new, large sanctuary. However, it had grown so much that there were five worship services a weekend. A large, active, and growing congregation seemed like the place to be. It was a fast-paced, stream-lined, and action-packed ministry.

But then, what ministry isn't the place to be? Regardless of the size of a congregation, people hurt, lives are broken, and humans sin. Big church or small church, the Sacraments need to be administered and the Good News of Jesus Christ needs to be proclaimed. Pastors have no small task, regardless of the size of congregation they serve. Ministry, wherever it is occurring, is the place to be. Large or little, growing or declining, the mission of the Holy Christian Church remains the same, right?

Unfortunately, not everyone sees it this way. The North American congregations of our time are facing a significant challenge. The challenge is to fully understand the mission of the Holy Christian Church.

There are no small amount of voices clamoring for the attention of congregations and what they are supposed to be doing. Right now, the Great Commission is often lifted up as an imperative and is used to determine whether or not your congregation is doing what Jesus commanded. This is not to mention the new words being employed. "Is your congregation a *missional* congregation?" "Does your congregation have *missional* leaders?" Thus, organizational and structural paradigms are being created to re-orient local congregations with the thought, "If you're inward-focused, you're not mission-focused, so let's get you missional-minded."

Others find this missional emphasis a curious oddity. For some, it is even a distraction from the greater mission of the Holy Christian Church—to preach the Word of God and administer his Sacraments—which, they assert, has always had the desire for the growth of God's kingdom.

Coupled with this is the continuation of the long-standing worship wars. Traditionalists look to the history of the Holy Christian Church as rationale to maintain its historic practices while contemporary enthusiasts assert that "doing" church a new way is necessary to reach the masses.

Subsequently, there is no small amount of confusion present in the North American church and her pastors today. The purpose of this book is to honestly and respectfully examine the historic mission of the Holy

Christian Church and provide some urgent and definitive perspectives for our time.

Perhaps you have your own understanding of the mission of the Holy Christian Church: what it is, what it is supposed to look like, and what it is supposed to do. I had studied it in a great deal of theory during my time at the seminary. However, when I began ministry, I was finally able to experience it firsthand. What did I find? The classroom did not have nearly as many complexities as the real thing. Nonetheless, I was determined to sweat it out and let the Lord make a pastor of me. What happened? Well, let's just say that I am still a work in progress.

But what I can tell you is that large or small, each congregation has its own challenges consistent with its own local setting. From balancing budgets to battling over governance styles, my first congregation gave me a lesson about the organizational trials congregations go through. From the unfortunate to the affluent, my first congregation taught me about the diversity and the divisions within a congregation. And from our large roster to our lack of an equally large, active discipleship, my first congregation taught me that big churches do not always mean deep discipleship.

But as I understood it, none of the above would change the mission of the Holy Christian Church. True, each local congregation has the flexibility to address the nuances and idiosyncrasies found in each local context. Nonetheless, big or small, declining or growing, the mission of the Holy Christian Church remains the same, right?

It was not until I began serving my second congregation that this understanding began to solidify and become especially clear, for it would be the circumstances and challenges of my second congregation that would bring about an epiphany regarding the historic mission of the Holy Christian Church.

First, to be clear, I was not looking to leave. My wife and I were very happy at First Immanuel. When we first arrived, the people filled our pantry. When our first child was born (Isabella), they lavished us with gifts. When we bought our first home, twenty people showed up and moved us from our rental home into our new home in a matter of three hours. When my brother and his unborn son were killed in a car accident, people cried with us, brought us food, and booked us airline tickets to fly home.

Nonetheless, there were the call documents sitting on my office desk. Zion Lutheran Church of Mayer, Minnesota, had called me to be their senior pastor. Like I said, I was not looking for a call. But the recent tragedies of life (my wife's second miscarriage and my brother's death) had me thinking in a new perspective. Experiencing tragedies has a way of making one long to be around family. Taking this call would put us much closer to family.

Yet that alone could not be the reason why I would take the call. In fact, I began looking for anything that could be used to decline the call. I liked where we were. We had just bought a new home. (I could hunt deer in my back yard!) We had made some very dear friends. I was growing as a pastor. Ministry was rewarding. And I was starting to like the Packers.

But a visit to the calling congregation proved to have the opposite effect I desired. The congregation was located in a small, historic, farm-based but now rapidly growing town, just 40 miles west of the Twin Cities and 20 miles from the suburbs. Three new housing developments were exploding and expanding the city limits. It had become a bedroom community to the Twin Cities.

The congregation was just over 800 souls. The church building was a historic, country-framed church over 100 years old with a small addition (narthex) made in the 1980s. They had a parochial grade school in an adjacent building. The congregation was growing, and according to the congregation's strategic plan, they were set to "build a new Christian Outreach facility that is technology oriented for Worship and Education, to meet needs of current and future generations."

I would be lying if I said that my ego and self-inflated aptitude did not come into play. (My wife usually carries a pin with her to keep my head from swelling too much.) I was only twenty-nine, and they wanted me to be their senior pastor. The congregation was budding. They were going to build! What aspiring and determined pastor would not want to lead them through this process?

They had rural farmers and suburbanites coming together. I had lived both. Growing up on a South Dakota dairy farm until I was seven and then living in large cities for the last eleven years, I knew I could relate to both. I had the degrees. I had the excitement. I had the experience (at least, I thought I did). I took the call.

The Lord has a way of humbling those who think too much of themselves. The next few years proved to be some of the very darkest times of my life. Very few know of the tremendous struggles and the utter despair I experienced during my first two years there. During my initial visit to the congregation, their best foot was put forward. When I arrived, it was a different story.

Congregational divisions over what land to purchase, a church and school split, intense staff and personnel strife, member suspicion, and organizational paranoia were vomited on to my lap. My intestinal fortitude was put to the test, quite literally. So intense was the unrest, so heavy were the pressures, so sharp were the struggles, so obvious was my inexperience, so many were my missteps, my internal and intestinal functions literally stopped working properly.

Ministry can be a very lonely place. Ministry can be a tremendous burden, especially when you try to bear it on your own. Those days were very dark.

Yet as I reflect on it, the Lord needed to have his way with me. Arrogance needed to be refined into confidence—confidence that was in the Lord of the church and his Word rather than on my fleshly ambition. As the apostle Peter reminds, "All flesh is like grass and all its glory like the flower of grass. The grass withers, and the flower falls, but the word of the Lord remains forever. ' And this word is the good news that was preached to you" (1 Peter 1:24–25).

Thus, it was to the preached and proclaimed Word that I turned. And it would be the preached Word that would lead the way, not only toward my own sanity and spiritual wholeness, but toward greater congregational unity and, ultimately, toward a greater understanding regarding the mission of the Holy Christian Church.

Amid all the challenges of the congregation, there was tremendous opportunity for refining. Through a combination of evaluation, some strategic planning trial and error, and finally the help of the church's historic confession of faith—the Apostles' Creed—the mission for our congregation began to come clear. And what I found was that it looked rather similar to what the mission of the church has been throughout the ages.

In short, this book endeavors to clarify the mission of the Holy Christian Church for our time. It will examine the recent trends present in the North American church through the lens of the historic confession of the church—the Apostles' Creed, especially its third article—in an effort to give focus and renewal to what has been historically the mission of the Holy Christian Church.

This book is admittedly shaped by its author's church affiliation. That's what I know, firmly believe, and regularly practice, though I am certainly familiar with other perspectives. This project is set forth in contrast to those perspectives with the hope of serving the greater church. There's a debate underway in the North American church today. My aim is to invite one and all to fraternal, collegial conversation. We need more light and less heat. My prayer is that the uniquely Lutheran perspectives I outline below will serve to promote theological honesty and integrity about the historic mission of the Holy Christian Church in our time.

Acknowledgments

WRITING A BOOK TAKES time and energy. I would like to give a special thanks to my congregation, Zion Lutheran Church and School, who first afforded me the time and opportunity to pursue these studies. I also want to thank the Rev. Dr. Harold Senkbeil for his constant encouragement and feedback. And finally, but most importantly, I couldn't have done it without the constant care, companionship, and support of my bride, Becca. Her encouragement has been invaluable and her love a blessing. She is precious to me.

Introduction

Missional Mandate or Missional Misunderstand?

"ARE YOU A MISSIONAL church?" "Are you a confessional church?" "Do you care about the lost?" "Do you care about doctrine?" So goes the questions for those in the churches of North America. This is especially so for pastors. The political climate within many North American churches has the tendency to create allegiances: *us* and *them*. "Which side are you on?" "Who do you support?" Or even more fun, "We have the Lord on our side. How about you?" As if somehow the Lord can be bent to any such allegiance!

Last time I checked, it was the Lord who gets to be the boss, and the way He went about being boss was by suffering upon the cross to die for our sins. Those who would come after Him are called to pick up their cross and follow Him—pastors, parishioners, and pagans alike.

However, it seems that the trouble comes among those in the Holy Christian Church when we begin defining what the church is, what it looks like, and how it should be done. Some say it is done through missions. Others say through faithful ministry. Some say through purity of doctrine, others through impassioned outreach. Must they be pitted against one another? Must they be done to the exclusion of the other? Doesn't all ministry, all mission, all doctrine, and all outreach happen within the Holy Christian Church—a church that is made up of real confessing and believing people, living real lives in the midst of a real culture, filled with real sins, real pain, and real joy? In my own church body, this uneasy tension has been present for decades.[1]

As a pastor and circuit counselor, it has been readily apparent to me that this tension remains.[2] But perhaps, in some ways, this is a good thing. The recognition of each extreme may help to maintain a healthy balance for those in the middle majority. It may also continue to provide needed dialogue regarding the orthodoxy (doctrine) and orthopraxy (practice) of twenty-first-century, North American congregations, pastors, and missionaries as they seek to be faithful to the mission of the Holy Christian Church.

However, the unfortunate practice has not always been to dialogue, but (at least in my own experience) to jostle for the power to control the dialogue and the perception of the church's mission. A return to collegial and honest theological dialogue would be beneficial to all involved.[3] However, I realize that not every question can be settled by means of a friendly discussion. I do not hold to the superstitious belief that dialogue is the infallible means to settling everything. I hold to the truth of God's Word, and his Word calls us to speak the truth in love and not arrogance (Eph 4:15). That is my aim here.

Yet it's not that dialogues aren't occurring. Indeed, they are happening. But as of late, it seems there is a tendency for theological honesty and respectful candor to be replaced by vitriolic cyber-disputations and uninformed electronic disdain. From heated and insulting blog posts to uncharitable and inflammatory emails, much of the church has lost the ability to have honest, collegial dialogue.

This ongoing tension has spurred on an interesting exhibition of wills in the churches across North America. It has been particularly

---

1. I am a member of The Lutheran Church—Missouri Synod (LCMS). Already in 1973, Dr. August Sueflow offered an essay prepared for the one hundred and twenty-fifth anniversary of the founding of The Lutheran Church—Missouri Synod entitled, "Recounting the Mercies," where he notes that there has been in our Synod's history a tension between what he called "twin focal points"—*preserve* the Gospel and *proclaim* the Gospel. Consequently, he observed that we have, at times, emphasized one over the other in the understanding of our purpose and mission. Noted in an article by Erwin J. Kolb, "The Primary Mission of the Church and Its Detractors," 127.

2. Our congregations are locally divided into clusters called circuits, where the circuit counselor convenes monthly meetings between the brother clergy.

3. In my own church affiliation, this would mean a return to mutually respectful and candid dialogue about genuine evangelical Lutheran theology, both its history and practice.

noticeable among my own church body. Some have claimed that "The Missouri Synod does not have a clear statement of its mission."[4] Yet others would contend this to be a curious claim. For within our guiding and conceivably binding, confessional documents (*The Book of Concord*), it states that, "The Church is the assembly of saints in which the Gospel is taught purely and the sacraments are administered rightly."[5] Even so, scores of convention resolutions—also supposedly guiding and conceivably binding (How *does* one tell?)—have been passed somehow to offer greater clarity to the purpose to the church.

Consider Resolution 1-02 of the 2001 LCMS convention, which required that the following final *resolve* be added to every resolution that remained for consideration: "*Resolved*, That all action taken in this resolution shall be used to carry out 'The Great Commission' and shall not in any way detract or distract from the primary mission of God's kingdom here on earth."[6] Such a guiding principle is not limited to my church body.

Perceivably, the so-called Great Commission (Matt 28:18–20) has now been thrust to the forefront of the church's identity as a sort of driving slogan to capture the hearts and minds of parishioners, pastors, missionaries, and seminary professors as the key factor that defines the church. It has the intent to give to the church one sole, clarifying purpose: to seek and save the lost. It is also what served as an emphasis to my second congregation's 2002 strategic plan "to build a new Christian Outreach facility that is technology oriented for Worship and Education, to meet needs of current and future generations," where written into the document was the statement: "We will follow Christ's command to obey the Great Commission."

It is also, I assume, what led one seminary professor to pen the following provocative words:

> Any theology which is not imbued with God's own passion to seek and save lost people is not pure theology without a missional attitude—it's just impure theology. Our theological work needs

4. Erwin J. Kolb, "The Primary Mission of the Church and Its Detractors," 126.

5 Kolb & Wengert, AC VII, § 1. In the "Concordia Tracts," *An Introduction to the Lutheran Church—Missouri Synod* also clearly states: "The primary mission of the Church, we believe, is the preaching of the Gospel and the administration of the sacraments," 13.

6. The Lutheran Church—Missouri Synod, *2001 Convention proceedings*, 5.

to be connected in visible, vital ways to the urgent task of making sure that every man, woman, and child know what God has done for them in Christ. If it isn't, then we are engaged (unwittingly, I assume) in nothing less than false doctrine, no matter how carefully we guard our formulae and arrange the loci and explore the ramifications. Mission is what theology is *for*. Theology pursued for some ultimate purpose other than God's mission of seeking and saving the lost is simply unfaithful theology.[7]

As a pastor who gives care to souls, this comes as no small assertion with no small potential implications. Pastoral ministry—the place where doctrine meets practice—is ministry done in a local congregation and community among real people with real problems, real dysfunctions, and real sins. It is, at best, an ordained burden and sanctified mess. At worst, it reduces pastors to "a quivering mass of availability,"[8] where they are simply trying to keep their head above water, let alone make every move of their ministry a missional move.

Nonetheless, the threat of being an unfaithful or impure practitioner of theology must be taken seriously. But to bear the burden of everything theological being absolutely missional and, therefore, every practice of theology necessarily missional is enough to crush a man, not to mention a congregation.

It is a particularly heavy assertion considering that the word *missional* is relatively new to the theological canvas. Alan J. Roxburgh and M. Scott Boren note that, "The word *missional* was introduced in 1998 because the definitions of *mission* and *church* [noted in their book] . . . are misleading and wrong. Adding the *al* to the end of *mission*, however, creates a new meaning we don't immediately see or understand. The word invites us to stop, check our assumptions, and ask if there might be a different way of being the church."[9] As such, the term *missional* lends

---

7. Schumacher, "Theology or Mission?," 117.

8. William H. Willimon in his book *Pastor: The Theology and Practice of Ordained Ministry* cited his collogue Stanley Hauerwas: "My colleague Stanley Hauerwas has accused the contemporary pastor of being little more than 'a quivering mass of availability.' Practicing what I have called 'promiscuous ministry'—ministry with no internal, critical judgment about what care is worth giving—we have become the victims of a culture of insatiable need. We live in a capitalist, consumptive culture where there is no purpose to our society other than 'meeting our needs,'" 60.

9. Roxburgh & Boren, *Introducing the Missional Church*, 30.

itself to identifying the latest Protestant trend as opposed to being a part of the historic orthodoxy and orthopraxy of the church.

However, I am not alone with my concern regarding the word. In their book *What is the Mission of the Church?*, Reformed pastor Kevin DeYoung and Baptist pastor Greg Gilbert express their concern for the word and what it means. They affirm the desire of those who simply want to be "on mission," but, "Nevertheless," they say, "it is not wrong to probe the word *missional*. It's a big trunk that can smuggle a great deal of baggage. Being suspicious of every use of the word is bad, raising concerns about how the word is sometimes used is simply wise."[10]

There are others as well. Taking a scholarly approach, Carl Raschke examines the word as it appears in the postmodern context and invites caution and reflection on what it truly means.

> One of the current buzzwords in what might be loosely char-
> acterized as the buzz marketing of the new and improved
> postmodern church is the adjective *missional*. These days every
> Christian community that wants in some legitimate sense to be
> au courant is beginning to define itself with this very adjective.
> The expression clearly is a direct adaption of the traditional and
> quite familiar ecclesiological word, "mission," from which we
> derive "missionary." The tacit implication in the present popular-
> ity of the term is that churches must be much more than simply
> self-standing and self-serving organizations attentive mainly to
> the needs and desires of their attendees. They must incessantly
> reach out to those who are beyond the fringes of established
> Christianity, and they must do so in a way that is integral rather
> than incidental to their mission and purpose. After all, is that
> not what the Great Commission ultimately comes down to? It
> is not more than a little ironic, however, that churches in the
> postmodern—or post-Christendom-world should have to mold
> themselves as "missional" at all? In its historic sweep Christianity
> has always been missional. The command to make disciples, rou-
> tinely confused by evangelical circles with planting churches, is
> seamlessly stitched with the command to love ones neighbor as
> oneself. Discipling shows what God's love in the person of Jesus,
> who is the Christ, is really all about. That is the true *missio Dei*.[11]

At a minimum, it gives cause to reflect on the missional reconsti-
tution of our theological language. Yet, to be fair, the above seminary

10. DeYoung & Gilbert, *What Is the Mission of the Church?*, 21.
11. Raschke, *GloboChrist*, 62.

professor does attempt to clarify by concluding, "It's not so much a question of finding and maintaining a balance between 'mission' and 'theology' as if these were two distinct elements which are both necessary. Rather, I think we need to realize that any theology-minus-mission is simply false theology, and any evangelism-minus-theology is no evangel at all."[12]

Still, that leaves us a host of questions. If the missional premise is to be true, what does that say about the theology and practice of worship, not to mention the theology and practice of preaching? What does it mean for the theology and practice of pastoral ministry, including parish pastors and chaplains—military, hospital, and nursing home? What does it say about the way congregations organize and govern themselves? Is a congregation that struggles to be outward-focused—whatever that means—disqualified from being faithful to the Lord?

Even more, what does it mean for the doctrine of vocation? Specifically, does a doctrine that expounds the hiddenness of God in ordinary tasks for the service of our neighbors—even lifting it up in utter celebration of God at work, independent of Gospel proclamation—now become invalid, unfaithful, and impure?

What does it do to considerations of orthodoxy and orthopraxy? Would new definitions need to be put into place? I believe a dialogue is in order. We need to have an honest and respectful conversation about this and what it means for the church today.

To be sure, seeking and saving the lost is what Christ came to do, did do, and continues to do through his church. But what this looks like and how it is done by His church today is really the question before us. I think it is a great oversimplification simply to identify the mission of the church as seeking and saving the lost. It is a true statement, but it lacks clarity and specificity, not only of the lost—their peculiarities and irregularities—but also regarding the means by which the church has been given to seek and save the lost. True, the Great Commission does offer clarity and specificity, but the question remains whether or not those so-called Great Commission verses (Matt 28:18–20) were originally meant to be pulled from their context and be given a life of their own.

Such a mission or purpose statement, wonderful as it is, would, at least in some theological respects, need to be squared with the historic understanding and use of it as a norming missional text within the Holy

12. Schumacher, "Theology or Mission?," 117–18.

Christian Church. But please understand that this is not meant to demean seeking and saving the lost. To be sure, the Lord's desire is that all people be saved and come to the knowledge of truth (1 Tim 2:4), and thus so is ours. My desire is that we simply maintain our theological integrity while we are reaching out to the lost.

If we are being honest, the recent missional trend among North American congregations and denominations has created, perhaps unintentionally, a serious threat to the theological integrity of the church and her practice of mission. In the desire to seek and save the lost, at times by all means necessary, some of those means have come to reconstitute the core of the church's theology.

But who am I to be making such a diagnosis? I'm not an academic teacher of theology, and I hold no position of notoriety. However, I am a pastor, and pastors are the ones who most frequently put theology into practice. We preach, we teach, we baptize, we commune, we admonish, we forgive, we evangelize, we marry, we bless, and we bury, amid all the fullness of life. We carry forward from one generation to the next the teachings of the Holy Christian Church. Thus, I think there is a legitimate opportunity for me to add to the dialogue.

Accordingly, where past ages of the church's history have demonstrated a precision for the marks of the Holy Christian Church—the most prominent being the bold and clear proclamation of the Gospel (along with the administration of the Sacraments, their number depending on your tradition)—the recent missional push has seemingly reconstituted the marks of the church to be that of obeying the Great Commission and that of making missional congregations, whatever that means.

Yet some may ask, "What's wrong with those behaviors as marks of the church? After all, don't we want the lost to be saved? Don't we want congregations to focus on seeking and saving the lost?" Absolutely! But for the moment, consider the proposition honestly and with all theological integrity. If the church is to be serious about her theology, such missional mandates reveal the very real danger of taking the free gift of the Gospel given in, by, and through Jesus Christ—His life, death, and resurrection—and potentially turning it into a law that must be obeyed. Should that be the case, it would be no small irony to note that Protestants, and especially evangelical Lutherans, both have namesakes that were forged out of a Reformation that protested against making the Gospel of Christ into a law to be obeyed.

Some might say I am simply misunderstanding the intent of what missional means. However, when missional-minded authors and church leaders have to regularly take to defending or redefining what it means—missional guru Alan Hirsch wrote an entire article defending and clarifying the word[13]—perhaps there remains a significant amount of uncertainty. And when coupled with the vast source material in the chapters ahead, it appears that confusion remains.

Consequently, I think it is time for honest, bold renewal and re-examination of the historic doctrine and practice of the church in light of the cultural changes and worldviews pressing upon the people of North America, all for the sake of the Gospel.

Such a re-examination invites a new lens for viewing and dialoging. But by this I do not mean to introduce some newly-discovered biblical insights never before considered, claiming that they will revolutionize the mission field. Rather, like the optometrist who provides bifocals to those entering a different age so that they can see old things anew, I intend to offer some historic bifocals with which to view our different postmodern age (and whatever is coming after it), so that we can see some old truths anew. The goal is to provide a common unifying framework in which to see the doctrine and practice of the Holy Christian Church, and to do so recognizing the very real mission and very real ministry that occurs among the very real people of North America (and the world), all of whom God "desires to be saved" (1 Tim 2:4).

These bifocals are set within the lens of the Apostles' Creed, where the third article of the Creed—"I believe in the Holy Spirit, The Holy Christian Church, the Communion of Saints, the forgiveness of sins, the resurrection of the body, and the life everlasting"—and its accompanying explanation set out in Martin Luther's *Small Catechism* serve as the actual bifocals. Since it is the Holy Christian Church with which we are dealing, the third article of this creed provides a natural lens in which to view the doctrine (orthodoxy) and life (orthopraxy) of the North American church.

Luther's explanation has a compact but deeply-insightful manner of describing what the Holy Christian Church is and what it does. Looking at the depth of the Holy Christian Church through the third

---

13 "Defining Missional: The word is everywhere, but where did it come from and what does it really mean?" December 12, 2008, www.christianitytoday.com/le/communitylife/evangelism/17.20.html?gclid=CMqdyNHrn6gCFUF95odgUltQw.

article of the Creed will radically celebrate the centrality of the Gospel in the life of the church. It will also increase the visibility and importance of the Christian's vocational life in the world as a natural and integral part to the mission of the church.

The doctrine of vocation is a profound component in evangelical Lutheran theology that, though sorely undertreated and rarely taught, is garnering some increased attention by a few authors.[14] If it would be regularly lifted up and celebrated by pastors and parishioners alike, it would, I contend, provide a further unifying understanding to the life of the church. The third article lens will help clarify and celebrate this profound possibility.

And just as bifocals help to correct a person's vision, these third article bifocals can also help correct the vision of the church. Where her vision has become blurred by competing claims that confuse the church or where her vision has been impaired by foreign movements sweeping through the church, it brings corrective clarity and faithful focus.

Therefore, chapter 1 will set out the creedal premise for this endeavor. It will examine the history of creeds in the church and their use today. Attention will be given to how the third article of the Apostles' Creed can bring clarity to the mission of the church and provide impetus for ongoing honest theological dialogue. Specific focus will also be put on the proclamation of the Gospel as the mission of the church as seen through both her worship and vocational witness. The first chapter will lay the foundation for all following considerations.

Chapter 2 will explore the comparatively recent trend by the churches in North America to use the Great Commission as the new defining missional motto for the purpose of the church. The text as it appears in the Gospel of Matthew will be examined. The historical use of the text, as well as a respectful but frank discussion on the hermeneutics and legitimacy of using it as a motto for the church today will then be considered. Here we will also engage in a candid but collegial assessment about the missional effectiveness of this motto. This will also provide framework for how the third article can be used as corrective lenses when the vision of the church has become blurred.

---

14. Consider Gene Edward Veith's *God at Work: Your Christian Vocation in All of Life*; Kurt Senske's *The Calling: Living a Life of Significance*; *Lutheran Spirituality: Life as God's Child*, Robert C. Baker, ed., 183–216; and *The Lutheran Difference: An Explanation and Comparison of Christian Beliefs*, Edward Engelbrecht, ed., 472–506.

Chapter 3 will examine the North American cultural landscape as influenced by postmodernism and its beginnings. Brief examinations of those considered to be the original postmodern thinkers will be offered, particularly Jean-François Lyotard, and how their thought has influenced the everyday North American culture. Using the third article as a lens to look through and examine postmodernism will demonstrate the significant opportunities for the church to engage postmodern people while remaining distinctly theologically grounded.

Chapters 4 and 5 will take an honest look at the contemporary church growth and emergent/emerging church movements in the North American church. They will explore how these movements are the respective results of modernity and postmodernity and offer some collegial but candid assessments. The aim will also be to demonstrate how using the third article as corrective lenses for the church can help stave off the unhealthy tendencies inherent in these movements.

Finally, chapters 6 and 7, the conclusion, and epilogue will provide an overview of the church by looking intently through the lens of the third article and the bifocals of Luther's explanation. These lenses will provide precision for the church's mission of Gospel proclamation and clarify the current confusion over the distinctive role of pastors and parishioners. They bring a picture of faithful worship and witness into sharper focus. They hone our vision for natural evangelistic growth through the doctrine of vocation, an approach to outreach that is, I contend, even more provocative and transforming than the current missional mindset of the organizational church.

Set along side of my own pastoral and life struggles, the goal of this book is to provide a point of collegial, honest, theological dialogue about the mission and ministry, the doctrine and practice, of the North American church. The hope is that North American congregations might find greater common ground in understanding the mission of the Holy Christian Church through the depth and the richness of what evangelical Lutheran theology confesses, all for the sake of the Gospel.

Chapter 1

The Great Confession

The Apostles' Creed

A DIFFICULT BEGINNING

WHEN I ARRIVED AT my second congregation, I encountered a number of significant challenges. Perhaps a more seasoned pastor would have handled them better. Nonetheless, the Lord saw to it he was going to make a pastor out of me. To be sure, I know he is not done yet, but my prayer is that I will never have to be refined as intensely as I was during my first two years serving the saints at Zion.

A few years before my arrival, the congregation had put together a strategic plan with the help of, as I was told, a "very expensive" church consultant. (I am not sure how expensive, but I do know German Lutherans are notorious for being extremely frugal.) It had as its bottom line the directive: "Through wise stewardship . . . build a new Christian Outreach facility that is technology oriented for Worship and Education, to meet needs of current and future generations."

Part of my role as senior pastor would be to ensure the congregation was outreach-oriented. That outreach was understood, at least initially, to occur primarily through the construction of the new technology-oriented outreach facility, as well as the proposed accompanying differing worship styles. The thought and verbal expression to me was, "If we build it, they will come."

Upon my arrival, the congregation was all set to buy sixteen acres of land on which to build the new worship facility. I was excited. The congregation was excited. We were all excited, that is, until another piece of land became available. The original sixteen-acre parcel was more centrally located in town but more expensive. However, when a twenty-acre parcel became available a half-mile or so outside of town, at what was thought to be a cheaper price, the congregation became intensely divided. (Did I mention that German Lutherans like to be frugal?)

At my first building committee meeting, I was politely but very directly encouraged to keep my mouth shut about my own opinion of which parcel might be better. I obliged. Thus, I listened as committee members battled it out for a number of hours. Then, a few weeks later, I experienced what would become one of many very heated congregational voters' assemblies. (To this day, I still have a hard time keeping a normal pulse at voters' assemblies.) In the end, the congregation elected to go with the cheaper land, though it was not by unanimous agreement. Unrest lingered. Hurt feelings remained. Challenges were imminent.

LORD, HAVE MERCY

As festering wounds can do, they began to grow. Unresolved strife became painfully apparent. There was a divide between the church and the school that I wasn't aware of when I took the call to serve the good people of Zion. The land issue only intensified this divide. Sides were taken. Parties were formed. Secret meetings took place. The troops were rallied. Paranoia developed.

Then it was budget time. (Oh, the joys of budget meetings!) Having money to buy land but not enough to keep the school operating in the black created hard feelings. Salaries were frozen. Expenditures had to be preapproved. More feelings were hurt. Mistrust only grew. The words of the Kyrie were often on my lips: "Lord, have mercy!"

I was reading every congregational leadership book I could find. I was putting out fires left and right, only to end up creating a few more on my own. I was working seventy hours or more a week and regularly telling my wife that it would get better the next week. (By the way, if you are a young, married pastor reading this, never go back to work on the same day your second child is born . . . or any child for that matter! Your wife will always remember it. I went back to work on the same day our second, Thaddaeus, was born. My thought was, "If I work harder, things will go better." They didn't. Please learn from my mistakes. Your vocations are ordered for your benefit—husband first, father second, and then pastor. Yes, there is always a balancing act to be done. But a wife needs her husband, and children need their father, particularly on those special days.)

In desperation, I encouraged the formation of an internal congregational Priorities Task Force to help study the congregation's situation and give some direction to the congregation. Numerous open forums and listening posts were held. Congregational surveys were administered. Opinions were recorded. In short, the task force identified three primary ministry desires of the congregation: (1) worship and discipleship, (2) outreach, and (3) Christian education (a parochial day school).

However, through the process the task force also discovered that the congregation had a distinct lack of funds to continue with the congregation's strategic plan to build a new outreach and worship facility. They were able to pay for the new land outright. However, there was a severe shortage of available funds to build a new facility, let alone try to build and continue to operate a parochial grade school.

THE GREAT CONFESSION

Amid all of the unrest, I continued to preach and teach. At one of the Bible classes I led, we were studying Matthew. Jesus's exchange with Peter came up, and it began to stick in my mind:

> Jesus said to them, "But who do you say that I am?" Simon Peter replied, "You are the Christ, the Son of the living God." And Jesus answered him, "Blessed are you, Simon Bar-Jonah! For flesh and blood has not revealed this to you, but my Father who is in heaven. And I tell you, you are Peter, and on this rock I will build my church, and the gates of hell shall not prevail against it. (Matt 16:15–18)

It set my mind in motion. The more I thought, the more I prayed, the more Scriptures seemed to come clear. Did we really need a fancy new building to be the church or to witness to others about Jesus? Sure, a new building and new technological toys would be great. After all, new buildings and growing congregations are a fun place to be. I certainly remembered from my first pastorate what it was like to be a part of a church that had all the bells and whistles. And, yes, constructing a new building was what the congregation's strategic plan called for, but bricks and mortar were not what Jesus built his church upon. Peter's confession of faith gave me a clear reminder of this.

In fact, dwelling on Jesus's words to Peter made the words of Peter's first epistle become all the more clear to me:

> As you come to him, the living Stone—rejected by men but chosen by God and precious to him— you also, like living stones, are being built into a spiritual house to be a holy priesthood, offering spiritual sacrifices acceptable to God through Jesus Christ. For in Scripture it says: "See, I lay a stone in Zion, a chosen and precious cornerstone, and the one who trusts in him will never be put to shame." (1 Peter 2:4–6)

It was plain to me. We did not need a new building to carry on the mission of the church. The building of Christ's kingdom came through his Word. Though I was certain of this fact, I was uncertain of what people would think about the implications that this might have for our congregation. Nonetheless, I shared my sentiments with the task force at one of our final meetings. It was received well. I was reminded that God's Word is powerful. It is not void. Yet, to be sure, the current financial condition of the congregation, no doubt, had a hand in it being received as warmly as it was.

Subsequently, the members of the task force and I encouraged the congregation to begin developing a new strategic plan that would focus on building relationships and the kingdom of Christ rather than being focused entirely on a new physical building. For the hard reality was that a new building would invariably create a significant and unsustainable financial burden on the congregation.

A NEW STRATEGIC PLAN

Thus, at a little over a year-and-half of serving the saints at Zion, we began to develop a new strategic plan. Again, a professional was consulted. (A congregational connection made this much more affordable and, therefore, much more palatable to the congregation.) More listening posts, open forums, surveys, and workshops were held, so that congregational input could be gathered. The congregation grew weary of these processes.

Nonetheless, from all of the data, a strategic plan was formulated. It was specific, detailed, and methodical. Unfortunately, it languished for two years, gaining no momentum, providing no real theological basis, and offering no real solution or unity.

Evaluation of the plan revealed that the congregation saw it to be too broad, too complicated and wordy, and offered no real tangible direction to unify the congregation. In reality, it was nothing more than a complicated peace treaty that tried to pacify the poles within the congregation. In that sense, perhaps it served its purpose.

As the context of Zion continued to change and my time as senior pastor at the congregation continued to increase, the time came for the congregation's strategic plan to be intentionally recast and theologically reshaped. I had enrolled in a doctoral program through one of our seminaries (with the blessing and support of my congregation) and was now at the point of beginning my dissertation.

During the course work portion of the degree, my congregational context was always on my mind. In fact, the design of the doctoral program was meant to be of value to the local congregation. Each class provided a venue for me to explore opportunities of how better to serve my congregation. As such, I began to consider how a simple, concise, biblical strategic plan might be received by the congregation.

A THIRD ARTICLE "AHA!"

My "aha" moment over Peter's confession of faith in Jesus from a few years earlier had stuck with me. It nudged me in the writing of one my early class papers. It was a paper on the church's great confession of faith, the Apostles' Creed, specifically the third article: *I believe in the Holy Spirit, the Holy Christian Church, the communion of saints, the forgiveness of sins, the resurrection of the body, and the life everlasting.*

For millennia, the church has stood with Peter, confessing her faith in Jesus Christ. In fact, the Apostles' Creed remained a regular part of our congregation's public confession of faith and worship life. It was quite familiar to them. It was historic. It had been handed down through the church for hundreds of years. It was taught in our parochial school. It was part of our catechetical instruction. There wouldn't be that much to debate about it. So the wheels of my mind started to turn.

With the addition of an associate pastor, other staff changes, along with the congregational governance council desiring clarity for members of the congregation, I began considering how a mission, vision, and strategy shaped by the third article of the Apostles' Creed might be able to serve, unite, and mobilize the congregation. So I began a deep study of one the church's great confessions of faith. What I found was absolutely invaluable.

A MULTISYLLABIC WARNING

First, a word of explanation: Much of the following explores the theological depth of the Apostles' Creed. Theological language can get adventuresome. It can get deep. It can become multisyllabic. And as pastors are prone to be wordy in sermons, theological authors are prone to be wordy in their explanations. They are prone to get lost in their academic thinking and the authors who think like them. Thus, I am grateful that my wife lets me know when I missed an opportunity to sit down in a sermon. And I am grateful for others who have let me know when I have become too academic in this project. Nonetheless, out of necessity, I do indulge in the depths of theology and her authors. But where I indulge, I do so for the benefit of clarity and consensus. My aim is to promote honest theological dialogue. And this necessitates talking theologically. I do my best to steady theology with application. However, theology will undoubtedly predominate. In a church culture that has lost the ability to talk theologically, we have to start somewhere. So let the multisyllabic adventure begin!

EARLY DEVELOPMENT OF CREEDS

If I were to sum up my findings in one sentence, it would be this: The church has always been accompanied by creeds. In order to provide a more helpful understanding, details are necessary. But I'm aware that not everyone is interested in the details. Some would prefer if I'd just give the big picture. However, anyone who's interested in the mission of the Holy Christian Church will be interested in the details. The history of the church reveals a constant presence of creeds that not only express the beliefs of the church, but help shape the life of the church. Details like these provide important brush strokes to the big picture. What follows unpacks those details.

At its simplest, a creed is a statement of belief. The word *creed* comes from the Latin *credo*, which means "I believe." Since the core of the New Testament Gospel is faith—belief in Jesus Christ—creeds could only be a natural result. However, I found the use of creeds goes well beyond statements of belief. History shows how they blossomed and grew to be used in the teaching of the faith, baptismal rites, worship settings, establishing standards of orthodoxy, and becoming treasured symbols of a faith community.

Creedal formulations can be identified already in the New Testament itself. From Peter's confession of Jesus as the Christ to numerous portions of Paul's epistles, J. N. D. Kelly, in his classic treatment of *Early Christian Creeds,* establishes that "the reader of the New Testament is continually coming across creed-like slogans and tags, catchwords which at the time of writing were being consecrated by popular usage."[1] In short, they were developed out of necessity.

Students of the New Testament observe this with regularity. Particular situations within the church's life lent themselves to the intentional and repetitious declaration of Christian doctrine. This was for the purpose of clarifying the faith, solidifying the faith, accurately passing on the faith, and expressing the faith in worship: "The day to day polemic of the Church, whether against heretics within or pagan foes without, provided another situation propitious to the production of creeds. Yet, another was supplied by the liturgy: solemn expressions of faith, in form of hymns, prayers and devotional cries, had a natural place there."[2] Consequently, Kelly declares, "That the Church in the apostolic age possessed a creed in the broad sense of a recognized body of teaching may be accepted as demonstrated fact."[3]

Later on, these declarations of faith became more formalized. People began using them as authorized common confessions that summarized and shaped what they believed to be true, real, and right. Allister McGrath says it this way: "The creeds emphasize that to believe is to belong. To become a Christian is to enter a community of faith whose existence stretches right back to the upper room in which Jesus met with his disciples (John 21)."[4] On the whole, then, we can say with certainty that creeds were carried forward with reverence and rejoicing. They played no small part in the life of the early church.

1. Kelly, *Early Christian Creeds*, 13.
2. Ibid., 14.
3. Kelly, *Early Christian Creeds*, 13.
4. McGrath, *"I Believe" Exploring the Apostles' Creed*, 16.

My interest in their use and function continued to intensify. Could the creed be utilized to shape a congregation's strategic plan? I wanted to dig deeper. How did the early church use them?

EARLY USE OF CREEDS: THE BAPTISMAL RITE

One of the vital roles creeds played was in the baptismal and initiation rites into the church. In his thoughtful and contemporary work, *The Creed,* New Testament scholar Luke Timothy Johnson notes that creeds were esteemed as signs or symbols of the church, particularly in their use with converts:

> In the early church, the creed was referred to as a *symbolum* because it was handed over to those being initiated into the community as a sign of their reception. Together with the Lord's Prayer and other practices of the community that were kept from catechumens until they had been instructed properly, the creed thus 'symbolized' the faith both of the church and of those being initiated, as they joined themselves together in the ritual of baptism.[5]

When we take a look at the church today we can see many traditions continue this practice. In my own, the Apostles' Creed is routinely confessed as a part of the liturgical baptismal rite. It also remains a formal part of our catechesis process (the teaching of the faith), as well as our rite of confirmation.[6] In this way, one generation to the next is shaped and informed by the details of the Christian life given in the creed.

MEASUREMENTS OF ORTHODOXY

Creeds have also had other uses throughout the history of the church. They've been used as measurements of orthodoxy, not always a popular word to invoke. But the orthodoxy of the church's teachings does have a significant history. Consider the development of the Nicene Creed. It was a creed wrought out of intense conflict and strife. The church was divided. But it was more than just a congregational divide. It was the whole of Christendom. Arius and his followers were on one side;

---

5. Johnson , *The Creed*, 52. Kelly emphatically concurs: "There can be no doubt that creeds have, historically speaking, been associated with baptism." *Early Christian Creeds*, 30.

6. For the LCMS, see *Lutheran Service Book*, 268–74.

the Trinitarians were on the other. Arius claimed God had created Jesus Christ. The Trinitarians, of course, did not. For them, as for the Scriptures, Jesus was very God of very God. He was begotten but not made. He was one substance with the Father, by whom all things were made. Truth won the day, and the Nicene Creed was crafted to embody that truth.

Jaroslav Pelikan, in his extensive modern analysis, details the many historical movements and developments of Christian creeds and confessions, not the least of which is the Nicene development:

> Already in the issuance of the first creed or statement of faith ever officially adopted to be binding on the universal church rather than merely on a local or regional church, the creed promulgated at the first ecumenical council, the Council of Nicaea in 325, under the watchful eye of the recently converted emperor Constantine I, the accompanying warnings and cannons make it clear that 'the catholic and apostolic church anathematizes' any and all those so-called Christians who presume to deviate from this creed or who take it upon themselves to alter it.[7]

After Nicaea, forms of confessional subscription were regularly practiced in various official forms. And depending on the time period and region in which you were, there were varying consequences for those deemed to be false teachers.[8] (I do recognize the ardent positions and, at times, unnecessarily harsh physical punishments some regions endorsed for punishment against false teachers. However, I do not fault the creeds for the uncharitable behavior of those desiring to uphold them, but rather the individuals who lacked reasonableness and biblical compassion.)

Nonetheless, the desire was that where there was right teaching (doctrine), right practice would follow. It is a useful insight for us to consider again amid the confusion present in today's church.

Johnson delicately outlines how a creed can, in fact, bridge orthodoxy and orthopraxy: "Because the creed constructs the world as one created by God the Father, saved by Jesus Christ his Son, and given life by the Holy Spirit, it also supports and guides the practices of the Christian community. It does not prescribe a full set of Christian practices. It does not tell Christians how to pray or act in the world. But it

7. Pelikan, *Credo*, 9.
8. Ibid., 249–77.

does establish the right belief (orthodoxy) that lets us recognize right practice (orthopraxy). By providing an epitome of Scripture, the creed provides a bridge between the complex witnesses of Scripture and the moral lives of believers."[9] Given the pluralism of the North American context, this bridge remains helpful for our time.[10]

THE TREASURE OF CREEDS

Creeds were a cherished, integral part of the lives of those in the early church. In fact, it has been observed that within the early church "the *tradatio* [tradition] and the *redditio* [proclamation] of the Creed was one of the most awe-inspiring events of the Christian Life. The creed was regarded as a treasure that contained truths absolutely vital for one's life with God. These were to be guarded and treasured throughout life."[11] From the inception of the Christian church then, creeds have played a vital and regular role. As we will observe, they continue to do so in many ways today, though perhaps on a smaller scale. So would it work to utilize a third–century baptismal rite to shape a twenty-first century strategic plan? I kept on digging.

CONTEMPORARY USE OF CREEDS

My own heritage has always been creedal. In fact, the first statements of belief included in our official confessional documents (known as the *Book of Concord*) are the three official creeds compiled during the formative years of the early church. They are the Apostles' Creed (third century AD), the Nicene Creed (fourth century), and the Athanasian Creed (fifth and sixth centuries). They are often called the ecumenical or church-wide creeds because they confess what all Christians have historically believed, taught, and confessed since the beginnings of the early church.

All three of these creeds are used in our liturgies. But it is the Apostles' Creed and the Nicene Creed that have regular roles. (The

9. Johnson, *The Creed*, 61.

10. Where creeds were used to measure orthodoxy, they are also used to provide precise definitions of doctrine. Consider the Athanasian Creed: "The longest of the 'big three' creeds is the Athanasian Creed, containing 656 words . . . this creed carefully addresses and defends the doctrine of the Trinity in a highly technical and in-depth way." *Lutheranism 101*, 238.

11. Arand, "'He Walks with Me and He Talks with Me,' Today's New 'Creeds,'" 373.

Athanasian Creed is typically used only once a year on Trinity Sunday.) And thanks to Martin Luther's *Small Catechism*, the Apostles' Creed is also an integral tool utilized by Lutherans for the ongoing teaching of the faith.

POSTMODERN USE OF CREEDS

In general, the creeds have remained a vital, though perhaps under-appreciated, part of the life of the contemporary church. In succinct terms, "The creed performs five distinct but interrelated functions for the Christian community in worship and in its life beyond that context. It narrates the Christian myth,[12] interprets Scripture, constructs a world, guides Christian practices, and prepares the Christian people for worship."[13] The more I dug, the more I began cherishing these treasures. But how would they hold up against the present North American postmodern context? Would they survive the scrutiny? More questions needed more answers.

Our present postmodern and bourgeoning post-postmodern condition[14] (which chapter 3 will examine in greater detail) seems to pose potential disdain for creeds. If, among other things, the postmodern era can be characterized by a general contempt for systems that claim any form of absolute knowledge or truth, what role can there be for these long-cherished creeds? Would the intricacies and complexities of our postmodern condition rule out the use of creeds? Would a congregation filled with postmodern people be willing to use an ancient creed for contemporary direction?

Jaroslav Pelikan, as only a historian of his stature can, offers careful, yet poignant encouragement. I admit being a bit indulgent here, but what he offers is particularly helpful.

> [T]he future of creeds is of fundamental importance for the future of belief and for the future of the churches as well, even of churches that might not be thought of as "confessional" in the

---

12. For simple clarity, the use of the word *myth* is here being used in the academic sense and according to Merriam Webster's online dictionary is defined accordingly: "a usually traditional story of ostensibly historical events that serves to unfold part of the world view of a people or explain a practice, belief, or natural phenomenon."

13. Johnson, *The Creed*, 58.

14. See Frederic W. Baue's book, *The Spiritual Society: What Lurks Beyond Postmodernism* for his description of what he calls the coming "Therian Age."

usual sense . . .Without minimizing in any way the likelihood that changes in worldview during the twenty-first and twenty-second centuries will be even more drastic than those of the nineteenth and twentieth have been . . . it is appropriate to be reminded by history that there has in fact been a vast diversity of worldviews, as well as creedal forms and confessional genres, during the two millennia of Christian History . . . For the history of conflict, compromise, and accommodation of Christian thought and teaching in relation to shifting worldviews suggests the following paradoxical generalization: there has never been any picture of the world, whether scientific or philosophical or even "mythological," with which the confession of the Christian faith has been entirely compatible, although undoubtedly it has found a better fit with some than with others; but there has also never been any picture of the world within which the confession of the faith has proved to be altogether impossible. It does not appear unwarranted to propose that this paradox will continue to apply to the confessions and creeds of the future, if any.[15]

I take this as an affirmation. Creeds do have a place in the life of the church today! What is more, paradox is just fine in my tradition, especially one that calls for boldness in our confession of faith. And since this is, in fact, the business of a creed, I see this as a clear invitation to remain audacious in the use of the creeds, particularly in a postmodern world. In so doing, we'll find just how versatile and powerful the creeds can be.

THE IMPACT OF A CREED

To that end, I wanted to know more. Exactly how could a creed be used in our times? Would it stand up to our postmodern condition? How could it impact the people and congregations of North America? Luke Timothy Johnson provides sage words:

The creed does not propose a philosophy of life but tells a story with characters and a plot. It is a story about God and the world, about God's investment in humans and their future. The fact that Christian belief is embedded in the story says more than any philosophy could about the Christian commitment to the world—visible and invisible—as created by God.[16]

15. Pelikan, *Credo*, 509–10.
16. Johnson, *The Creed*, 58.

It's more profound encouragement! His words hack away at any postmodern accusations—both within the church as well as from outside it. They bear witness to the vibrancy of what others have considered to be dead (ineffective) orthodoxy. It's a detail worth sharing.

But what do we do when postmodernism seeks to deconstruct everything? In the words of the angels to the shepherds, "Fear not." The Good News of Jesus Christ is true whether others believe it or not, whether others deconstruct it or not. And what this means is that we're simply called to a greater awareness of our postmodern surroundings. This awareness frees us to be bold in living the creed rather than trying to convince people that it is true. Here again, Johnson offers a helpful and detailed explanation:

> Not every construction of the world can be true. God either creates all that is, or God doesn't. But humans are not in a position to adjudicate between competing world constructions. Contemporary Christians—who have been brought to this awareness more sharply than in any previous age— recognize that their world is not everybody's world. The world as constructed by Hinduism or Confucianism is simply not the same world that is constructed by the Bible and the Christian creed. Christians must acknowledge, furthermore, that they cannot demonstrate the superiority of their world to that of others. They must, therefore, live in the tension inherent in what has been called the "post-modern condition:" they affirm the truth of the world as expressed in the creed even as they know that other creeds construct other worlds that are just as believable—just as "livable"—as the Christians.[17]

In other words, the Christian faith is one that is confessed and lived, not in arrogance, but with authenticity. It is something the church and this world of unbelievers desperately need, people who believe their faith and live their faith. The role of a creed then is not to seal faith into the confines of nostalgic certitude, but to give it a living voice—one that has historic familiarity and authentic sincerity—that can be seen and heard in the life of the Christian.

The historic creeds can also address the ailments of a postmodern influence on the Christian mind, specifically by serving "the need for our intellectual healing because they [the creeds] objectify the Gospel message in the Christian's way of thinking about God and life, a contrast

17. Johnson, *The Creed*, 60.

with the myopia of any contemporary reading of the meaning of life in our time."[18] Thus, there is in the creeds a story that has been told and retold—rehearsed and confessed over and over for millennia—that situates us in the very midst of that story every time we confess it. And as we confess it and live it, we invite others to be a part of it.

CREEDAL THEOLOGY

Suffice it to say, the use of creeds in our times, or perhaps especially in our times, remains entirely desirable. Indeed, they can address the issues of postmodernism. They can form and inform people in the faith. Thus, it seems they would also be quite usable to shape a congregation's strategic plan. But now the question: Can they also revive the art of theological dialogue?

Jaroslav Pelikan, in his vast diversity of skills, again gives us hope. But this time, he does so by setting up the creedal tradition as a backdrop to formal biblical interpretation. Pelikan's biblical commentary on Acts was the first available in the new series of Brazos Theological Commentaries on the Bible—in his eightieth year no less!

What is so significant about this commentary series is that it is designed to be distinct and unique in comparison to traditional exegetical (text interpretation) commentaries. It is specifically meant to be theological in nature. The premise of the series is that doctrine clarifies rather than confuses. The editor's preface alone demonstrates this: "This series of biblical commentaries was born out of the conviction that dogma clarifies rather than obscures. Brazos Theological Commentary on the Bible advances upon the assumption that the Nicene tradition, in all its diversity and controversy, provides the proper basis for the interpretation of the Bible as Christian Scripture."[19] A breath of fresh creedal air has just been breathed back into the lungs of the church. She's been invited to speak with a voice rich in history and sweet with theology.

The editor further clarifies that it is "to theologians and not biblical scholars that we have turned" precisely because they maintain that the Nicene tradition more properly prepares one for biblical interpretation.[20] In scholarly terms, and here comes some of the multisyllabic language,

18. Eyer, *They Will See His Face*, 102.

19. Pelikan, *Acts*, 13–14.

20. Ibid., 14.

the approach is aimed at the shortcomings of modern historical-critical study of the Bible.[21] The series is designed to be an experiment in "reconstructive" rather than "reactionary" approaches to "postcritical doctrinal interpretation" wherein the commentaries are *not* to be written "according to the settled principles of a well-functioning tradition."[22] The "tradition," therefore, refers to the style of linguistic interpretation, not the theological tradition.

Perhaps it is a bit technical, but the basis of this interpretive approach was deemed necessary because the European and North American intellectual culture has been de-Christianized. The unfortunate effect was that each dimension of a "formerly unified Christian practice" was fractionalized into independent functioning. Consequently, the editor laments: "Theology has lost its competence in exegesis. Scripture scholars function with minimal theological training. Each decade finds new theories of preaching to cover the nakedness of seminary training that provides theology without exegesis and exegesis without theology."[23] It is an intentional and formal effort to resurrect the interpretative tradition of the historic creedal church. It is an approach appreciated by other scholars as well.

James W. Voelz seems to offer a tacit, though qualified, agreement about this interpretive approach. In his hermeneutics textbook *What Does This Mean? Principles of Biblical Interpretation in the Post-Modern World,* he concludes by stating:

> The church has always recognized the interpersonal nature of textual interpretation and said that it can only truly be done within the church ('within the church' being understood to include personal faith as well as community context). Thus a confessional posture, one which specifically endorses a given

21. At the risk of oversimplifying, the historical-critical method is a controversial interpretive approach that treats the Scriptures as simple pieces of ordinary historical literature rather that as the inspired Word of God. It provides for no historical norming measures to be applied to the interpretive process. Thus, the approach investigates and attempts to explain the origin of the Bible in that same way as any other historical phenomenon. It deals only with the human aspects of the Bible. It will neither deny nor affirm a supernatural dimension of historical phenomena since the supernatural is not amendable to investigation by the procedures of this discipline. This approach, therefore, limits interpretation to those aspects of the Bible that can be investigated by this method.

22. Pelikan, *Acts*, 16.

23. Ibid., 15.

community/faith understanding of the Scriptures as congruent with the understanding of the historic Christian church which produced and received those documents, is a completely responsible one after all.[24]

Again, it is a bit academic in explanation, but it is a detail that is worth noting.[25] The point has been to demonstrate how the creeds—or in this case, the creedal tradition—has been recently used to re-examine the Scriptures in light of a postmodern age that seeks to deconstruct, and perhaps disassociate altogether, the historic community and the Scriptures that give it life.

The creeds breathe life back into the lungs of theological discussion. Not only was I finding that the creeds could be utilized for a congregational strategic plan, but they could very well serve the greater church in a like manner.

CREEDAL LENSES

It is in this same vein that I propose using the Apostles' Creed, and especially the third article of this creed, as lenses to re-examine not the Scriptures of the church *per se*, but rather the life and mission of the church today.

Where Brazos observes the European and North American intellectual culture has been de-Christianized, my observation is that the North American church culture has been de-doctrinized. In short, the historic teachings (doctrine) that have guided the church and her mission are slowly being stripped away. And where Brazos observes that "theology

24. Voelz, *What Does this Mean?*, 340.

25. The evangelical Lutheran perspective is one that is deeply rooted in theological and exegetical traditions that are complementary to one another. In fact, they were the fundamental principles that gave rise to the Lutheran identity. But while Lutherans do have a tradition of interpretation, this is so only insofar as the Scriptures remain the source and norm of this tradition. Lutherans find it important to maintain the teaching authority of the Scriptures, not as a matter of tradition, but because the Scriptures call for it. Here the primary difference in interpretive approaches (maybe more subtle for some than others) could be found between evangelical Lutherans and the framework established by the Brazos Theological Commentary series. Though great similarities can be found between the two, there is an underlying fundamental difference that could potentially impact the treatment of the Scriptures and, inevitably, the theology of the Word of God itself (i.e., where any church tradition itself is put on par with the Scriptures). As a result, the way the Scriptures are approached will also necessarily impact the longevity of all doctrine and theological traditions.

has lost its competence in exegesis," my observation is that theology has lost its competence in practice. A surge of new movements have been sweeping through the church and, though perhaps well-meaning, have cast a great deal of theological confusion and practical uncertainty in the church. I will say much more on this later, but for the moment, let us check out what life looks like through creedal lenses.

THE APOSTLES' CREED

The Apostles' Creed is the oldest and shortest of the formalized creeds. It is possibly also the most familiar, at least to North American Christians. In my tradition, it is a deeply cherished treasure of the church and an integral part of her catechesis (forming and informing of disciples). Divided into three articles (respectively on the Father, Son, and Holy Spirit), it provides a short but profound confession of faith:

> I believe in God the Father Almighty, maker of heaven and earth. And in Jesus Christ, His only Son, our Lord, Who was conceived by the Holy Spirit, born of the Virgin Mary, suffered under Pontius Pilate, was crucified, died, and was buried. He descended into hell. The third day He rose again from the dead. He ascended into heaven and sits at the right hand of God the Father Almighty. From thence He will come to judge the living and the dead. I believe in the Holy Spirit, the holy Christian Church, the communion of saints, the forgiveness of sins, the resurrection of the body, and the life everlasting. Amen.

Martin Luther saw the tremendous value of it and so implored its use in both his Small and Large Catechisms, even noting that, "For as long as we live we shall have enough here in the Creed to preach and learn."[26] And to be sure, what he had to say about the creed has stood the test of time. His explanation of the creed has brought meaning to lives across epochal boundaries. Originally written to engage and encourage sixteenth-century sinners with the Gospel, twenty-first-century sinners are no less engaged. Not only does it provide a confession of faith for the believer, but it also provides a curriculum for witnessing to his neighbor. "I believe" invites the believer to proclaim what it is he believes. And the content of what he believes, as given expression through Luther's explanation to each article of the creed, invites him to take his neighbor

---

26. Kolb & Wengert, LC, Third Article, § 70.

where that person is at—notably, in creation, enduring the curse of sin, and searching for fulfillment in life, and assure them all are in this life together.[27] Where they may be looking for hope, the creed lets people locate where it is found—God the Father, Son, and Holy Spirit.

In short, Luther uses each article to describe three ways in which God's "recreative word" has identified us as children of God.[28] Each article takes a different starting point to unpack God's love, goodness, and care for his human creatures. They are apt points for us to consider as we engage our postmodern neighbors in today's world.

For Luther, the Apostles' Creed is good news. It "brings pure grace and makes us righteous and acceptable to God."[29] Where the Ten Commandments show us God's law, the creed shows us God's grace. Hence Luther ordered his *Small Catechism* in this way (i.e., the Ten Commandments first and the creed second) to contrast how the commandments "teach us what we ought to do" while "the Creed tells us what God does for us and gives to us."[30] It was a design for pastors as much as it was for the family.[31] I was finding that the usefulness of the creeds was only continuing to grow.

CRISIS: THE NEED FOR A CREED

In the preface to his *Small Catechism*, Luther writes:

> The deplorable, wretched deprivation that I recently encountered while I was a visitor has constrained and compelled me to prepare this catechism, or Christian instruction, in such a brief, and simple version. Dear God, what misery I beheld! The ordinary person, especially in the villages, knows absolutely nothing

27. Robert Kolb offers this assessment: "Luther's treatment of the Apostles' Creed offers a program for meeting our neighbors 'where they are,' for engaging their formulations regarding what human life is all about. For, like all fallen human creatures, we and our contemporaries are on a pilgrimage through this life, longing to find home, wherever and whatever it might be. Today, as in every age, our spirits are restless, and Luther's explanations to the article of the Creed lead their hearers to find rest in God." "'That I May Be His Own,'" 29. See also Kolb's *Speaking the Gospel Today*.

28. Kolb, "'That I May Be His Own,'" 30.

29. Kolb & Wengert, LC, Third Article, § 68.

30. Ibid., § 67.

31. Luther's *Small Catechism* was designed particularly for the family even as it was for the greater church. The heading of each of its six chief parts reads: "As the head of the family should teach in a simple way to his household."

about the Christian faith, and unfortunately many pastors are completely unskilled and incompetent teachers. Yet supposedly they all bear the name Christian, are baptized, and receive the holy sacrament, even though they do not know the Lord's Prayer, the Creed, or the Ten Commandments![32]

Out of necessity, Luther designed and crafted a simple and clear tool for instructing people in the faith. I found that its design was pure genius.

The condition of the church and her pastors during Luther's time was such that the Gospel and its proclamation were in a dire condition. In their book, *The Genius of Luther's Theology,* Robert Kolb and Charles Arand make an important observation, particularly for our discussion:

> The Reformation Luther led with his colleagues at the University of Wittenberg arose out of the crisis of pastoral care that plagued the late medieval church. That crisis had its roots in a crisis of proclamation: there was too little preaching in the fifteenth century, largely because pastors were ill trained or not trained at all. Most knew little theology and, had little idea of how the Gospel might make a difference in people's lives.[33]

Luther recognized action was needed, so action was taken. But what I also found (and I'm indulging again) was that there are those who have argued that the church today is suffering a similar crisis. Stanly Hauerwas and William Willimon began calling attention to what they considered a denomination-spanning crisis in 1989 with their seminal work *Resident Aliens*. It was quite compelling for its time. They described the fall of the church this way: "What we call 'church' is too often a gathering of strangers who see the church as yet another 'helping institution' to gratify further their individual desires."[34]

David Wells resolutely began following suit in 1993 through 2008, citing the maladies of North American evangelicals in no less than five scholarly works. Laboring over the culture and condition of the evangelical church, he laments its ultimate and interminable decline. A brief excerpt from his 2005 work, *Above All Earthly Powers: Christ in a Postmodern World*, demonstrates his stark but telling assessment:

32. Kolb & Wengert, LC, Third Article, Preface to SC, § 1–3.
33. Kolb and Arand, *The Genius of Luther's Theology,* 11.
34. Hauerwas and Willimon, *Resident Aliens,* 138.

The indicators of decline and weakness, I believe, are already beginning to appear, though as so often happens to those who see themselves as still in the flush of success, these indicators seem not to be there. I can now only attempt to illustrate my judgment in one particular area, that of the new ways of "doing church," though my concern here is obviously selective. What I shall argue is that in this area, the lure of success is the very means by which success is actually disappearing and, in the next generation, we will see the bitter fruit appearing more evidently than we can see it now. And the irony which today is almost completely lost on evangelicals is that in this new quest, this new way of "doing church," those who once stood aloof from the older liberalism are now unwittingly producing a close cousin to it. By the time this becomes so evident that it will be incontrovertible, it will be too late.[35]

To be sure, it is a sad prediction, but it is one that must be addressed, not just for evangelicals, but for all those church bodies who follow the "new ways of doing church."

But even before these voices were put into print, Gerhard Forde was calling the church to task. In 1987, he observed that Lutherans (my own tradition!) were suffering from what he called an "identity crisis," even blatantly chiding that Lutherans "seem to be looking for someone to sell out to."[36] Ouch!

Ultimately, he identifies the malady facing the church to be a crisis of Gospel proclamation. That is, churches were having church, but there was no Good News being proclaimed. Churches were compromising their message. The Gospel was too offensive. It had to be reshaped. Sadly, churches began giving in. Churches were selling out.[37] What had plagued the church of Luther's day had returned, though now colored with a few more subtleties. Churches had preaching, training, and theology for pastors, but as Forde asserts, it is, sadly, too often of the compromising kind. Doctrine was being displaced. Preaching was no longer proclamation.

35. Wells, *Above All Earthly Powers*, 264–65.

36. Forde elaborates: "The continuing crisis for anyone who is grasped by that radical Gospel comes both from the fact that the world and its church cannot do other than resist and attack that Gospel (as a matter of self-defense), and from the fact they cannot escape the constant temptation to make compromises which disguise or blunt the sharp edges of its radicality." "Radical Lutheranism," 1–2.

37. Ibid., 8.

BLURRED VISION

It remains much the same today. However, voices of reason continue to blare out. Tullian Tchividjian (cha-vi-jin), grandson of Billy Graham and senior pastor at the famed Coral Ridge Presbyterian Church in Fort Lauderdale, Florida, puts the continued maladies of the contemporary North American church bluntly:

> Absorbing this narcissistic assumption, the modern church is all too often guilty of producing worship services that are little more than motivational, self-help seminars filled with "you can do it" songs and sermons . . . Preachers these days are expected to major in "Christian moral renovation." They are expected to provide a practical to-do list, rather than announce, "It is finished." They are expected to do something other than, more than, placarding before their congregation's eyes Christ's finished work, preaching a full absolution solely on the basis of the complete righteousness of Another. The irony is, of course, that when preachers cave in to this pressure, moral renovation does not happen.[38]

Summing it up, by more than one diagnosis, the church's vision is blurred. By more than one assessment, her eyesight is impaired. Her focus is distorted. However, with a voice of clairvoyance, Forde directs the church back to the purity of the Gospel. "If Lutheranism is to recover a sense of its identity and mission today, it must begin to consider what it means to preach the Gospel in radical fashion."[39] Yes, it is directed at Lutherans, but there is broader application for the contemporary North American church.

This is why I believe an intentional return to the genius of Luther's theology remains altogether desirable. His insights on the Apostles' Creed, particularly the third article, offer a lasting foundation—corrective

38. Tchividjian, *Jesus + Nothing = Everything*, 50, 117.

39. Forde, "Radical Lutheranism," 11. See also Forde's subsequent book, *Theology is for Proclamation*, 8: "What the church has to offer the modern world is not ancient history but the present-tense unconditional proclamation. The strategy of accommodation and defense has resulted in the sentimentalization and bowdlerization of almost everything. It is time to risk going over to the offense, to recapture the present tense of the Gospel, to speak the unconditional promise and see what happens. To do that it will be necessary to construct a theology that is for proclamation, for going over to the offense, not for defense."

even—that provides a historic paradigm for the church's mission and life.[40] It clarifies the important details. Let's take a closer look.

THE THIRD ARTICLE OF THE APOSTLES' CREED: BIFOCALS FOR THE CHURCH

With the words of the third article of the Apostles' Creed, there is confessed the belief in the "Holy Spirit, the Holy Christian Church, the communion of saints, the forgiveness of sins, the resurrection of the body, and the life everlasting." (Now we're really going to start digging deeper into some theological language.) There are five profound realities created by the one Holy Spirit. Each element brings clarity to the mission of God: what it is, what it gives, how it is accomplished, and who will do it. Luther offers the details with his explanation to this article:

> I believe that by my own understanding or strength I cannot believe in Jesus Christ my Lord or come to him, but instead the Holy Spirit has called me through the Gospel, enlightened me with his gifts, and made me holy and kept me in the true faith, just as he calls, gathers, enlightens, and makes holy the whole Christian church on earth and keeps it with Jesus Christ in the one common true faith. Daily in this Christian church the Holy Spirit abundantly forgives all sins—mine and those of all believers. On the Last Day the Holy Spirit will raise me and all the dead and will give to me and all believers in Christ eternal life.[41]

In short, Luther here details the mission of God. God the Holy Spirit begins the mission through the living voice of the Gospel. In the midst of human living, mouths speak the Word of God and unbelievers are "called" into believers—adult, child, worker, and foreigner. Yes, there is a context. Yes, people have needs. But the Word of God is what the Holy Spirit uses in those contexts and amid those needs. As Paul told the

40. In the theological sense, it clarifies the *missio Dei*—the mission of God—as opposed to the confusing missional imperative being put upon the church. "Speaking of mission as *missio Dei* signifies a theological shift from the common perception of mission as substantially a human endeavor to a theocentric approach that makes God, and not humans, the sources and initiator of mission." Schulz, *Mission from the Cross*, 88.

41. Kolb & Wengert, SC, Third Article, § 6. Though this is the current translation, I will often summarily refer to the explanation with the older translation that was learned by so many in catechesis (confirmation): "I believe that I cannot by my own reason or strength . . ."

Romans, the Gospel "is the power of God for salvation to everyone who believes" (Rom 1:16).

Interestingly, the Holy Spirit then "gathers" these believers into a specific, identifiable community called the Christian church and the communion of saints, again by the Gospel. Luther emphasizes that they are "the community of saints" in his *Large Catechism*.[42] And it is through this community of saints that God the Holy Spirit "daily" and "abundantly" forgives sins. This too is done by the Gospel. This goes on day by day, week after week, year after year. The life of believers—the community of saints—center on the Gospel, up to the Last Day, where dead bodies are raised and "all believers in Christ" are given "eternal life."

Without question, the creed and its explanation emphasizes that the Gospel is the power of God for the salvation of everyone who believes. This is the *missio Dei*. It is the Gospel of Jesus Christ at work in the lives of sinners. As Luther says, "This is most certainly true." Using it as a lens (or in this case as bifocals) to examine the life of the North American church provides a foundation to address the confusion happening in her midst. It will also, as I have noted, provide a provocative and transforming paradigm for the outreach of the church.

A CLOSER LOOK

In his explanation of the third article of the Apostles' Creed, Luther provides believers the joy of giving credit where credit is due. The Holy Spirit alone works faith. This He does by nothing other than "calling through the Gospel." No self-help. No attitude adjustments. No personal decisions. Faith in Christ is the work of the Holy Spirit speaking through the Word of God, irrespective of the particular mouth being employed to speak it. As the Scriptures say, "Faith comes from hearing, and hearing through the word of Christ" (Rom 10:17).

Again, I recognize the relational aspects of sharing the Gospel and will touch on those in greater detail in chapters 6 and 7, and the conclusion, but as the Scriptures declare, the Gospel alone is the power of God for the salvation of souls (Rom 1:16). Thus, Luther locates the Holy Spirit where the Holy Spirit wants to be found: in the Word of God, both

---

42. "Likewise, the word *communion*, which is attached to it, should not be translated 'communion' but rather 'community.' It is nothing but a comment or interpretation by which someone wished to explain what the Christian church is." Ibid., LC, The Creed, Third Article, § 49.

spoken and sacramental. No emotions. No visions. No nebulous force floating in the air. Rather, the Holy Spirit blows fiercely and mightily through the living voice of the Gospel. "No one can say 'Jesus is Lord' except by the Holy Spirit" (1 Cor 12:3b).

Since a congregation is made up of believers and the Holy Spirit is the one who makes believers, Luther's explanation also celebrates that it is the Holy Spirit who makes a congregation "church." Constitution committees beware! This, too, the Holy Spirit does through the Gospel. As Luther put it, "calling, gathering, enlightening and making holy the whole Christian church on earth."

To make sinners holy is no small thing. But that would only be the natural work of the Holy Spirit. The way he works is not secret. It is not hidden, but open and specific. Luther is clear on this. Commenting on the third article in his *Large Catechism*, he writes:

> [T]he Holy Spirit effects our being made holy through the following: the community of saints or Christian Church, the forgiveness of sins, the resurrection of the body, and the life everlasting. That is, he first leads us into his holy community placing us in the church's lap, where he preaches to us and brings us to Christ . . . Therefore being made holy is nothing else than bringing us to the Lord Christ to receive this blessing, to which we could not have come by ourselves.[43]

Believers are made holy and, therefore, the church is holy. Luther then ends his sentence by noting that the Holy Spirit propels the church forward by "keeping it with Jesus Christ in the one common true faith." Thus, we could say that the things that don't keep the church "with Jesus Christ in the one common true faith" are not the work of the Holy Spirit.

But that is the issue, isn't it? What constitutes keeping the church with Jesus? Is a growing church more "with Jesus" than a shrinking church? Is a doctrinal church more "with Jesus" than a missional church? Such questions seem to be spurious alternatives, but they are the ones being asked today.

Fortunately, Luther gives some direction here. What is central to the work of the church, he says, is the forgiveness of sins: "Daily in this Christian church the Holy Spirit abundantly forgives all sins—mine and those of all believers." Thus, at a minimum, "with Jesus" there is the "forgiveness of sins."

43. Kolb & Wengert, LC, The Creed, Third Article, § 37–38.

This is good news! In fact, again in his *Large Catechism*, Luther reminds us that this is the reason that the Holy Spirit appointed a community of believers: to ensure that this good news gets delivered! "[T]he Holy Spirit continues his work without ceasing until the Last Day, and for this purpose he has appointed a community on earth, through which he speaks and does all his work. For he has not yet gathered together all of this Christian community, nor has he completed the granting of forgiveness."[44] It's a certain reference to what we today call seeking and saving of the lost. Thus, hopefully it is clear that theological dialogue is not anti-evangelism. Nor is it impractical. It merely seeks to keep things duly ordered.

CRISIS OF VOCATION

The community of saints on earth is made up of individuals who are placed in various vocations of life to serve others. Those vocations very often place them in relationships with unbelievers. And it is through these relationships that the Good News can be most naturally and frequently delivered.

But here's the challenge: the crisis of Gospel proclamation is not solely a lack of preachers preaching the Gospel. It also stems from a lack of pastors teaching about the role the community of saints plays in the world and with one another through their various vocations.

To be sure, the theology of vocation can be traced back to the creed through two places (I know . . . more theological indulgence here.): (1) to the first article, God's care of creation; (2) to the third article, "the community of saints" situated in creation.

However, here's the rub. In the context of all the missional talk, is the doctrine of vocation a pure or impure theology? Remember, the charge was made "that theology pursued for some ultimate purpose other than God's mission of seeking and saving the lost is simply unfaithful theology."[45] True, our vocations put us in relationships with others who may be unbelievers, which then gives us the opportunity to witness to them. But is that the primary or sole purpose of vocation? What if some or all the elements of the doctrine of vocation are not designed

44. Ibid., § 61–62.
45. Schumacher. "Theology or Mission?," 117.

for actually spreading the Gospel? What then? Is it an impure doctrine? Again, more light and less heat is needed for this conversation. So here goes.

VOCATION AND MISSION

Vocation, simply put, is a person's station in life. From family to community, workforce to congregation, people have multiple vocations as they go through life. But as has been asked, how does the community of saints situated in their daily vocations rate in view of all the missional talk? Is there any value to developing a theology that speaks of God's hidden work among the ordinariness of life?

Luther thought so.[46] Robert Kolb is quick to demonstrate Luther's insight: "Service to God is expressed in every aspect of human life, as it is lived out in homes, workplaces, communities, and congregations of God's worshipping and witnessing people. The importance of the congregation dare never be overestimated: Luther's insight into the godliness of every human calling, in family, occupation, political state and local neighborhood, as well as in the congregation, is vital for the practice of the rule of Christ in the lives of His people."[47] But does every earthly vocation (i.e., every station or order that a person has in life) inherently include the proclamation of the Gospel? If not, again I ask the question, is this impure doctrine? Even more, are Christians sinning by pursuing such a theology and taking solace in it?

Gustaf Wingren would seek to put Christians at ease as he unpacks the details of Luther's profound understanding of vocation. At the same time, he broadens the understanding of God's mission:

46. From his December 27, 1534, Christmas sermon: "Here is another excellent and helpful lesson, namely, that after the shepherds have been enlightened and have come to a true knowledge of Christ, they do not run out into the desert—which is what the crazy monks and nuns in the cloisters did! No, the shepherds continue in their vocation, and in the process, they also serve their fellowmen. For true faith does not create people who abandon their secular vocation and begin a totally different kind of living . . . Christ did not come to change external things, nor to destroy his creation nor to transform it. Therefore you should clothe your body, provide it with sustenance, and use it to do some honest-to-goodness labor. That is God's creation and order, and he hasn't changed that order; he did not come to change that arrangement. When or if it becomes necessary, we are free to make minor adjustments, of course . . . The real change which Christ came to effect is an inward change of the human heart." Klug, *Complete Sermons of Martin Luther, vol. 5*, 148–49.

47. Kolb, "'That I May Be His Own,'" 38.

What is effected through these orders of society is not due to an inner transformation of the human heart. The corruption of the heart is amended in heaven, through the Gospel of Christ. There the human being is a "single person" and there inquiry is made into his inner wickedness, even if on earth it has been ceaselessly repressed and hindered from outer expression. On earth and in relation to his neighbor he fulfils an "office"; there the main point is that creation is sustained, e.g., that children receive food, clothing and care. This work of love God effects on earth through the "orders"— the order of marriage, of teacher and pupils, of government, etc. Even persons who have not taken the Gospel to their hearts serve God's mission, though they be unaware thereof, by the very fact that they perform the outer functions of their respective stations.[48]

Even unbelievers, he says, are used to serve God's mission! And according to Wingren, it is a mission that is broader than seeking the lost. So I will pose this question for you to think about: Could the doctrine of vocation be a part of the Holy Spirit's enlightening of the whole Christian church on earth (to use Luther's words) as it participates in God's greater mission? To be sure, the creed reminds us that the primary role of the Holy Spirit's enlightening is "the forgiveness of sins, the resurrection of the body and the life everlasting." However, to be called by the Gospel, and thus given the "abundant life" of Christ (John 10:10), doesn't remove one from the earthly stations of life. Rather, it enlightens believers with the fullness of the Gospel so that we might live this life to the full—here in time and there in eternity. Thus, while we're here in time, this living goes on precisely within the vocations of each believer.[49]

THE VOCATION OF DAILY LIVING

Gene Edward Veith is a more recent champion of Luther's explanation of vocation. He does a superb job of celebrating the details of how God is actually at work through our vocations. There is great joy and freedom in recognizing this:

> What is distinctive about Luther's approach is that instead of seeing vocation as a matter of what we should *do*—what we must

48. Wingren, *Luther on Vocation*, 6–7.

49. "The same Spirit who calls us to faith through the externality of his word also calls us to life in creation." Pless, "Contemporary Spirituality and the Emerging Church," 362.

do as a Christian worker or a Christian citizen or a Christian parent—Luther emphasizes what *God does* in and through our vocations. That is to say, for Luther vocation is not just a matter of Law—though this is a part of vocation that neither Luther nor this book will neglect; rather, above all, vocation is a matter of Gospel, manifestation of *God's* action, not our own, In this sense, vocation is not another burden placed upon us, something else to fail at, but a realm in which we can experience God's love and grace, both in the blessings we receive from others and in the way God is working through us despite our failures.[50]

This understanding frees the community of saints to live out their lives with the fullness of God's mission in mind. I'll put it simply: in the midst of knowing God's desire for all people to be saved, life must still be lived out—diapers changed, cows milked, papers graded, teeth cleaned, fires doused, and criminals arrested. The ordinariness of life (our day-to-day, routine activities) by necessity and by divine ordering takes up a large part of our living. We cannot minimize this reality. It's simply a part of life. It's a part of God's creative ordering and continual care of His creation.

But we cannot forget that mixed in with this are the spiritual afflictions we face as we're situated in a fallen creation.[51] Christians face spiri-

---

50. Veith, *God at Work*, 23–24.

51. Kolb and Arand capture it all well. "As believers return to creation, they encounter some harsh realities. The creator's sovereignty is disputed on every front by the devil, the world, and their own desires, which reject God's lordship and design. Believers find themselves surrounded by sin, evil, death, and decay. Christians find their faith under constant assault by events suggesting that God is not in control. Drawing false conclusions from a false correlation of evil and God's intention toward his creatures, some Christians throughout history have concluded that the world is too corrupt a place in which to live, much less in which to work out their sanctification. Creation and our responsibilities in creation are not good enough to attain true holiness. According to this view of life, creation is no more than our stepping-stone to the life hereafter. Once I am saved, I can begin saying good-bye to this world. It ceases to be of strong interest or concern to me. Thus, Christians are tempted to live only as aliens or strangers in this world, pilgrims who are making the journey through this life. Such a belief argues that it is necessary to retreat from the world. Thus, the enticement of a creation-denying, world fleeing, self-depriving spirituality has confronted Christians of every age. We are always on our way somewhere else, to an idealist heaven where there is no change or decay or flesh or sex or children and all that, or to a utopia, to Solla Salloo, where they never have any troubles, or at least very few. While Christians do discipline their lives and avoid excessive indulgences, ever ready to make sacrifices for others, they confess that this world belongs to their Father and their family. Therefore, they feel free to use his created gifts in ways that please him." *The Genius of Luther's Theology*, 107.

tual afflictions that tempt them to doubt the meaning of their earthly purpose and presence. However, the first article of the Apostles' Creed ("I believe in God the Father Almighty, maker of heaven and earth") reminds us that the earth was created by God the Father, who orders it and places his creatures in it for his purpose and His mission. The third article ("I believe in the Holy Spirit") then reminds us how his human creatures are made aware of their Creator and his purpose for them. This is how vocation flows out of the first article of the Apostles' Creed and into the third article of the Apostles' Creed. We find that it does, in fact, create doctrine and, therefore, godly life for the community of saints as they live on this earth.

VOCATION AS OUTREACH

But it is also here that an approach to outreach even more provocative and transforming than the current missional mindset of the organizational church is provided. Namely, where there is a renewal and celebration of our God-given earthly vocations, there is a corresponding renewal and celebration of our Christian vocation seen in our lives as the worshipping and witnessing community of saints.

They are lived out naturally, in tandem, and not at the expense of the other. Here we can, as Eugene Bunkowske invites, "gossip the Gospel" and "make and multiply disciples by positively and naturally introducing our good friend Jesus to other people in our everyday life."[52] In this way, homes, workplaces, and neighborhoods become places of mission when, in the course of natural conversations and service to those around us, we have the opportunity to share the Good News of Jesus Christ, where, through the "gathering" of the Holy Spirit, others are invited into the community of saints.

I offer this is in contrast to the present missional movement. The primary modes of outreach in this movement are seen to be the so-called appealing and culturally relevant forms of worship, coupled with the reorganization of congregations around missional leadership. Pastors are encouraged to re-invent, re-shape, and re-imagine the historic and creedal way that worship services have been done, so as to market the church and thus interest, attract, relate to, and (hopefully) evangelize unbelievers. Pastors are also invited to use consultants and

52. Bunkowske, "A Hand of Life Giving Love," 26–28.

organizational gurus to help them better structure and mobilize their congregations. The idea is to be focused on missional leadership, where the invariable goal is to make everyone a missionary.

So what's wrong with that, you ask? Is it really that bad to have everyone sharing their faith? Let me be clear. No! I am, after all, proposing a model that does, in fact, aim at everyone being better equipped to share their faith. My point is that it does not have to occur at the expense or the devaluing of our vocations or the reordering of the historic practices and purposes of the church. It also recognizes that not everyone is necessarily or equally equipped in discipling others. And even when that is the case, it does not reduce the value of their daily vocation or threaten their faithfulness to Christ.

What is more, the model I am proposing aims to uphold the depth of the historic creedal practices and teaching of the mission of the church. In fact, if I am being honest, the model is actually nothing new. Rather, it is simply a continuation of how the early church grew. In fact, study of the New Testament early church seems to affirm the nature of vocational outreach as a more transforming and, if one wants to use such a word, *effective* way of witness to the Gospel: "When the early Christians themselves recount how they learned of the Gospel, they usually confess that their faith was the result of casual contact with the 'way of life' . . . The work was not done by people who called themselves missionaries but by rank-and-file members. The least among men, even the unknown, are indeed the greatest in the Kingdom of heaven."[53]

I recognize that the missional movement has great zeal. It is certainly well-meaning. And I appreciate the great and sincere love they have for reaching people with the Good News of Jesus Christ. In fact, I do think they have something to offer the church in this way. However,

---

53. Engelbrecht, *The Church from Age to Age*, 13. Also consider Michael Green in his book *Evangelism in the Early Church*, which makes five observations about the first Christians worth noting, particularly in view of our consideration of vocational witness and the Third Article. Some may be more significant than others, but they are interesting observations to note nonetheless: "First, they did most of their evangelism on what we would call secular ground. You can find them in the laundries, at the street corners and in the wine bars talking about Jesus to all who would listen . . . A second priority of the early Christians seems to have been personal conversations with individuals . . . Third, it is very noticeable that the home provided the most natural context for gossiping the Gospel . . . A natural development of the home meeting is church planting . . . Finally, it is worth noting what emphasis the first Christians put on the work of the Holy Spirit," 23–25.

as we will find, and if we are being honest, it has not been as effective as its supporters claim. In fact, there is growing evidence that the movement has actually had adverse effects upon the church and her mission. I think it is important we have an honest, collegial conversation about this. We will leave the vitriol at home. We will avoid demonizing language. But we do need to be frank. We do need to be candid. I think that is what it means to speak the truth in love.

To start this conversation, we will address the core of the missional emphasis. It has been rooted in the so-called Great Commission of Matthew 28:18–20. Therefore, in the next chapter, we will take a careful look at this text, its uses and misuses, along with some assessments on the effectiveness of the current missional movement.

Chapter 2

Great Commission or
Great Confusion?

MY FATHER-IN-LAW, THE OPTOMETRIST

I HAVE TERRIBLE EYESIGHT. Without my contacts or classes, everything is a massive blur and I am easily confused. My eye doctor tells me that part of my affliction comes from a slight astigmatism in my right eye. I am not an eye doctor. I do not know what that means. I ask. "Astigmatism is an optical defect where your vision blurs because your eye can't bring an object into a sharp focused image on your retina. This happens either because of an irregular curvature of your cornea or the lens of your eye."[1] Now I know.

Eye doctors are amazing! I, for one, am thankful for their vocation. Without them, I certainly would not have been able to type these words, shoot my bow, admire my wife's pretty face, or see the faces of my members when I preach. (Maybe the last option wouldn't be all that bad. Every preacher knows the distracting faces that people can make. From the yawning mouth to the sleeping eyes to the perpetually itchy nose, such faces can cause a preacher to lose his focus. I digress.)

BLURRED VISION

It is my contention that the North American church is suffering from astigmatism. In an attempt to try to help focus the mission of the church,

---

1. Dr. Robert E. Swanson, O.D., who is also the author's father-in-law.

the so-called Great Commission of Matthew 28:18–20 has been elevated to what seems like a supreme, all-defining symbol and purpose statement of the church. But ironically, there is evidence that it has actually caused the church to lose her focus instead.

Church bodies, local congregations, and pastors alike have rallied behind this mantra. Good or bad, I, along with many other pastors, have preached more than one sermon using the Great Commission—the actual text of Matthew 28:18–20 as well as the phrase "Great Commission"— as a forced set of marching orders for the church. What is more, my congregation is just one of many who have at one time or another used the Great Commission to shape its strategic plan and purpose for being. In fact, whole church bodies have passed official resolutions using the Great Commission as rationale for their directives.

Some may ask, "What's wrong with that? How bad can it be to have Scripture as a guiding principle? After all, is not the Great Commission the very words of Jesus?"

Scripture is certainly good, especially verses that focuses on the Gospel. It is, as we noted in the last chapter, how the Holy Spirit "calls, gathers, and enlightens the whole Christian Church on earth." However, as well-intentioned as this attempt at greater focus may be, I contend it has actually blurred the vision of the church and created significant confusion. I would like to show you how.

I contend that using this text as a motto and quasi-purpose statement of the Holy Christian Church has caused the North America church to lose the ability to clearly see the mission of God (*missio Dei*). It has created an irregular curvature of the church's eye, causing the church to have blurred vision. I know; it sounds a bit presumptuous. And who am I to be making such a diagnosis? Like I have said, I am not an academic teacher of theology, and I hold no position of notoriety. But I am a pastor who preaches, teaches, evangelizes, baptizes, communes, admonishes, forgives, marries, blesses, and buries. So I think there is a legitimate opportunity for me to add to the dialogue.

AN EYE EXAM

I will start the dialogue with a candid examination of my own tradition. We need to start somewhere, and I am not about to take pot shots at churches just because they are outside my own tradition. My aim is to engage all of us in the conversation. Thus, I begin with my own tradition.

In his book *Evangelical Style and Lutheran Substance,* David Luecke lifts up the centrality of the Great Commission as an imperative to the church. He also urges Lutherans to find "new ways" to receive power from God in order to do evangelism:

> Matthew is led to emphasize how Jesus left his followers with the command, "Go and make disciples of all nations." That this imperative is a command is even more apparent in the additional charge that we are to teach them to obey all that He commands. Through his encounter with God in Christ, Matthew was motivated to obey the instructions given him by his commander. With him, we today continue the divinely appointed mission of extending to all people of the world what we know and believe . . . Christians must always heed the Great Commission passed on by Matthew . . . Lutheran evangelism can be improved by finding new ways to receive the power from on high to share the joy that flows from it.[2]

The Great Commission is certainly Christ's words, which do, in and of themselves, convey some profound truths. However, evangelical Lutheran theology is uncertain about "finding new ways to receive the power from on high" when it has historically confessed it to come through nothing other than the Word of God and the Sacraments.

Consider the aforementioned emphasis at the 2001 LCMS Synod convention where Resolution 2–01 was adopted. It required that a Great Commission final *resolve* be added to every resolution that remained for consideration: "*Resolved,* That all action taken in this resolution shall be used to help carry out 'The Great Commission' and shall not in any way detract from the primary mission of God's kingdom here on earth."[3] A result of this has been that many Lutheran congregations, ministries, missions, pastors, and laymen are often being assessed on their faithfulness to the Great Commission—whatever that means.[4]

---

2. Luecke, *Evangelical Style and Lutheran Substance,* 44, 45.

3. The Lutheran Church—Missouri Synod, *2001 Convention Proceedings,* 5.

4. For example, consider the following emphasis intended for all congregations of my regional district to utilize and adopt: "*What is a Missional Congregation?* The members of a 'missional congregation' think, plan and act in alignment with God's calling in the Great Commission. The vision, mission, staffing, policies, priorities and budget are intentionally determined in light of the congregation's role to share the Gospel of Jesus Christ to their community. This key 'missional' aspect is as important as serving the needs of their own existing members." MN South District of The Lutheran Church—Missouri Synod, *A Missional Congregation: What does this mean?,* workshop handout,

Commenting on the potential shortfalls of this Great Commission emphasis, Harold Senkbeil succinctly states: "The central focus in preaching is often 'go and tell,' while the redemptive work of Christ upon his cross seems to have gone out of focus."[5] In other words, blurring has occurred. And it is impairing the church, her mission, and her theology. Senkbeil elaborates, "This emphasis on style over substance and method over message prompted one prominent Lutheran evangelist to remark already some years ago that in the Missouri Synod the so-called 'Great Commission' has become the material principle of theology."[6]

In short, there are apparent pitfalls that need to be addressed when using the Great Commission as a motto. But first, let me be clear: I recognize that the core of a Great Commission emphasis is certainly the desire to seek and save the lost, a desire we all share. Yes, I do want the unbelievers to know Jesus. Yes, I do care about them. And yes, we do need to go to great lengths to love them and reach out to them! (I just spent $500 today bailing a man out of jail for a DWI. He is a community member who is unchurched and an unbeliever. His wife called in desperation. She didn't have enough money to post bail. He had already been in jail for a week. He would lose his job if he did not get out. He was broken and contrite. He was desperate for forgiveness. He longed for a new beginning. Five hundred dollars from our congregation's help-a-neighbor fund was a small price to pay so that he could see and hear about the love and forgiveness of Jesus Christ.)

However, if we are being honest, the recent Great Commission emphasis has a reoccurring tendency to lose sight of the Gospel itself and subsequently create significant confusion within the church. I say this not to be antagonistic to the movement but as one dissatisfied with the movement's theology.

Thus, like an eye doctor who diagnoses blurred vision and provides corrective lenses to see clearly, I propose the third article and its explanation as corrective lenses to help bring the mission of God back into sharper focus, not at the expense of the lost, but rather, for the sake of the Gospel. It is the process that I journeyed through with my own congregation.

lines 1–4. Also on the district website, 12/13/11. http://mns.lcms.org/LinkClick.aspx?fi leticket=RLzxIFHDJbw%3d&tabid=186&mid=711.

5. Senkbeil, "Till the Trumpets Sound," 18.

6. Ibid.

But before we look through those lenses, an assessment of the Great Commission and its contemporary use is warranted. Thus, this chapter is fourfold in nature. It will consider the following: (1) a very brief exegetical look at the text (i.e., the actual translating of the original text, (2) the hermeneutical approach to the text (i.e., the interpretive principles used while translating and considering the text), (3) the historical treatments of the text as the "Great Commission," and (4) some practical implications and assessments for the church today.

AN EXEGETICAL LOOK

I offer a brief examination of the original Greek text below. However, I realize that not every reader will know the Greek. (My father-in-law is a great eye doctor, but whether it is Latin, Greek, or Hebrew, he gets a kick out of saying, "It's all Greek to me!") Therefore, I put my parsing and translation rationale in the footnotes and have the English Standard Version's translation underneath the Greek text. My translation rationale is implicitly integrated into the conversations on the text in order to avoid it becoming unduly academic or inaccessible to readers.

MATTHEW 28:18–20

18 καὶ προσελθὼν ὁ Ἰησοῦς ἐλάλησεν αὐτοῖς λέγων, Ἐδόθη μοι πᾶσα ἐξουσία ἐν οὐρανῷ καὶ ἐπὶ [τῆς] γῆς. 19 πορευθέντες[7] οὖν μαθητεύσατε[8]

---

7. πορευθέντες verb part (imper) aor pass dep nom masc 2nd per pl, from πορεύομαι go, proceed; travel, journey; NOTE: This verb should not be taken independent of μαθητεύσατε. "When two actions are connected with a single event, Matthew puts the aorist participle of the preparatory action before the aorist of the main verb. This sentence construction is so common that it may be designated a characteristic of Matthew's style." Adolf Schlatter, translated by David J. Bosch, "The Structure of Mission," 229. This means that *poreuthentes* and *matheteusate* (make disciples) refer to *one* event. Its use here is in the *pleonastic* sense. The "going" is not separate from the event expressed in the verb in the imperative mood.

8. μαθητεύσατε verb imper aor act 2nd per pl, from μαθητεύω trans. make a disciple of; intrans. (or pass.) be a disciple. NOTE: This verb only occurs four times in the NT: Matt 13:52; 27:57; 28:20; and Acts 14:21. This is the only instance when this verb occurs in the imperative mood. The thrust here is that "discipleship is determined by the relation to Christ himself, not by conformity to an impersonal ordinance." Bosch, *Transforming Mission*, 67.

πάντα τὰ ἔθνη⁹, βαπτίζοντες¹⁰αὐτοὺς εἰς τὸ ὄνομα τοῦ πατρὸς καὶ τοῦ υἱοῦ καὶ τοῦ ἁγίου πνεύματος, 20 διδάσκοντες¹¹ αὐτοὺς τηρεῖν¹² πάντα ὅσα ἐνετειλάμην¹³ ὑμῖν· καὶ ἰδοὺ ἐγὼ μεθ' ὑμῶν εἰμι πάσας τὰς ἡμέρας ἕως τῆς συντελείας τοῦ αἰῶνος.

ESV TRANSLATION

"And Jesus came and said to them, 'All authority in heaven and on earth has been given to me. Go therefore and make disciples of all nations, baptizing them in the name of the Father and of the Son and of the Holy Spirit, teaching them to observe all that I have commanded you. And behold, I am with you always, to the end of the age.'"

HERMENEUTICAL APPROACH

As Greek New Testament students learn, any translator of the New Testament must be mindful of Matthew's first-century community. They need to read these verses as he intended them to be understood by his first readers with all the fullness of what they encompassed. Any present-day pastor, missionary, or theologian does well to teach these verses with that context in mind.

As such, Jeffery Gibbs characterizes Matthew's account this way:

> Addressing a broad audience of Jewish and Gentile worshipping communities in Syria and Palestine during the middle of the first century AD, Matthew the apostle extended the Scriptures of

9. ἔθνη noun acc neut pl, from ἔθνος, ους n nation, people; τὰ ἔ. non-Jews, Gentiles; pagans, heathen, unbelievers ("no homogenous units implied—*panta ta ethne* is to be interpreted without any restriction whatsoever." Bosch)

10. βαπτίζοντες verb part (imper) pres act nom masc 2nd per pl , from βαπτίζω baptize; wash NOTE: This modal participle is taken as subordinate to μαθητεύσατε, and describes the manner in which disciple making occurs.

11. διδάσκοντες verb part (imper) pres act nom masc 2nd per pl, from διδάσκω (aor. pass. ἐδιδάχθην) teach NOTE: This modal participle is also taken as subordinate to μαθητεύσατε, and describes the manner in which disciple-making occurs. Further, "The teaching of verse 20 refers to the communication of the total revelation which God has given in Jesus and not only the call to faith." Scaer, "The Relation of Matthew 28:16–20 to the Rest of the Gospel," 256.

12. τηρεῖν verb inf pres act , from τηρέω keep, observe, obey, pay attention to.

13. ἐνετειλάμην verb ind aor mid dep 1st per sing , from ἐντέλλομαι (fut. ἐντελοῦ μαι; aor. ἐνετειλάμην, ptc. ἐντειλάμενος ; pf. ἐντέταλμαι) command, order: NOTE: What might the direct and understood referent be for this? See Matt. 19:21; 22:37–40.

Israel by authoritatively narrating how the end-time reign of God
had broken into the world through the historical deeds and the
words of Jesus of Nazareth, God's Son, and God's Christ.[14]

In other words, the whole of Matthew's Gospel account had something profound to say in terms of who Jesus was and what God had
done through him, not just in a few words, but in a complete picture
and total narrative. It was a prolific message of salvation that was for all
nations. But it was one that needed to be proclaimed in its entirety and
was greater than any one or two verses might imply. Present-day congregations, pastors, and missionaries are encouraged to note the depth
of this Gospel.

In fact, the renowned South African missiologist David Bosch
has much to say about this particular text, its relation to the rest of the
Gospel, and its relation to missions. First, he says:

> Any Christian can read and understand the Bible, but in this
> process "short-circuiting" inevitably occurs. It then becomes the
> theologian's responsibility to call the reader back to the context
> and intention of the biblical author and to draw attention to the
> distance that separates the present situation from that of the bib-
> lical story. A creative tension must be maintained between these
> two contexts, and we do ourselves a disservice if we immediately
> read our own situation back into the Bible.[15]

Thus, according to Bosch, simply utilizing these verses as an imperative and proof text for the church mandate to be missional would
not be exegetically or hermeneutically appropriate.

Accordingly, readers should see all the preceding verses and chapters that had been recorded by the evangelist as the referent to these
culminating verses of Matthew. As David Scaer observes:

> Matthew is clearly referring to what he has just set down in his
> Gospel and nothing else. His written Gospel is the "all things
> whatsoever" which Jesus taught. The reader is invited, not to go
> on to any other writings, but to return in a circular fashion to
> reread what he has just finished reading. "Scripture interprets
> Scripture," but here Matthew's Gospel, in the mind of the evange-
> list, is a satisfactorily complete document in itself.[16]

14. Gibbs, *Matthew 1:1—11:1*, 1.

15. Bosch, "The Structure of Mission," 226.

16. Scaer, "The Relation of Matthew 28:16–20 to the Rest of the Gospel," 256.

It becomes clear, then, that Matthew 28:18–20 should not be read and understood on its own, but only against the background of the entire first Gospel and of the constraints of the community to which the author belonged.

In fact, Bosch gives a clear and profound word of caution to those who might simply lift this verse out of its context as a mere motto or slogan:

> Today scholars agree that the entire Gospel points to these final verses: all the threads woven into the fabric of Matthew, from chapter 1 onward, draw together here. All this means that the way the "Great Commission" has traditionally been utilized in providing a biblical basis for mission has to be challenged or at least modified. It is inadmissible to lift these words out of Matthew's Gospel, as it were, allow them a life of their own, and understand them without any reference to the context in which they first appeared. Where this happens, the "Great Commission" is easily degraded to a mere slogan, or used as a pretext for what we in advance decided, perhaps unconsciously, it should mean.[17]

At a minimum, these words should give us pause to consider the integrity with which this text is used. One particular case in point would be to contrast the Great Commission text of chapter 28 with Matthew's account of Jesus's first commissioning (or sending) of the disciples in chapter 10. It would seem to stand that this first commissioning is a part of the Great Commission's "teaching them to observe all that I have commanded you." Yet, Jesus's first sending of the disciples is undeniably burdensome, filled with hardship and peril, not too family friendly, and, to be sure, not a strategic plan for success:

> And he called to him his twelve disciples and gave them authority over unclean spirits, to cast them out, and to heal every disease and every affliction. . . .These twelve Jesus sent out, instructing them, "Go nowhere among the Gentiles and enter no town of the Samaritans, but go rather to the lost sheep of the house of Israel. And proclaim as you go, saying, 'The kingdom of heaven is at hand' . . . And if anyone will not receive you or listen to your words, shake off the dust from your feet when you leave that house or town. Truly, I say to you, it will be more bearable on the day of judgment for the land of Sodom and Gomorrah than for that town. Behold, I am sending you out as sheep in the midst

17. Bosch, *Transforming Mission*, 57.

of wolves, so be wise as serpents and innocent as doves. Beware of men, for they will deliver you over to courts and flog you in their synagogues, and you will be dragged before governors and kings for my sake, to bear witness before them and the Gentiles . . . Brother will deliver brother over to death, and the father his child, and children will rise against parents and have them put to death, and you will be hated by all for my name's sake. But the one who endures to the end will be saved. When they persecute you in one town, flee to the next, for truly, I say to you, you will not have gone through all the towns of Israel before the Son of Man comes . . . Do not think that I have come to bring peace to the earth. I have not come to bring peace, but a sword. For I have come to set a man against his father, and a daughter against her mother, and a daughter-in-law against her mother-in-law. And a person's enemies will be those of his own household. Whoever loves father or mother more than me is not worthy of me, and whoever loves son or daughter more than me is not worthy of me. And whoever does not take his cross and follow me is not worthy of me. Whoever finds his life will lose it, and whoever loses his life for my sake will find it. Whoever receives you receives me, and whoever receives me receives him who sent me (Matthew 10).

Consequently, I think it is important for us to note that when Jesus sends the disciples on their second and expanded mission "to all nations" in Matthew 28, he retracts nothing of chapter 10. Rather, he simply adds the fullness of the Gospel promise to his directive to teach and baptize: "Baptizing them in the name of the Father and of the Son and of the Holy Spirit, teaching them to observe all that I have commanded you. And behold, I am with you always, to the end of the age." Thus, whether we like it or not, the realities of the mission given in chapter 10—persecution, division, rejection, and suffering—will also come with the expanded mission given in chapter 28. But now the promise that Jesus gives is that even when this happens, he is with us "always, to the end of the age."

Stanley Hauerwas, in his recent commentary on *Matthew* written for the previously noted *Brazos Theological Commentary Series*, gives an implicit critique of those who would forget this reality and assert the Great Commission as an imperative for the growth and success of the church. Commenting on Matthew 10, he writes:

Jesus' instruction for the disciples' mission, however, remains true for any understanding of Christian evangelism. Too often concerns for the status of the church tempts some to employ desperate measures to insure that the church will remain socially significant or at least have a majority of the population. But the church is not called to be significant or large. The church is called to be apostolic. Faithfulness, not numbers or status, should be the characteristic that shapes the witness of the church. Indeed it may well be the case in our time that God is unburdening the church so that we can again travel light.[18]

Hauerwas' final sentence is no doubt a biting criticism of various movements in the North American church, some of which will be examined in greater detail in chapters 4 and 5. Nonetheless, the point has been that from an exegetical and hermeneutical perspective, the popular use of this text as a self-standing mission mantra is highly questionable, to say the least.

MATTHEW 28:18–20 IN THE LUTHERAN CONFESSIONS

The use of the Great Commission as a proof text for the mission of the church remains a relatively recent phenomenon. Yet its dominant status can be detected across the spectrum of church bodies. How it came to have this status is an interesting story. What we will find is that it did not arise out of deep theological reflection, but rather one man's deep personal conviction needing some scriptural backing.

But before we take a look at that story, I want to take a brief look at how the theological documents of an established and long-standing church have treated the Great Commission text itself. In this case, conveniently I will admit, I will use my own Lutheran tradition. The extensive theological documents of this tradition have been officially recognized since 1580 and have been compiled in *The Book of Concord*.[19]

18. Hauerwas, *Matthew*, 107.

19. The title page of the original compilation of documents reads: "Concordia: Christian, Recapitulated, Unanimous Confession of the Teaching and Faith of the Undersigned Electors, Princes, and Estates of the Augsburg Confession and of their Theologians [Whose Names Are Subscribed at the End of the Book.] With an Appended declaration—Well-Grounded in the Word of God as the Only Guiding— of Several Articles about Which Controversy and Strife Occurred after Dr. Martin Luther's Blessed Death. Prepared for Publication by the Unanimous Agreement and Order of the Aforementioned Electors, Princes, and Estates for the Instruction and Admonition of Their Lands, Churches, Schools, and Descendants." Kolb and Wengert,

It, therefore, serves our discussion as the oldest and most well-defined protestant tradition. How it treats this particular text will provide a helpful perspective both in what it says and what it does not say.

To begin, the Great Commission is not referenced as the Great Commission in the Lutheran Confessions. To be sure, the biblical text of Matthew 28:18–20 is certainly referenced, but not as the sole means to establish the mission of the church. The emphasis placed on this text within the body of the confessions surrounds two general issues: (1) the authority that has been given to the resurrected Christ and (2) Christ's instruction on baptism. For brevity, the references below note each respective section where the text is cited.

- Apology of the Augsburg Confession, Article IX, Baptism, 2.

- The Small Catechism, Baptism, 4.

- The Large Catechism, Preface, 21–22 & Fourth Part: Concerning Baptism, 4.

- Treatise on the Power and Primacy of the Pope, 31 (discussing the nature of "authority").

- Formula of Concord, Epitome, Article VIII, *Concerning the Person of Christ* (especially v. 18 "all authority") and Solid Declaration, Article VII *Holy Supper* & Article VIII, *Person of Christ,* (v. 18 "all authority").

In sum, the Lutheran confessions take the Scriptures as a whole. The Great Commission does not separately or formally have a part of defining the work and mission of the church apart from the greater context of the Scriptures in which it occurs. This is why Article VII of the Augsburg Confession simply states: "The Church is the assembly of saints in which the Gospel is taught purely and the sacraments are administered rightly."[20] Much like the third article of the Apostles' Creed, it confesses the Gospel, the community of saints, and the sacraments.

True, there is an emphasis on *purely* and *rightly*. However, that is not license to focus on the rigidity and propriety that each adverb could afford, lifting up a pharisaical attitude of purity and correctness to the exclusion of reaching out to the lost. Nonetheless, *purely* and *rightly* does carry a necessary expectation. As we noted in the third article of the

---

Book of Concord, 3.

20 Ibid, AC VII, § 1.

Apostles' Creed, those things that do not keep the church "with Jesus Christ in the one common true faith" are not the work of the Holy Spirit. Neither would they constitute church teaching and practice *purely* or *rightly*.

At a minimum, when a long-standing and well-defined theological tradition offers no commentary on this text as mandating mission text, perhaps there is cause for us to pause and consider how we are using it.

HISTORY OF THE GREAT COMMISSION

In a recent volume titled *The Great Commission: Evangelicals and the History of World Missions,* contributing author Douglas Sweeny observes: "The 'Great Commission' found in Matthew 28 has shaped our evangelical movement as much as any passage of Scripture. Though entrusted by the Lord Jesus Christ to His disciples before His ascension, it suffered sore neglect from most believers through the ages. During the past few hundred years, however, thanks in large part to the work of evangelical missionaries, it has played a powerful role in the rapid spread of the Christian faith—numerically, culturally, and geographically."[21] It's a bold claim.

But whether this is actually the case seems questionable since other present studies have revealed that such intense mission fervor by the church has not actually yielded the rapid success espoused above. Consider what Detlev Schulz offers:

> Christianity has voiced its optimism of those who have and continue to envision total world evangelization . . . Many evangelical groups conceived of mission in unrealistically optimistic terms . . . Today, this optimism has surfaced again. In the late 1980s many denominations and movements prepared for global evangelization in the forthcoming decade (the 1990s) which they declared to be the decade of evangelism. Denominations and movements of every kind—whether Protestant, Evangelical, Ecumenical, Roman Catholic, or Pentecostal/Charismatic—launched global plans and made solemn pledges to complete Christ's commission on earth in that decade. But as Barret points out, the results of such campaigns were disappointing. The envisaged ten-year period of unstoppable expansion of Christianity did not materialize. Despite an overall increase in expenditure

21. Sweeney, *The Great Commission*, 1.

during that period (topping more than $70 billion), Christianity made no substantial progress.[22]

The contrasting claims are fascinating, to say the least. To be sure, "the rapid spread of the Christian faith" would be a wonderful event indeed. But given the substantiated, and much less triumphal assessment by Schulz, could the "rapid spread" referenced above be more about the spread of the Great Commission itself, rather than "the rapid spread of the Christian faith— numerically, culturally, and geographically?"

The following is a brief compilation on the history and use of the Great Commission, particularly as it has emerged primarily out of protestant evangelical thought. Its appeal is portrayed as profound. But given the confusion that exists in the church today it is debatable on just how effective the Great Commission as motto actually really is. In fact, there is evidence that there have been adverse affects from using it as a motto for the church.

GREAT COMMISSION AS MOTIVATION

Most present-day evangelicals regard Matthew 28:18–20 as the major, if not sole, motivation for mission. However, what do we know about the use of this text prior to the sixteenth century, or in the early church for that matter? Once again, David Bosh is invaluable:

> The first point that strikes the careful reader is that none of the passages which are usually referred to as parallels to the Matthean Great Commission (Lk. 25:45–49; John 20:21; Acts 1:8) contains a *command* to do mission work. As a matter of fact, the Great Commission does not function anywhere in the New Testament. It is never referred to or appealed to by the early church. It is therefore quite clear that the early church did not embark on the mission to Jews and Gentiles simply because it had been told to do so. This would place mission in the context of legalism. Mission would then have been depersonalized . . . As Roland Allen (1962 and 1968) and Harry Boer (1961) have argued cogently, the early Christian mission was an essential result of Pentecost. It was this event that became the driving force for mission. The "debt" or "obligation" Paul had to Greeks and non-Greeks (Rom 1:14) was the debt of *gratitude,* not of *duty.* Newbigin aptly said, "we have regarded witness as a demand laid upon us instead of seeing it as a gift promised to us" (1979). Or, with reference to Acts 1:8, "The

22. Schulz, *Mission from the Cross,* 7.

word, 'You shall be my witnesses,' is not a command to be obeyed, but a promise to be trusted (Newbigin, 1978; Allen, 1962).[23]

Also, recognizing that the Great Commission "does not function anywhere in the New Testament," Rolland Allen also makes a thoughtful observation: "Had the Lord not given any such command, had the Scriptures never contained such a form of words . . . the obligation to preach the Gospel to all nations would not have been diminished by a single iota. For the obligation depends not upon what he orders, but upon what He is, and the Spirit of Christ is the Spirit of Divine love and compassion and desire for souls astray from God."[24] It becomes apparent then that the Great Commission was not used as a directive for the early church or even for subsequent centuries of church history.

ORIGINS OF A MANDATING TEXT

It was not until the late eighteenth-century that the Great Commission was first considered as a mandating text. It was the renowned Baptist missionary William Carey who brought this text to light. Carrying a deep conviction for world missions, he was the first to make inroads into what was considered to be a prevalent apathy about this mission in his famous, *An Enquiry into the Obligations of Christians to Use Means for the Conversion of the Heathens* (1792).

Carey's logic, notes Bosch, was simple: "If the commission to make disciples of all nations were restricted to the apostles' then the command to baptize (Mt. 28:19) and the promise of Christ's abiding presence (Mt. 28:20) should be subject to this limitation! Carey won the argument, and a large-scale Protestant missionary enterprise was launched from Europe and North America. Ever since, it has been customary to base missions on the Great Commission."[25]

However, it remains curious how a relatively recent and primarily evangelical development—one that did not have any specific New Testament, early, medieval or Reformation church tradition—came into regular practice by the majority of North American churches.

23. Bosch, "The Structure of Mission," 219–20.
24. Allen, *Missionary Principles*, 31.
25. Bosch, "The Structure of Mission," 218.

CONTEMPORARY USE OF THE GREAT COMMISSION

In 1979, the Constitution of the Evangelical Foreign Missions Association in the USA explicitly affirmed obedience to the Great Commission as the primary motive for mission. In 1980, students who applied to the Student Consultation on Frontier Mission in Edinburgh were asked to sign a declaration which read, in part, "I will make the Great Commission the commanding purpose of my life for the rest of my life."[26] In short, many churches in North America regard it as the *Magna Charta* of mission. A brief survey of recent authors and their appeal to the Great Commission will demonstrate its constant and repeated use.

In 1995, Rick Warren published his *Purpose Driven Church*. At the core of every church's purpose, he claims, should be the Great Commandment and the Great Commission: "A Great Commitment to the Great Commandment and the Great Commission will grow a Great Church."[27] It is a neat little slogan.

He then follows that by identifying the five tasks he says Christ ordained as purposes of the church from these two texts: "A *purpose-driven* church is committed to fulfilling all five tasks that Christ ordained for his church to accomplish . . . 1) Love the Lord with all your heart. 2) Love your neighbor as yourself. 3) Go and make disciples. 4) Baptizing them. 5) Teaching them to obey."[28] It became a standard for many with countless authors following suit.

In 2000, Mark Mittelberg published *Building a Contagious Church*. His appeal to the Great Commission was fervent and frequent:

> [T]he words of Jesus in the Great Commission are seared in our minds . . . This mandate was given for all churches of all time, so it includes every one of us who is a part of those congregations. Since we all agree we are supposed to be carrying out the Great Commission, why aren't we doing more about it?[29]

> We were made to fulfill the Great Commission. I believe evangelizing is the primary reason God left us here on the planet. We can spend all of eternity worshipping God, learning from his Word, praying to him, and encouraging and edifying one

26. Bosch, "The Structure of Mission," 243.

27. Warren, *The Purpose Drive Church*, 103.

28. Ibid., 103–6.

29. Mittleberg, *Building A Contagious Church*, 20.

another. But only here and now do we have the chance to reach the lost people for Christ.[30]

Jesus gave us our universal mission statement in the Great Commission, and any church that neglects any aspect of it—including the "making disciples" part—is disregarding his divine mandate.[31]

What about your church or ministry? Is your mission clear? Is it aligned with the Great Commission? Is it known by your people and in the minds of your leaders?[32]

The Great Commission is portrayed as a law that must be obeyed on pain of divine disobedience. Many others have similar portrayals.

In his 2003 book *The Present Future,* Reggie McNeal states that, "If we are not focusing on Missiology then we are being disobedient to the Great Commission."[33] Thom Rainer, in his 2005 book *Break Out Churches,* says, "It is a sin to be good if God has called us to be great. Christians refer to Matthew 28:18–20 as the Great Commission, not the Good Commission."[34] (He then unpacks and measures "greatness" in terms of church attendance where a "break out" can be tracked.)

In their 2006 book *Breaking the Missional Code,* Ed Stetzer and David Putman note, "Jesus gave four directives that outline the missional mandate of the church. They challenge his followers with the call to be on mission, and they serve as the instruction manual for missional ministry. Each time Jesus gave a sending command, it was spoken to a group of his disciples. These commands are still in effect for the church today, his current disciples."[35]

Paul Borden's *Direct Hit: Aiming Real Leaders at the Mission Field* (2006) asserts that, "Effective congregations—defined by the ability to fulfill the Great Commission— have outstanding leaders. This is true for new church plants, growing congregations, or congregations who desperately need transformation. Some might say this principle is

---

30. Ibid., 21.
31. Ibid., 25.
32. Ibid., 26.
33. McNeal, *The Present Future,* 51.
34. Rainer, *Break Out Churches,* 15.
35. Stetzer and Putman, *Breaking the Missional Code,* 30.

self-evident, but with so many dying and ineffective churches, is it really obvious that the leader is key?"[36] There are countless others.

Each quote demonstrates the continued affinity for using the Great Commission as a missional imperative for the church today. Ironic is the insinuation that somehow the church has lost its purpose and that these few verses have now clarified the real purpose and meaning of the Holy Christian Church. It has become an infectious claim. Without question, it is present among my own church body. Congregations, pastors, leaders, and teachers continue to hear about these claims regarding the Great Commission.

In a January 2008 paper at the *Transforming Congregations Network* conference, LCMS California-Nevada-Hawaii District President Robert D. Newton attempted to bring some thoughtful Lutheran considerations to this issue when he raised the following question:

> Is the call for Christians to participate in Christ's mission Law or Gospel? That's not the way we ordinarily hear that question. The question goes more like: Is the call for Christians to obey the Great Commission Law or Gospel? Note the difference in "obey the Great Commission" and "participate in Christ's mission." I think it's equally important not only to answer the question biblically but to ask it biblically. In this case it's much more appropriate or accurate to speak about participating in Christ's mission rather than our obeying the Great Commission . . . In the business of obeying the Great Commission, the word *obedience* must be understood in the same way we speak of obedience in reference to the Gospel. Often we refer to saving faith as obedience to the Gospel. That is, we receive by faith the gift of eternal life won for us by our Lord Jesus Christ. We are able to disobey the Gospel promise only by refusing to receive it. We are also able to obey it only by believing it and embracing it as our own. That is not a law. That is faith born by the Gospel of our Lord Jesus Christ. Justification by faith alone is the centerpiece of Lutheran theology.[37]

Though he attempts to defend the use of the Great Commission from a Lutheran law/Gospel perspective, it is, nonetheless, another example of how the Great Commission as directive for the church continues to be a pervading issue.

36. Borden, *Direct Hit*, 19.
37. The paper was entitled "Accountability and Faithfulness in Reaching the Lost."

IS IT WORKING?

To be sure, motivation to seek and save the lost is a good thing. And again, let me be clear, I do care for the lost and want them to come to the knowledge of salvation. However, the question being asked is: at what theological cost does this motivation come? Is there any evidence to suggest that using the Great Commission as the motivating and defining purpose of the church has any actual negative consequences? Consider Fred W. Beuttler's evangelical insider assessment about Great Commission congregations:

> The great progress of the past century of American missions has stressed evangelism and individual conversion, illustrated by a recent sermon in a Pentecostal congregation interpreting the Great Commission as "evangelism, evangelism, evangelism." But evangelism is not mentioned in Matthew 28:19–20; rather it is a call to "make disciples." Over the past generations the Church has learned the meaning of *ethne*. Perhaps this generation will focus on the discipling task as we seek to obey for the next "great century."[38]

At a minimum, the implication is that the church has lost sight of making disciples in her zeal to reach the lost. It appears her vision has become blurred.

Also consider original *Church Growth* pioneer Donald McGavran and his approach to the verses of Matthew 28:18–20 (see specifically his works *How Churches Grow: The New Frontiers of Mission*, 1966; "How about that New Verb 'to disciple?'" from *Church Growth Bulletin 15:5*, May, 1979; and *Understanding Church Growth*, 1980). In short, notes Bosch, *discipling* is used by McGavran as a synonym for *evangelizing*, and it consists, in his view, of going to unreached people with the Gospel and persuading them to "turn from idols to serve the living God." It therefore concerns only the initial conversion experience of a homogenous group of people. Any further activity toward building up these converts is covered by Jesus's "teaching them all things" and is designated as "perfecting," which is a term found in Eph 4:12.[39] Zeal for the lost is good, but again, not at the expense of discipleship.

---

38. Beuttler, "Evangelical Missions in Modern America," 132.
39. Bosch, "The Structure of Mission," 231.

But are these isolated incidences, or is there more to this? Current literature and recent blogging suggests the latter. In fact, recent church studies reported by *Christianity Today* actually show the potential shortcomings of using a Great Commission as a missional motto as well as how such mentalities, zealous as they are, can actually contribute to a lack of discipleship:

> After modeling a seeker-sensitive approach to church growth for three decades, Willow Creek Community Church now plans to gear its weekend services toward mature believers seeking to grow in their faith. The change comes on the heels of an ongoing four-year research effort first made public late last summer in *Reveal: Where Are You?*, a book coauthored by executive pastor Greg Hawkins . . . Since 1975, Willow Creek has avoided conventional church approaches, using its Sunday services to reach the unchurched through polished music, multimedia, and sermons referencing popular culture and other familiar themes. The church's leadership believed the approach would attract people searching for answers, bring them into a relationship with Christ, and then capitalize on their contagious fervor to evangelize others.
>
> But the analysis in *Reveal*, which surveyed congregants at Willow Creek and six other churches, suggested that evangelistic impact was greater from those who self-reported as "close to Christ" or "Christ-centered" than from new church attendees. In addition, a quarter of the "close to Christ" and "Christ-centered" crowd described themselves as spiritually "stalled" or "dissatisfied" with the role of the church in their spiritual growth. Even more alarming to Willow Creek: About a quarter of the "stalled" segment and 63 percent of the "dissatisfied" segment contemplated leaving the church . . . As Willow Creek expanded its research into churches of varying geographic locations, sizes, and ethnic and denominational backgrounds, the church said the same general pattern emerged, an indication that the problem extends beyond Willow Creek.[40]

Willow Creek is to be applauded for their willingness to take stock and self-assess. It is always good for churches to reflect on what they are teaching and confessing. But it appears that they are not the only ones in need of doing some self-assessment.

40. Branaugh, "Willow Creek's Huge Shift," May 15, 2008, http://www.christianity-today.com/ct/2008/june/5.13.html.

MOUNTING EVIDENCE

To that end, evaluations of the recent "missional" emphasis continue to be offered. Most notable are those being made by the pioneers and practitioners of the movement itself. Consider the following September 14, 2011, post from the popular evangelical website *www.vergenetwork.com* titled, "Why the Missional Movement Will Fail," written by missional guru Mike Breen:

> It's time we start being brutally honest about the missional movement that has emerged in the last 10–15 years: Chances are better than not it's going to fail. That may seem cynical, but I'm being realistic. There is a reason so many movements in the Western church have failed in the past century: They are a car without an engine. A missional church or a missional community or a missional small group is the new car that everyone is talking about right now, but no matter how beautiful or shiny the vehicle, without an engine, it won't go anywhere.[41]

What is the engine that is missing? Without question, Breen says, it is discipleship. In short, he says that the North American church has become so obsessed with getting the message out (i.e., being missional) that they are failing to get the message right. Consequently, they are failing to make true disciples. He notes: "We took 30 days and examined the Twitter conversations happening. We discovered there are between 100–150 times as many people talking about mission as there are discipleship (to be clear, that's a 100:1). We are a group of people addicted to and obsessed with the work of the Kingdom, with little to no idea how to be with the King."[42]

Breen goes on to cite an intriguing post from another popular missional website (www.outofur.com) written by Skye Jethani and titled, "Has the Mission Become Our Idol?" Here too there is an internal alarm being sounded about the recent missional push by the North American church. Jethani offers no small indictment: "[M]any church leaders unknowingly replace the transcendent vitality of a life *with* God for the ego satisfaction they derive from a life *for* God." Then he adds this provocative note:

---

41. Breen, "Why the Missional Movement will fail," September 14, 2011, http://www.vergenetwork.org/2011/09/14/mike-breen-why-the-missional-movement-will-fail/.
42. Ibid.

> When we come to believe that our faith is primarily about what
> we can do *for* God in the world, it is like throwing gasoline on
> our fear of insignificance. The resulting fire may be presented to
> others as a godly ambition, a holy desire to see God's mission
> advance—the kind of drive evident in the Apostle Paul's life.
> But when these flames are fueled by fear they reveal none of the
> peace, joy, or love displayed by Paul and rooted in the Spirit.
> Instead the relentless drive to prove our worth can quickly be-
> come destructive.[43]

It is no small admission when the missional movements' own leaders are sounding such alarms. Still, it is not that they are necessarily
giving up on the movement. They want to offer a course correction to
the overall missional movement's perceived correction for the greater
church. However, it is interesting that the course correction they are urging is what historic creedal theology has long maintained to be a part of
the mission of the church: "the making of disciples."

Breen's sentiments echo this: "While the 'missional' conversation
is imbued with the energy and vitality that comes with kingdom work,
it seems to be missing some of the hallmark reality that those of us who
have lived it over time have come to expect: Mission is messy. It's humbling. There's often no glory in it. It's for the long haul. And it's completely unsustainable without discipleship."[44] These are powerful sentiments
that we cannot afford to ignore.

GETTING THE MESSAGE OUT OR GETTING THE MESSAGE RIGHT?

Nonetheless, the notion of "getting the message out" (as opposed to "getting the message right") remains an intense push among many North
American congregations,[45] so much so that, as we'll note in chapters 4

43. Jethani, "Has the Mission Become Our Idol?," July 18, 2011, http://www.outofur
.com/archives/2011/07/has_mission_bec.html.

44. Breen, "Why the Missional Movement will fail," September 14, 2011.

45. Note Raschke's insight: "The Great Commission, as many close readers of the
Gospel text itself have emphasized, is not really about getting the message out. It is not,
as hucksters have tended to spin it, simply about marketing the distinctive name brand
we call Christianity from Toronto to Timbuktu in much the same way that fast-food
or consumer commodities are promoted and sold in a variety of different cultures. It is
about manifesting and making real the meaning of the paradox of the incarnation and
the miracle of Christ's resurrection. The Great Commission, when all is said and done,
rests upon the great postmodern preposition—the 'with' of divine relation as contrasted

and 5, it is motivating some to take increasingly confusing steps toward that end. But is there any evidence that the priority of "getting the message out" has somehow morphed into getting the message wrong?

Christian Smith's 2005 book *Soul Searching: The Religious and Spiritual Lives of American Teenagers* answers in the affirmative. In the largest survey ever of its kind, Smith and his team assessed the faith life of American teens and their families. What he found is that despite all the concerted efforts of Evangelicalism to Christianize American culture for the last three decades, America has its own unique religion. Called "moralistic therapeutic deism," people "believe God exists" but only to "help them when they are in need," yet "wants them to be good, fair, and nice," but is otherwise "uninvolved in their life." But in the end, "Good people go to heaven when they die."[46] When this is compounded with what missional guru Skye Jethani observes about the profound pressure people feel to be missional, the potential to get the message wrong continues to grow:

> Sometimes the people who fear insignificance the most are driven to accomplish the greatest things. As a result they are highly praised within Christian communities for their good works. This temporarily soothes their fear until the next goal can be achieved. But there is a dark side to this drivenness. Gordon MacDonald calls it "missionalism." It is "the belief that the worth of one's life is determined by the achievement of a grand objective." Missionalism starts slowly and gains a foothold in the leader's attitude. Before long the mission controls almost everything: time, relationships, health, spiritual depth, ethics, and convictions. In advanced stages, missionalism means doing whatever it takes to solve the problem. In its worst iteration, the end always justifies the means. The family goes; health is sacrificed; integrity is jeopardized; God-connection is limited.[47]

---

with the 'is' of doctrinal propositions. God is never what he is 'in himself.' God is always *mit uns* (with us) or *für uns* (for us), as Luther insisted. He is what he is *in relation to us*. The Great Commission, which Jesus pronounced at the same location where he delivered the Sermon on the Mount, transforms the Christian faith into something that is much more than a new torah, or instruction, from on high. It is not divine revelation so much as it is divine relation, a relationship that is 'with us always.' It is relation that must be propagated until the 'end of time.'" Rascke, *GloboChrist*, 48.

46. Smith, *Soul Searching*, 162–63.

47. Jethani, "Has the Mission Become Our Idol?," July 18, 2011.

The evidence is significant. Confusion exists. Uncertainty is present. Vision is blurred. A corrective is in order. To spur such an endeavor on, David Bosch comes to the following conclusion:

> Mission (or disciple-making) avoids becoming a heavy burden, a new law, a command to obey. The disciples' involvement in mission is a logical consequence of their being "discipled unto Jesus" and of the "full authority" given to him (notice the "therefore" in Mt. 28:19). "You are my witnesses *because* you have been with me" (Jn 15:26). To be involved in mission is to receive a gift, not to obey a law; to accept a promise, not to bow to a command. Christ's promised presence (Mt. 28:10) "is not a reward offered to those who obey: it is the assurance that those who are commanded will be able to obey." So the Great Commission is not a commission in the ordinary sense of the word, but rather a creative statement, in the manner of Genesis 1:3 and elsewhere, "Let there be . . ."[48]

Speaking of the Great Commission with *gift* language begins to focus things back to the wider mission of God. It also provides a beginning corrective to the myopic nature of missionalism, and it focuses on keeping the church, as Luther writes, "with Jesus Christ in the one common true faith."[49]

FOCUSING THE MISSION

In the end, keeping the Great Commission in the context of Matthew's Gospel account, as well as in the greater context of the whole Gospel message, gives focus and faithfulness to the this mission. Klaus Detlev Schulz notes the broader significance of this Matthew text and, in fact, argues for the elevation of multiple Great Commission texts. He contends they are all to be seen in the light of their New Testament context, not to mention the greater history of the Holy Christian Church:

> Representatives in mission should carefully consult Scripture for the validity of a shift in strategy. "Old fashioned" ideals of what missionaries once did are perhaps not that outdated after all. It seems as if the Great Commission texts point out a method that should remain with the Church for all times. They encourage

48. Bosch, "The Structure of Mission," 243.

49. Kolb and Wengert, SC, Third Article, § 6, Luther's Small Catechism explanation on the third article of the Apostles' Creed.

the sending of individuals authorized to make disciples through Baptism and instruction (Matthew 28) and of imparting the forgiveness of sins through preaching and absolution (John 20).[50]

When the texts of Scripture are treated in this manner, the mission stays clear and the message stays focused.

Stanley Hauerwas's Brazos theological commentary on *Matthew* gives a complementary example of this. He keeps Matthew 28:18–20 in the context of all Jesus's ministry, not once mentioning the phrase Great Commission, and paints a distinct picture of the mission of the Holy Christian Church:

> [Jesus] alone has the authority to send the disciples to the world to make disciples of all the nations. He first sent the disciples only to Israel (10:5–6), but now he sends the disciples to all the world to baptize them in the name of the Father, Son, and Holy Spirit.
>
> What had been hidden from the foundation of the world, what has been hidden from the wise, is now revealed by the Son. The God of Israel is the God of all nations. The disciples are now equipped to be sent to the nations, baptizing them into the death and resurrection of Jesus to make them citizens of his death-defying kingdom. Israel is not to be left behind, but rather its mission now continued in a new reality called church. Through the church all nations will learn to call Israel blessed.
>
> The church, moreover, is but the name of a people who have been formed to worship the Father, the Son, and the Holy Spirit. To worship that God is to live a life described by Jesus in the Sermon on the Mount. Therefore, Jesus commands his disciples to teach those whom they baptize to obey all that he has commanded. Jesus's death and resurrection cannot be separated from the way he has taught us to live. The Sermon on the Mount, how we are to serve one another as brothers and sisters, the forgiveness required by our willingness to expose the sin of the church, is salvation. The teaching and the teacher are one. The salvation that Jesus entrusts to his disciples is the Gospel of Matthew.
>
> The disciples are to remember that the mission on which Jesus sends them is not one on which they must go alone. He is the resurrected Lord who will always be with those entrusted to witness to him and his work. He was in the beginning, which means that he can promise to be at the end of the age. But the age that he will be present at the end of is the age inaugurated by his birth, ministry, death and resurrection. On that basis and that

50. Schulz, *Mission from the Cross*, 9.

basis alone Christians are sent to the world with the message: "Repent, for the kingdom of heaven is present.[51]

Hauerwas keeps it all connected. From Jesus's Sermon on the Mount to Jesus's first sending of the disciples, from Israel to all nations, everything remains connected to the life, death, and resurrection of Jesus Christ. In this way, the life Jesus gives His church to live and the mission He sends His church on are inextricably bound to the entirety of who Jesus is. The mission of the church is, therefore, the mission of God as it flows from the Gospel, given to those entrusted to pass it on through the communities of saints called "church" and witnessed in the lives that they live.

But with all of that said, I do recognize that the influences of postmodernism have also created massive confusion for the church in North America. Its influences have yielded an "emerging" church growth movement that has precipitated the recent missional movement (and its corresponding nomenclature). Therefore, as we journey toward looking at the church through creedal lenses (and third article bifocals), we will first need to take a look at the postmodern culture of North America and its impact on the church and how it might influence a strategic plan.

51. Hauerwas, *Matthew*, 249.

Chapter 3

Postmodern Confusion

THE CULTURE OF OUR TIMES

As I CONSIDERED HOW to craft a theologically based strategic plan, I realized it had to communicate a practical way of doing outreach. The congregation's 2002 strategic plan had focused on the construction of a new, technology-oriented outreach center. It provided the congregation with what was thought to be a very concrete way of doing outreach. I wanted to continue that perception. But I wanted to do it in a way that flowed more naturally out of our confession of faith and in a way that was consistent with my bourgeoning affirmation of the historic mission of the church.

I recognized that as our postmodern (and, by some standards, post-postmodern) society pressed forward, new technology uses and gadgets were coming on the scene every day. It is certainly a sign of our times. It is also certainly how a good number of people communicate and interact. However, just as constructing a new building to try to make connections with people seemed incomplete, the idea of relying solely on becoming technologically savvy did not seem the most accurate.

Yes, congregations certainly need to be aware of technology and utilize it. We committed to a website overhaul, created a Facebook page for our school, integrated Smart Boards into all of our school classrooms, and use all appropriate technology to aid our worship services. But that still could not be the bottom line for our strategic plan.

Considering the nature of the third article of the Apostles' Creed, I finally saw an obvious connection staring me in the face: the community of saints. The Holy Christian Church is certainly a community of people who are regularly in relation to others, and very often it is with others who are not a part of the Christian community. At home, at work, or in the local community, the Holy Christian Church is made up of relational people. Recognizing this and desiring to explore how we might best reach out to unbelievers, I set out to investigate the culture of our times.

I was familiar with the North American postmodern ethos, but the deeper I dug, the more fascinated I became, not only with the spiritual confusion of our times, but also by the tremendous opportunity to reach out to the people of our culture.

WHEN I WATCH TV

To be sure, I became no expert on postmodernism, although I am certainly conversant about it. I recognize the academics who live and breathe it are far more apt at describing all the nuances, intricacies, and certainties (or perhaps better said, the uncertainties of it). Nonetheless, thanks to my eye doctor and the corrective lens he has prescribed for me, I can regularly watch postmodernism. In fact, it would be rare for a person living in North America not to see it. They may not be aware they are seeing it, but they are seeing it nonetheless.

As Gene Edward Veith has noted, "The entertainment industry spreads postmodernist ideology into every home with a TV set."[1] Add in YouTube, Hulu, TiVo, DVRs, and the massive influx of satellite and cable TV, and it is a significant proliferation. "Television, in general, is considered to be postmodern because it is like a tornado of images that whirl by with such velocity that they have been stripped of all meaning—referring only to other images—the audience having reached the point of total saturation as the meaningless images glow and flicker, making the viewer into a kind of mindscreen."[2] Anthropologists and TV commentators alike are having a heyday in observing how technology is aiding the expansion of a philosophy.

---

1. Veith, *Postmodern Times*, 95.
2. Powell, *Postmodernism for Beginners*, 143.

A February 24, 2009, CNN report headline read, "*TV Viewing at an All Time High*."[3] The report cited "the Nielsen Company's latest 'three screen' report," noting that "the average American television viewer is watching more than 151 hours of television per month—an 'all-time' high—up from more than 145 hours during the same period the previous year." The increase in television watching is "part of a long-term trend," which has been attributed to a greater availability of televisions as well as online viewing.

In a telling observation, the Nielsen spokesman noted that, "The average household has more televisions than people." Increased viewing was also attributed to the substantial amount of what was called "niche programming" because of the "many, many more cable channels than before." The report noted that "digital recorders, DVR and TiVo devices" have also contributed to the increase as they "allow viewers to watch programs at their leisure rather than during the show's slated time slots." Add in movie rentals, instant movies from Netflix and Blockbuster, along with any movie theater going hours, and there is no small exposure to the contemporary entertainment industry.

It should be no surprise, then, that the people of North America are influenced and shaped by what they watch. For example, in the 1990s, the most popular comedy show (and for two years, the most popular overall TV show) was *Seinfeld*. It was self-admittedly a show "about nothing." It often focused on the inconvenient minutia of life and the trivial details of relationships. Yet the show was such a cultural phenomenon that in 2002 TV Guide named it the best show of all time. The irony is uncanny. What is it that made a show about nothing so popular to almost everyone?

SHOWS ABOUT NOTHING

In his book *Shows About Nothing*, Thomas Hibbs examines *Seinfeld* along with other shows like *Ally McBeal* and *The Simpsons,* as well as movies like *Seven*, *LA Confidential*, and *Pulp Fiction* to explore the growing nihilism (meaninglessness) in pop culture.[4] He then elaborated on his observations at a university lecture:

3. CNN online article, "TV Viewing at an All Time high,"1/10/11, http://articles .cnn.com/2009-02-24/entertainment/us.video.nielsen_1_nielsen-company-nielsen-spokesman-gary-holmes-watching?_s=PM:SHOWBIZ.

4. Hibbs, *Shows About Nothing*. Nihilism is from the Latin *nihil* that means

> Seinfeld is a way of thinking through what nihilism really means
> . . . it's devoid of fundamental meaning or final purpose . . .
> Compared to the basic, classical structure of older sitcoms, such
> as *The Honeymooners* or *I Love Lucy*, *Seinfeld* marks a decisive
> break. *Seinfeld* goes for the art of the unhappy, but the very funny.[5]

He continued by noting how the role of the modern family also comes under this meaningless analysis. Where older shows concentrated on the family unit, Seinfeld focused primarily on single individuals. He further noted how shows like *The Simpsons* combine family and nihilism (meaninglessness) through the development of their characters. Consider how Homer is more of a child than he is a father figure. As Hibbs notes, he is "barely rational," "inarticulate," and displays a "primitive, subhuman state of nature."[6]

Thus, while the nihilistic sitcom formula "destroys the possibility of the family," Hibbs said it is secondary to the relationships themselves. He observes, "Cold calculations replace love and romance," where the characters deal with trivial things in relationships. For instance, Jerry breaks up with a woman because she has "a man's hands." Thus, the idea of a perpetual adolescence compels the *Seinfeld* characters. The goal, says Hibbs, is to attain the advantages of an adult while retaining the responsibilities of a child. But the characters fail to achieve this, and very little of everything else they want, which leads to the show's theme and overwhelming skepticism about the pursuit of happiness.[7] It is a fascinating analysis, particularly for those of us who grew up watching these shows.

What is more, though these shows were being reported on at the end of the 1990s and we are now into the second decade of 2000s, the *Simpsons* still remain a part of regular programming and in syndication.[8] *Seinfeld* also remains in regular syndication. And online video services like *Netflix* and *Blockbuster*, as well as Hulu, YouTube, and satel-

---

"nothing." In philosophical terms, it is the study of meaninglessness.

5. Reported on by John Huston, "Hibbs examines 'Senfeild,' other shows about 'nothing,'" in *The Observer Online*, 2/7/11, http://www.nd.edu/~observer/12031999/News/5.html.

6. Ibid.

7. Huston, "Hibbs examines 'Senfeild,' other shows about 'nothing.'"

8. As of October, 2011, FOX renewed *The Simpsons*, the longest-running comedy in television history, for an incredible 24th and 25th season.

lite and cable TV, ensure they can be brought into the homes of North Americans all the more.

TV shows today continue to pick up on the minutia and mundane aspects of life. But now they add a sense of existential fantasy and the surreal. Consider the more recently ended comedy series *Scrubs.*[9] The show ran for seven seasons on NBC and then on ABC for two more. The show's title is a play on surgical scrubs and a term for a low-ranking person. (At the beginning of the show, most of the main characters were medical interns, one of the lowest ranks in the medical hierarchy.)

Scrubs follows the often-irreverent lives of several employees of the fictional Sacred Heart teaching hospital. It features fast-paced screenplay with slapstick, surreal, and almost schizophrenic vignettes presented mostly as the daydreams of the central character, Dr. John Dorian (J. D.), who is played by Zach Braff.

In every episode, J. D. has many comical daydreams. However, the comedy is brought about through the nature of the superficial, nonsensical, random, and self-indulgent nature of the daydreams, which constantly remain as an existential background for each show's theme.

J. D. is constantly trying to find the balance of his daydream world and the world in which he exists, often reminiscing on an indulgent daydream come true. The daydreams are often portrayed in such a way that the viewer does not necessarily know how to discern which world is more real.

Moral dilemmas are cast into the realm of relativity, lifting up a common human predicament but often letting the idiosyncrasies of each character establish what, in the end, is right. At the end of most episodes, J. D. summarizes the episode's themes in a sequence of shots that show how it has affected each of the characters. It is not so much the lesson learned that is being emphasized, but rather the experience that has been shared.

In this case, the underlying emphasis of the show is not so much on nihilism, though it certainly can be detected at various times (i.e., "Ted," the pathetically inclined hospital lawyer), but rather on the individual relative perspective of each character within his shared experience, even if it is outrageous.

It is a progression in the line of postmodern expression. And though some contend we are now moving beyond postmodernism (becoming

---

9. It was officially canceled on May 14, 2010.

post-postmodern to Therian to pseudo-modern or something else),[10] any such determined and definitive cultural assessment has not yet been uniformly agreed upon. As such, the prevailing postmodern diagnosis remains the context in which we will speak.

Accordingly, the above TV series and movies would seem to remain consistent with Veith's observations of the postmodern aesthetic toward the arts. He cites Terry Eagleton for a succinct description:

> There is, perhaps, a degree of consensus that the typical post-modernist artifact is playful, self-ironizing and even schiziod; and that it rests to the austere autonomy of high modernism by impudently embracing the language of commerce and the commodity. Its stance towards cultural tradition is one of irreverent pastiche, and its contrived depthlessness undermines all metaphysical solemnities, sometimes by brutal aesthetics of squalor and shock.[11]

This is the culture pervading the people of North America. It is one of fantasy, irreverence, skepticism, materialism, relativism, nihilism (and any other "ism" one can think of) as well as indulgent, superficial, empty, uncertain, searching, and yet altogether unconcerned. It is, by one description, postmodern. However, I realize that the mission of the Holy Christian Church is not, in the end, concerned with postmodernism per se but with the people living in the postmodern culture. But even so, understanding the basics of postmodernism becomes essential to reaching out to the lost people of our culture.

10. See Frederic W. Baue's book *The Spiritual Society: What Lurks Beyond Postmodernism* for his description of what he calls the coming "Therian Age." Also consider what Dr. Alan Kirby notes in his article "The Death of Postmodernism and Beyond." He asserts that postmodernism is dead and buried, where in its place comes a new paradigm of authority and knowledge formed under the pressure of new technologies and contemporary social forces: "This pseudo-modern world, so frightening and seemingly uncontrollable, inevitably feeds a desire to return to the infantile playing with toys which also characterises [*sic*.] the pseudo-modern cultural world. Here, the typical emotional state, radically superseding the hyper-consciousness of irony, is the *trance*—the state of being swallowed up by your activity. In place of the neurosis of modernism and the narcissism of postmodernism, pseudo-modernism *takes the world away*, by creating a new weightless nowhere of silent autism. You click, you punch the keys, you are 'involved', engulfed, deciding. You are the text, there is no-one else, no 'author'; there is nowhere else, no other time or place. You are free: you are the text: the text is superseded." From *Philosophy Now: A Magazine of Ideas*, issue 58, 2006, online edition, http://www.philosophynow.org/issue58/The_Death_of_Postmodernism_And_Beyond.

11. Veith, *Postmodern Times*, 94–95.

WHAT DOES THIS MEAN?

Certainly, there are a host of opinions on postmodernism. Regardless of the critiques, the aim is to keep the proclamation of the Gospel to postmodern people the central focus. But care must be given in this task. We must engage the people of this culture with the Gospel and not remodel the Gospel to appeal to the culture.

Lutheran culture critic Gene Edward Veith is initially rather pessimistic about postmodernism as a whole: "This book is critical of postmodern*ism*, but remains open to the post modern."[12] At the same time, Lutheran exegete James Voelz had a more favorable opinion: "[I]t is the contention of this author that postmodernism, for all of its excesses, is not our enemy but a sort of friend, a later 20th century discovery that, in so many ways, the perspective of the early church was right: only believers can truly interpret the sacred books of God."[13] Yet in Veith's recently revised edition of *The Spirituality of the Cross,* he has provided a subtle second take about how "an interesting apologetic for Christianity has arisen" from our postmodern condition:

> Postmodernist thinkers go so far as to say that all religions, ideologies, and cultural institutions are nothing more than "constructions" designed to impose power over other people. These metanarratives—stories that purports to account for reality—are all about power. But in response, an interesting apologetic for Christianity has arisen. There is one metanarrative that is not about power. It is about the abnegation of power, centering on a powerful God who emptied Himself to become a poverty stricken, homeless baby in a manger and who was killed by torture as a criminal. And yet, strangely, this death redeems us, as we, too, give up our power and accept His free gift. This one metanarrative is *not* about power and is *not* a human construction. The other metanarratives *are* constructions by corrupt human beings asserting their selfish will to power. But this one is so different, it must be true.[14]

Both Veith and Voelz seem to point toward a distinct way of theologically approaching postmodernism. I think they are right. And it is my contention that the distinct way to look at postmodernism and the

12. Veith, *Postmodern Times,* 24.

13. Voelz, *What Does This Mean?,* 11–12.

14. Veith, *The Spirituality of the Cross,* 11–12.

mission of the Holy Christian Church is to do so through the bifocals of the third article of the Apostles' Creed.

As we continue on our way to look through those lenses, we will first examine what postmodernism brings to the culture in this chapter and then discuss a few of the reactionary movements that resulted in the church in the next two chapters.[15] Thus, this chapter will provide brief acknowledgements of those considered to be the early postmodern thinkers and engage in some abbreviated philosophical considerations. We will primarily engage in a dialogue with postmodernism as it manifests itself among the people of North America. But we will also demonstrate how, despite all of postmodernism's excesses and confusion, the Gospel is still able to transcend any perceived cultural limitations brought about by postmodernism.

POSTMODERN THINKERS

Given the nature of postmodernism as a subject of study and the sophistication of those who write about it, it is difficult for discussions not to become overly academic. However, in the interest of balancing understanding and brevity, we will venture forward.

It has been said that, in the end, "The postmodern world is merely an arena of dueling texts."[16] It is a short sentence upon which thousands of pages have been written. A longer and still yet insufficient summary describes postmodernism this way:

> In the postmodern world, people are no longer convinced that knowledge is inherently good . . . [P]ostmodernism replaces the optimism of the last century with a gnawing pessimism... The Postmodern mind refuses to limit truth to its rational dimension and thus dethrones the human intellect as the arbiter of truth. There are other valid paths to knowledge besides reason, say the postmoderns, including the emotions and the intuition. Finally, the postmodern mind no longer accepts the Enlightenment belief that knowledge is objective . . . reality is relative, indeterminate, and participatory.[17]

15. For reactionary movements, see chapters 4 and 5 on the church growth movement and the emergent church movement.

16. Grenz, *A Primer on Postmodernism*, 7.

17. Ibid.

As helpful as summaries can be, postmodernism is not always the easiest to summarize. It has a dynamic state of being mixed with a complexity of deep thought. The curious thing about trying to evaluate postmodernism is that no one particular postmodern thinker or author is entirely definitive of the philosophy. Each of the so-called early influences of postmodern thought—whatever that maybe—has a distinct contribution, expansion, or focus that collectively defines postmodernism.

Consequently, we need to look at some of the movement's major influences with a significant emphasis on one in particular: Jean-François Lyotard. His contributions provide further rationale for the use of the third article of the Apostles' Creed as a framework for re-examining the mission of the church. (However, be advised: Postmodern philosophers do have a tendency to make one's head hurt when reading them. Brevity and clarity is my aspiration. But perhaps a couple of Tylenol still might be good to have nearby.)

THREE FRENCHMEN PLUS ONE

Many note that the most influential early postmodern philosophers were Frenchmen: Jean-François Lyotard, Jacques Derrida and Michel Foucault. Each provides a distinct contribution to the development of postmodern thought. However, American philosopher Richard Rorty should also be mentioned as he provided postmodernism with a new pragmatism. Each of these men were reacting against the modernist way of thinking, which is often characterized by its scientific approach to the certainty of knowledge. It is the idea or theory that there are absolute truths in life that are scientifically verifiable. It is what postmodern thinkers came to revile.[18]

MICHEL FOUCAULT

First is Michel Foucault. His thinking is intense but profoundly distinct. In short, he helped fuel the idea that, "What's true for you may not be true for me. It's only true for those in power." He was an ardent disciple of nihilist thinker Friedrich Nietzsche and argued that knowledge is

18. "Postmodernism can be understood as the erosion of confidence in the rational as sole guarantor and deliverer of truth, coupled with a deep suspicion of science—particularly modern science's pretentious claims to an ultimate theory of everything." Smith, *Who's Afraid of Postmodernism?*, 62.

produced through the operations of power. This meant it would change fundamentally through different historical periods, somewhat like the bully on the playground telling kids what to think and do . . . until the next bully comes along and changes the rules. Foucault's claim was that language triggered the dissolution of humanity. In intellectual terms, it was "the loss of humanity as an object of our knowledge." His point was that we are now realizing that humanity is nothing more than a fiction "composed by the modern human sciences," for which the Western view of history is to blame and is itself really nothing more than a "myth" that needs to be laid to rest.[19]

He was not one to mince words (although actually being able to comprehend them is often the issue.) His point was that objective truth was not possible because it is simply the result of an arbitrary construction of the thought process defined by those in power. What the bully thinks and says is what goes.

JACQUES DERRIDA

Next is Jacques Derrida. His thinking is also intense. He is the father of what is known as deconstruction, and he practiced philosophy as a form of textual criticism.[20] (In culinary terms, it is like making lasagna by cooking every ingredient separately and then only placing them together when you finally serve it. All the ingredients are there, but it's nothing like Mom's lasagna!) He criticized Western philosophy as privileging the concept of "presence" and *"logos"* (word), as opposed to "absence" and "markings" or writings. Derrida claimed to have deconstructed Western philosophy by arguing, for example, that the Western ideal of the present *logos* is undermined by the expression of that ideal in the form of *markings* by an absent author. (I know. My head hurts too. In simple terms, it is like you reading the words I typed on this paper in my absence. How can you know what I really mean unless I am there to tell you?)

To emphasize this paradox, Derrida reformulated human culture as a disjointed network of proliferating markings and writings with the

19. Grenz, *A Primer on Postmodernism*, 129–30.

20. Deconstruction: I would define it as the practice of pursuing the meaning of a text to the point of exposing the supposed contradictions and internal oppositions upon which it is founded, supposedly showing that those foundations are irreducibly complex, unstable, or impossible.

author being absent.[21] Putting it more simply and to help our heads stop hurting, he helped give rise to the notion, "Truth is relative." (He also gave rise to the notion that Tylenol is necessary when reading his work.)

RICHARD RORTY

Richard Rorty, though entirely postmodern, was a different character altogether, not only by what he wrote but by how he wrote.[22] But his thinking is no less intense. Rorty developed a novel form of pragmatism in which scientific and philosophical methods are merely contingent vocabularies that are abandoned or adopted over time according to so-cial conventions and usefulness. But in so doing, he denied the nature of self-refuting relativism, which was developed by the two previously noted French philosophers.[23] (Take the Tylenol!) In plain terms, there are some knowable truths that can be conveyed and understood.

(In sports terms, it's like the recent switch to rally scoring in volley-ball. Rally scoring had been formerly reserved for overtime. It is where a point is awarded with every serve regardless of who wins the side out. The previous scoring method required a team to be in control of the serve before they could score a point. But the game was not as excit-ing. A "practical" and "useful" solution was needed to increase the pace and excitement of the game. The change from the conventional scoring method changed the number of points required to win a game, and it changed the strategy to get those points. The players and fans still talk about the score of a volleyball game, but it is fundamentally different from what it once was. There is a new way of keeping score, but the important reality or truth is that there is still a score being kept.)

JEAN-FRANÇOIS LYOTARD

Finally (and hopefully the Tylenol has kicked in by now), consider Jean-François Lyotard. He is largely concerned with the role of narrative (sto-ry) in human culture. Particular for him was how the role of narrative

21. Grenz, *A Primer on Postmodernism*, 138–50.

22. "If Foucault is difficult to understand and Derrida nearly impossible to compre-hend, Rorty's clear prose is a breath of fresh air." Ibid., 151. "In Contrast to the seem-ingly bleak implications of others, Rorty's pragmatism appears refreshingly hopeful. Unlike the anti-utopia of Derrida and the negative utopia of Foucault, Rorty leads his followers into a new postmodern utopianism." Ibid., 159.

23. Ibid., 151–60.

has changed as we have left modernity and entered a "postindustrial" or postmodern condition. (Take a breath for this next sentence.) In his relatively short yet intensely sophisticated work, *The Postmodern Condition: A Report on Knowledge,* he argues that modern philosophies legitimized their truth claims not on logical or empirical grounds—as they themselves claimed—but rather on the grounds of accepted metanarratives[24] about knowledge and the world. (The French words for *metanarratives* are *grand reçits*—literally, "big stories.")

As such, Lyotard states, "Simplifying to the extreme, I define postmodern as incredulity toward metanarratives."[25] He is intentionally skeptical about any overarching story or truth claim about the human condition or history. Lyotard goes on, "This incredulity is undoubtedly a product of progress in the sciences: but that progress in turn presupposes it."[26] To explain this, he uses Austrian Philosopher Ludwig Wittgenstein's concept of *language games.*[27]

In plain terms (and with the help of a few more Tylenol), Lyotard claims we cannot necessarily know if the overarching rules of society or the record of our history is actually objective and true. His claim is that we have simply constructed them on ideas that we have created over time within each respective culture of people, rather than on the existence of truths that transcend time. His aim is to question all claims of absolute truth.

Lyotard argues that these metanarratives (big stories) no longer work to legitimize truth-claims. He suggested that in the collapse of modern metanarratives, people are developing a new language game: one that does not make claims to absolute truth, but rather celebrates differing perspectives. In simpler terms, it is a world of ever-changing relationships. (Like the TV show *Scrubs,* it is not so much the lesson learned but the experience shared.)

---

24. These are sometimes also referred to as "grand narratives" or grand, large-scale theories and philosophies of the world, such as the progress of history, the knowability of everything by science, and the possibility of absolute freedom.

25. Lyotard, *The Postmodern Condition,* xxiv.

26. Ibid.

27. "What he [Wittgenstein] means by this term is that each of the various categories of utterance can be defined in terms of rules specifying their properties and the uses to which they can be put – in exactly the same way as the game of chess is defined by a set of rules determining the properties of each of the pieces, in other words, the proper way to move them." Ibid., 10.

In short, he argues that there is no longer the belief that grand narratives are adequate to represent and contain everyone. Lyotard says that people are now sensitive to difference diversity and the incompatibility of aspirations, beliefs, and desires. Consequently, postmodernism is characterized by an abundance of "little narratives" or micronarratives (little stories).[28]

PAYOFF FOR THE PAIN

But here is the payoff for all of the pain: It is precisely within the context of these little narratives that the Christian narrative can legitimately speak and exist in a postmodern society. In particular is the narrative expressed by the Apostles' Creed and lived out by the Holy Christian Church and the community of saints as confessed in the third article of the creed.

What Lyotard unwittingly, and most likely unwillingly, provides the church is the catalyst for a bold narrative confession of the faith. The community of saints becomes a little narrative whose intent is not to convince the world of the truth it has, but rather to simply confess the truth that this community believes to the world. Yes, it does speak from a grand narrative of truth. However, the grand narrative does not necessarily need to be imposed into the midst of witnessing to the way, the truth, and the life of Jesus Christ. Rather, simply confessing the truth of Christ through the narrative of the Gospel will provide the opportunity for the grand narrative to fall into place. I will say more on this in chapters 6 and 7, and the conclusion.

THE SUBLIME

There is an additional thought that Lyotard develops that is quite useful for our conversation. His treatment of the sublime within the aesthetics (the arts) provides a window into our current entertainment industry.[29]

---

28. "We no longer have recourse to the grand narratives—we can resort neither to the dialectic Spirit nor even to the emancipation of humanity as a validation for postmodern scientific discourse. But as we have just seen, the little narrative [*petit recit*] remains the quintessential form of imaginative invention, most particularly in science." Ibid., 60.

29. *Sublime* here refers to the experience of pleasurable anxiety that we experience when confronting depictions of wild and threatening sights, such as the scene of a massive and roaring waterfall looming terrifyingly in our vision as if we were soon to go

It is particularly useful for understanding TV shows like *Seinfeld*, *The Simpsons*, and *Scrubs*, as well as movies like *The Matrix* trilogy or the 2010 Oscar-nominated and popular film *Inception*,[30] and the resulting fascination, obsession, and even personalization of them by people in North American society.

Lyotard's treatment of the sublime is certainly sophisticated. (Keep the Tylenol bottle close.) However, it is worth exploring as it gives significant insight into the entertainment industry's impact on our culture.

> [M]odern aesthetics is an aesthetic of the sublime, though a nostalgic one. It allows the unpresentable to be put forward only as missing contents; but the form, because of its recognizable consistency, continues to offer to the reader or viewer matter for solace and pleasure. Yet these sentiments do not constitute the real sublime sentiment, which is in an intrinsic combination of pleasure and pain: the pleasure that reason should exceed all presentation, the pain that imagination or sensibility should not be equal to the concept.
>
> The postmodern would be that which, in the modern, puts forward the unpresentable in presentation itself; that which denies itself the solace of good forms, the consensus of a taste which would make it possible to share collectively the nostalgia for the unattainable; that which searches for new presentations, not in order to enjoy them but in order to impart a stronger sense of the unpresentable. A postmodern artist or writer is in the position of a philosopher: the text he writes, the work he produces are not in principle governed by pre-established rules, and they cannot be judged according to a determining judgment, by applying familiar categories to the text or to the work. Those rules or categories are what the work of art itself is looking for. The artist and the writer, then, are working without rules in order to formulate the rules of what *will have been done.*[31]

---

over it. Our sensibility is incapable of coping with such sights, but our reason can assert the finitude of the presentation.

30. It is an utterly thrilling and visually stimulating yet complex and intricate movie. Leonardo DiCaprio plays Dom Cobb, a specialized spy or corporate espionage thief. His work consists of secretly extracting valuable commercial information from the unconscious mind of his targets while they are asleep and dreaming. Unable to visit his children, Cobb is offered a chance to regain his old life in exchange for an almost impossible task: "inception," the planting of an idea into a target's subconscious, which can only be done through the most complex series of a dream within a dream within a dream.

31. Lyotard, *Postmodern Condition*, 81.

A demonstration of this, in addition to the TV shows and movies already mentioned, is the cable TV station MTV. Its basis of presentation has long been a disconnected flow of images that blur the lines of reality and fantasy. The viewer has to sort out what is more real: the surreal life portrayed on the screen and replayed over and over in the mind, or the rules of society that impinge upon that fantasy and begrudgingly bring them back to reality, which, in turn, tempts the viewers to construct their own new surreal realities.

THE SPREAD OF POSTMODERNISM

In the end, each of these philosophers provides intricate details into the utterly brilliant capabilities of the human mind. (And how they can make our heads hurt!) However, they are the elite of society. In other words, they are not demonstrative of the average man or women on the street or in the pew. Nonetheless, as Veith notes, the intellectual climate of a culture often "finds its full expression in the arts," that which, when seen in the "fine arts of the 'high culture,'" often "provide clues to where our culture is heading."[32]

Hence, in a perpetually video-screened, plugged-in, WiFi, video-gamed society, it can only stand to reason that the "entertainment industry spreads postmodernist ideology into every home with a TV set." But now, thanks to home computers, laptops, portable DVD players, iPhones and iPads, *Xbox, Play Station,* and *Nintendo,* that ideology can be spread into every car, bus, subway, plane, or any place there is a battery, a signal, or a video screen.

The people of North America are being shaped with postmodern minds and postmodern behaviors that flow out of their favorite TV shows, movies, and YouTube videos, which, in the case of YouTube videos, are sometimes simply the home video or video phone recordings of a lived-out fantasy previously seen in another venue. It is a reality that the community of saints needs to face as they go about the mission of God.[33]

32. Veith, *Postmodern Times,* 94.

33. "Those who think that postmodernism is a figment of the academic imagination, a passing fad, could not be more wrong. Postmodernism has flowed right out of the musty corridors of academia into the world of popular culture; it is on the pages of youth magazines, on CD boxes and the fashion pages of *Vogue.*" Dave Tomlinson, *The Post-Evangelical,* cited by Dan Kimball in *The Emerging Church,* 55.

For these reasons, it is helpful for the church and her leaders (pastors and parishioners) to be aware of postmodernism. In this way, the community of saints can maintain informed and reasoned conversations with the people and movements of society as they go about confessing and living the faith.

In fact, one fascinating current example of utilizing the sublime, surreal, and postmodern comedic nature of video is Lutheran pastor Jonathan Fisk who creates a twice-a-week webcast at *www. WorldviewEverlasting.com*. In MTV-like fashion, various images that often abstractly visualize what he is talking about flash within the screen, while he himself is seen speaking about confessional Lutheran theology and the life of faith in a choppy, edited, Max-Headroom-like fashion. He uses a playful, comedic, and whimsical irreverence to deliver deep theological and exegetical truths to teach and to challenge his viewers, which only endear him all the more to his loyal viewers.

ASSESSING THE CONDITION

So, what have Christian thinkers and theologians been saying about this postmodern condition? Many have decried postmodernism as an evil and many elements of it rightly so.[34] However, more Christian authors have begun to develop a hermeneutic that aims thoughtfully to engage postmodernism and, therefore, the people living in the midst of it, but not without first dealing honestly with the condition of the church at the same time.

Robert Jenson is one such individual. He observes that not only is North America postmodern, but it is most certainly also post-Christian.[35] And when asking, "Who is a post-Christian?" Jenson answers with an indictment:

34. For example, see Charles Colson's "The Postmodern Crackup: From Soccer Moms to College Campuses, Signs of the End," *Christianity Today*, December 2003, as well as D. A. Carson's *Becoming Conversant with the Emerging Church: Understanding a Movement and Its implications.*

35. "Thus to be post-Christian is to belong to a community—a polity or civil society—which used to be Christian and whose habits of thought and policies of action are determined by that very fact. One can therefore be a post-Christian without knowing anything about Christianity—and many in the West's great cities are now in just that condition." Jenson, "What is a Post-Christian?" in *The Strange New Word of the Gospel,* 21.

> There are whole immense congregations, of all denominations or none, that are post-Christian at least in their public self-presentation. Their theology is a collection of clichéd abstractions—"love" and "acceptance" and "empowerment" and "peace-and-justice" (one word), and so on—and they could easily make any hero or mythic figure at all be the loving or accepting or empowering one, or the guru of peace-and-justice, instead of Jesus, and sometimes do.[36]

What is his recommended solution? "First, we must purge our churches themselves of almost-nihilism and abstracted Christianity. Or rather, we must pray God to purge us of them, for we plainly are not going to do it voluntarily. If God is thus merciful, our churches will of course get much smaller than they are."[37] His point: Abstracted Christianity is really no Christianity at all.

Some might question if this purging mentality constitutes a legitimate theology, since it would seem to be counter to seeking and saving the lost. Not to worry, for Jenson is unequivocal that "the West is now a mission field."[38] Even his colleague Carl Braaten notes, "As we enter the third millennium we are still the people elected to bring the Gospel and build the church in this post-Christian, post modern, post-communist, post denominational, post-whatever kind of situation in which we find ourselves."[39] A dose of reality, even if it stings, does not diminish the *missio Dei*. The church must still be the church whatever the age. The age cannot become the church. As Jenson warns, abnormal abstractions are the result.

POSITIVES OF POSTMODERNISM

One author who speaks positively about the ability of postmodernism to serve faith is Crystal Downing. In her book *How Postmodernism Serves (My) Faith,* she sets forth a sophisticated paradigm of putting faith into postmodern terms. Again, brevity and understanding will be the endeavor.

---

36. Ibid., 28.

37. Ibid., 29.

38. Ibid.

39. Braaten, "The Future of the Apostolic Imperative: At the Crossroads of World Evangelization." in *The Strange New Word of the Gospel,* 174.

Downing demonstrates that, for the postmodernist, empirical explanations of reality, as we have noted, are subject to question. Recognizing that this presents a very real threat to Christian claims of reality, she explores some "postfoundationalist"[40] constructions of Christianity looking for alternatives.

She argues for a Christian faith built on "moving foundations."[41] That is to say, Christian faith is essentially dynamic rather than static. Like a building made to withstand an earthquake, the ability of the foundations of orthodox Christianity to move within certain limits makes it unmovable:

> I would argue that the foundation of Christianity stands in a four-sided pit dug into a bedrock of belief. One side that limits extreme movement is lined with the Bible; another side is lined with church tradition; the third side is a wall of reason; and personal experience (which includes cultural situatedness) makes up the fourth wall . . . Because foundation is placed on rollers of faith, it can move as we employ reason to assess empirical data in the light of biblical teaching and traditional dogma. But this also means that we need to assess our understanding of the Bible and church tradition by reasoned assessment of science and culture to keep our foundation intact by allowing it to move.[42]

After creating this dynamic foundation, she concludes, "Christians today, then, can sing with confidence 'The Church's one foundation is Jesus Christ her Lord,' knowing that they join myriad others throughout the last two millennia to confirm that just as our One God is three, so our One Foundation is plural: the body of Christ kept alive in numerous bodies of believers, whose faith is bona fide *because* it moves."[43]

Any opportunity to sing, "The Church's One Foundation Is Jesus Christ Her Lord" is cause for rejoicing. However, a word of caution is urged, at least from my perspective. Downing's "moveable foundation" is concerning. It is an interesting consideration, and in some ways, it is very helpful in promoting the creedal tradition (i.e., her lines of the Bible and tradition). But she is perhaps more generous in allowing reason and experience to play the definitive role that is does. It goes beyond what

40. For instance, truths that are not self evident apart from a culture.

41. Downing, *How Postmodernism Serves (My) Faith*, 118–20.

42. Ibid., 119.

43. Ibid., 120.

some of us are comfortable with. Such elements are not inimical to the tradition of faith. However, many people (my tradition included) would not be comfortable with them being part of the norming norm of faith.

Nonetheless, her overall aim is laudable. Her desire is for honest dialogue: "Only by confronting our complicity in postmodernism, I will argue, can Christians establish an identity worthy of our name, employing the best of postmodernism to 1) rethink how we read the Bible and 2) lovingly relate the truth of Christ."[44] Honest dialogue and intentional assessment are always appreciated. It offers us a good way forward. I am hoping that this book makes a significant contribution toward that dialogue in North America.

GIDDINESS FOR POSTMODERNISM

Another individual who has a favorable disposition, perhaps even giddiness, towards postmodernism is James K. Smith. He is a series editor and beginning contributor of a book series on the church and postmodern culture that aims to highlight what are considered the potential helpful qualities of postmodernism.

> The goal of this series is to bring together high-profile theorists in continental philosophy and contemporary theology to write for a broad, nonspecialist audience interested in the impact of postmodern theory on the faith and practice of the church. Each book will, from different angles and with different questions, undertake to answer questions such as, What does postmodern theory have to say about the shape of the church? How should concrete, in-the-pew and on the ground religious practices be impacted by postmodernism? What should the church look like in postmodernity?[45]

The series attempts to answer his questions. To date there are five books in this series. Smith's *Who's Afraid of Postmodernism?* was the first and most openly direct and helpful. Next was John D. Caputo's potentially thoughtful yet politically laced and ultimately disenfranchising *What Would Jesus Deconstruct?*,[46] followed by Carl Raschke's

44. Ibid., 209.

45. Smith, *Who's Afraid of Postmodernism*, 10–11. From the *Series Preface*.

46. Caputo is sincere in his attempt to demonstrate that deconstruction is not necessarily antithetical to Christianity. However, in an effort to demonstrate this possibility he engages in criticism of the Christian Right, which, though warranted by the Right's

enlightening *GloboChrist: The Great Commission Takes a Postmodern Turn.* Next came Merold Westphal's hermetical endeavor of *Whose Community? Which Interpretation?* and finally the deep work (but also political critique) of Graham Ward's *The Politics of Discipleship: Becoming Postmaterial Citizens.*

True to the series preface, there was no shortage of different angles and different questions. However, the accessibility of each of the books may not be as broad as the "non-specialist audience" noted in the series preface. Nonetheless, two were substantially helpful in considering the potential positive perspective of postmodernism, as well as building a creedal approach to re-examining the doctrine and life of the church.

James Smith's work was distinct in this regard. In his first chapter, he "introduces the questions that the phenomenon of postmodernism poses for the church and suggests a strategy for engagement that avoids simple dichotomies of either demonizing or baptizing postmodernism."[47] He sets out to engage the reader with the three French philosophers

---

abuses, can tend to alienate the reader from his larger point, particularly when coupled with his play on the Right's "What would Jesus do?" by asking "What would Jesus deconstruct?" Here he gives special attention to abortion and the homosexual agenda, which, in the end, only seem to betray his attempt of legitimizing deconstruction, reraising the red flags about postmodernism, and portraying a whimsical yet seemingly self-indulgent diatribe that merely succeeds in fortifying his own left-leaning agenda. Consequently, I feel he significantly devalues the legitimacy and lasting potential of his work as well as any possibility for wider appeal. Consider the following quote: "In my view, even if there is a dominant view against homosexuality in the Scriptures and tradition—and as a deconstructive reader, I would always insist on a full hearing for all the nondominant views, of which there are plenty—I would argue that on this point the Greeks were right and the dominant tradition among Jews and Christians is wrong, just as the Scriptures are wrong to underwrite slavery and the oppression of women . . . Were Jesus alive today and familiar with the pros and cons of the contemporary argument, his centeredness on love would have brought him down on the side of the rights of what we today call the 'homosexual' difference . . . After my friends on the Right have regained consciousness, they will perhaps want to hear my reasons for saying this. Jesus systematically took the side of the outsider, of those who are excluded and marginalized and made to suffer for their marginalization by the powers that be, those whose names are blackened by their difference from the mainstream. Based on the Gospel of love by which he was driven, he would today have found love in homosexual love and a mission among the advocates of gay and lesbian rights."

"What is revealed in the Scriptures is not a literal picture to hold up against the present like a mechanical template but a living Spirit whose inner force is to be brought to bear in a loving and living dialogue with the circumstances of the present." *What Would Jesus Deconstruct?*, 109–11.

47. Smith, *Who's Afraid of Postmodernism?*, 15.

previously noted above. His claims regarding Derrida and Lyotard are intriguing:

> *Derrida.* Deconstruction's claim that there is "nothing outside the text" can be considered a radical translation of the Reformation principle sola Scriptura. In particular, Derrida's insight should push us to recover two key emphases of the church: a) the centrality of Scripture for mediating our understanding of the world as a whole and b) the role of community in the interpretation of Scripture.
>
> *Lyotard.* The assertion that postmodernity is "incredulity toward metanarratives" is ultimately a claim to be affirmed by the Church, pushing us to recover a) the narrative character of Christian faith, rather than understanding it as a collection of ideas, and b) the confessional nature of our narrative and the way in which we find ourselves in a world of competing narratives.[48]

A return to the Reformation principle of *sola Scriptura* is welcome indeed! Evangelical Lutherans have long maintained this as the formal principle of faith. For them, the material principal—the narrative that expresses all doctrine and life of the Scriptures—is nothing other than the Gospel.[49] Smith's positive assessment of Derrida and Lyotard provides a profound consideration for the North American church to intelligently engage postmodernism and, therefore, postmodern people. As such, given the communal nature of the creedal paradigm put forth in chapter 1, it would certainly appear to provide an adequate lens in which to view the doctrine and life of the church.

48. Smith, *Who's Afraid of Postmodernism?*, 23.

49. Thus, for Lutherans the point at which all theological thinking begins is the article of justification by faith or, more simply put, the Gospel of Jesus Christ: his death and resurrection to forgive the sins of the world. From this article emanates all thinking and understanding of Scripture and the other doctrines that Scripture puts forth. As the Formula of Concord states: "This article concerning justification by faith is the chief article in the entire Christian doctrine, without which no poor conscience can have any firm consolation or can truly understand the riches of the grace of Christ" Kolb and Wengert, Solid Declaration, Article III, § 6. It is important to understand the distinction and balance that is to be maintained between the two. "The charge is sometimes made that Lutheranism overstresses the doctrine of justification by faith alone so much that it loses sight of the significance of other doctrines, such as sanctification . . . But genuine Lutheran theology, while maintaining a careful distinction between the various doctrines, e.g., justification and sanctification, will never permit a separation of Christian doctrines into isolated compartments." F.E. Mayer. *The Religious Bodies of America*, 147. In other words, it maintains them as an integral whole or perhaps, more aptly, a narrative whole.

A POSTMODERN ETHOS OF THE CHURCH

As Luther's explanation of the third article of the Apostle's Creed reminds us, the community of saints is both "called and gathered" by and around the Gospel. They confess with their mouths and believe with their hearts the narrative of Jesus Christ. They do so amid the plurality of postmodern beliefs. In fact, the incredulity toward what is considered an imperialistic metanarrative of the church can now be softened by the authenticity and humility of those who simply confess and live by this truth.

This is not meant to suggest a timid confession of faith or a lack of outreach to the lost. Rather, just the opposite! In the midst of an unbelieving world, we still confess the faith. That is, we simply live the narrative our faith confesses. Boldness for sharing this faith is then seen in the community of saints as they gather for sacramental worship and live out their daily vocations. Such forthright expression of doctrine and practice seems to be exactly what Smith is advocating:

> So far, I have been suggesting that a properly postmodern theology will be dogmatic, not skeptical. This is not to advocate a return to an uncritical fundamentalism or the triumphalist stance of the Religious Right. Rather, it is to affirm that our confession and practice must proceed unapologetically from the particularities of Christian confession as given in God's historical revelation in Christ and as unfolded in the history of the church's response to that revelation. To be dogmatic then, is to be unapologetically confessional, which requires being unapologetic about the determinate character of our confession, contra the Cartesian anxiety exhibited by much postmodern theology. This should translate into a robust appropriation of the church's language as the paradigm for both thought and practice.[50]

> The church is the site where God renews and transforms us—a place where the practices of being the body of Christ form us into the image of the Son. What I, a sinner saved by grace, need is not so much answers as reformation of my will and heart. What I describe as the practice of the church include the traditional sacramental practices of baptism and Eucharist but also the practices of Christian marriage and child-rearing, even the simple

---

50. Smith, *Who's Afraid of Postmodernism?*, 123.

but radical practices of friendship and being called to get along with those one doesn't like.[51]

Said another way, what the church has always done and always confessed is to continue being what the church does and confesses. Postmodernism need not dictate something new for us. In fact, what is even more intriguing is Smith's call to return to the ancient ritual of liturgy.

> If we want to be postmodern in some sense, we must recover elements of ancient ritual and practice, for it is liturgy that honors our fleshliness. But this is not a merely traditionalists fiat; it stems from the very way we think about the world and what it means to be human. In other words, an incarnational affirmation of liturgy and the aesthetics of worship is the fruit of an incarnational ontology (an account of the nature of reality) and a holistic anthropology (an account of what it means to be human).[52]

This is wholly refreshing for those liturgical churches desiring to uphold the practice of the historic liturgy. It is particularly so when there remains a strong contingent within many North American churches that are continually urging the abandonment of the liturgy—in the name of postmodern cultural and missional relevance no less.

CULTURAL RELEVANCE

Carl Raschke, in his work *GloboChrist*, has much to say about the church's movement toward cultural relevance. Combating this urge, he juxtaposes the culturally relevant church with the Apostles' Creed to demonstrate what true relevancy means. "The church can never be relevant, however, when it seeks mainly to be attractive to a particular focus group or demographic constituency. It can only be relevant when it is the catholic church, as confessed in the Apostle's Creed."[53] Thus for Raschke, relevancy for the church comes not through the culture, but by confession and by a confession that has been historically confessed throughout the ages. He then goes on to echo Smith's incarnational plea:

> The postmodern church can no longer foster its identity merely in a Western countercultural guise, for a counterculture is still a

51. Ibid., 30.
52. Ibid., 136.
53. Rascke, *GloboChrist*, 168.

particularist culture. Indeed, it is just a subculture that mirrors darkly what it has set its face against. Wandering in the wide-open "smooth spaces" of globalization, the postmodern church must no longer take its cues from the twilight broodings of the West or from American culture wars. It must become the incarnational church that knows no cultural boundaries.[54]

In other words, a confessing church speaks through the culture; it does not unduly subject itself to culture. There is a distinct difference between the two. But right now there is a significant amount of confusion about this distinction within the Church.

However, Smith, too, remains resolute, dealing honestly with those who urge for cultural relevancy while also articulating a postmodern ancient ethos for the church:

> The postmodern church resists the tendency of pragmatic evangelism, which tries to "dumb down" the story to make it accessible or attractive to the culture. Instead, the postmodern church affirms the timelessness (and timeliness) of the biblical narrative as it is told. Rather than trying to translate the biblical story into a contemporary, more "acceptable" narrative (which usually ends up compromising the narrative to culture), the postmodern church seeks to initiate listeners into the narrative. Authentic Christian worship both invites outsiders into the Gospel story and provides a significant means for the formation of disciples of Jesus Christ.[55]

The means of this formation, then, is the confessional creedal tradition, which, as Smith noted, has been historically bound to Word and Sacrament liturgical worship set within the liturgical church year.[56]

---

54. Ibid., 167.

55. Smith, *Who's Afraid of Postmodernism?*, 77.

56. Lutheran liturgist and exegete Arthur Just encourages Lutherans to simply do some thoughtful reflection: "Is there an alternative between the 'culture friendly' and 'culture critical' camps that will allow us to be faithful to our liturgical tradition, while at the same time contemporary in our expressions? Yes! Lutherans have a liturgical tradition that mediates between the two extremes and still maintains a liturgical ethos that is incarnational and sacramental. Luther restored the historic liturgy in a relatively simple setting, especially when compared to other liturgical traditions. Lutheran liturgy is liturgical without being ceremonial, timeless without being inaccessible. Instead of seeking after greener liturgical pastures, we should look at our own tradition, learn it, and discover its riches." *Liturgy and Culture*, 1/10/11, http://www.lcms.org/pages/internal .asp?NavID=837. (No longer associated with the link as the website was overhauled.)

There is a deep timelessness and timeliness about this ritualized worship. It is framed around the life and time of Christ while administering the timely—here and now—distribution of His gracious gifts. It is being lifted up, not simply out of mere preference, but out of the divine narrative it is and the divine truth it gives.

The narrative of the liturgy and the liturgical church year weave the community of saints into the story of Jesus Christ, week after week and year after year. Where postmodernism permits micronarratives, it would seem that the liturgy and the liturgical church year become quintessential narrative marks for the worship and witness of the Holy Christian Church.

They are essential in all of their fullness. As Robert Jenson puts it, "In the postmodern world, if a congregation or churchly agency wants to be 'relevant,' here is the first step: it must recover the classic liturgy of the church, in all its dramatic density, sensual actuality, and brutal realism, and make this the one exclusive center of its life. In the postmodern world, all else must at best be decoration and more likely distraction."[57] Thus, understanding the effectiveness of the church's message begins not in how much the world likes it or thinks it to be hip, but in how consistently and faithfully it confesses what it has historically been confessing and how it has historically been worshipping throughout the ages.

CONFESSING JESUS IN A POSTMODERN WORLD

David Lose, in his work *Confessing Jesus Christ: Preaching in a Postmodern World,* articulates this in more succinct terms. He emphasizes how the *confession* of faith and the *confessing* of faith must accompany the proclamational identity of the church. They must remain central to the formation of the liturgical narrative marks of the church and the formation of the community of saints, particularly as they live out their vocations.

> Without confession accompanying and supporting the proclamation, there is no proclamation. By confessing faith in Christ through celebration of the sacraments, sermons, hymns, witnessing, and daily life, those gathered in the name of Christ speak the word of God to each other and to the world. This public confession of faith in Christ through the pluriform speaking of the word is *the central constitutive mark of the church.* It is through this that the church lives as church and manifests itself externally

57. Jenson, "How the World Lost Its Story," reprint, 5–6.

as church. Although such confession is admittedly always a result or effect of the "word," just as faith, too, is a result or effect of the "word" (see Rom. 10:8–10), the "word" is proclaimed in no other way than this pluriform confessing. The confession of faith of one person leads to that of others thereby constituting the church.[58]

This dynamic duality affirms the life of the Holy Christian Church as confessed in Luther's explanation of the third article of the Apostles' Creed: "Not by reason or strength" but by the "Holy Spirit" who calls, gathers, and enlightens "the whole Christian church" by the Gospel.

Lose's ultimate assertion is that postmodernism is not an all-out evil, but rather, "far from threatening the life of the church, postmodernism presses us to release deceptive foundational securities and live, once more, by faith alone."[59] Sola Scriptura, faith alone, communal, narrative, and incarnational—all are invoked as significant to developing a postmodern ethos of the church. All flow naturally out of the Apostles' Creed and can be brought into sharper focus through the bifocals of the third article of the Apostles' Creed.

The ancients knew what they were doing. Their confession of faith was bold: "I believe in the Holy Spirit, the Holy Christian Church, the Communion of Saints, the forgiveness of sins, the resurrection of the body, and the life everlasting." This bold confession has been passed on from generation to generation, transcended the Dark Ages and on through the Middle Ages as well as the age of rationalism (modernism), and it will continue to be passed on even amid the challenges of the postmodern age. Thus, as I considered using it to help frame a strategic plan, I continued to find it entirely desirable.

However, before we explore all the details of this postmodern creedal ethos and how it might help direct a congregation's strategic plan, we first need to take a look at a few of the current alternative responses occurring in the North American church: the church growth movement (decidedly a product of modernity but now trying to acquiesce to postmodernism) as well as the emergent church movement (a direct reaction against the certitudes of the church growth movement and an adaption from postmodernism). By exploring the details of these movements, we can uncover the origin of a good bit of the church's present confusion.

58. Lose, *Confessing Jesus Christ*, 86.

59. Ibid., 5.

Chapter 4

Church Growth Confusion

PASTOR'S GOT A GUN?

W HO DOESN'T LIKE TO have new stuff? A new house, a new car, new golf clubs, or, if you're a hunter like me, a new shotgun . . .

I recently picked up a new-to-me "over-and-under" bird-hunting shotgun. Though it would have been nice to go with a top-of-the-line, brand new, over-and-under Browning Citori, our fourth child was on the way. So a used, inexpensive, off-brand model was the way to go.

Sure, new stuff is fun to have. It looks pretty, and it is more appealing—church buildings included. But are they essential? Are they necessary? A top-of-the-line Browning Citori would be great, but I am pretty sure my off-brand, used shotgun will do the trick. In fact, when I took it out for target practice the first time, I hit 22 out of 25 clay pigeons.

I know my congregation would still love to construct a new building. The urge is certainly still there. Some members still wonder why we have not started building. They are confused why our 20 acres still remains crop land.

Once a commitment to build is made, it is hard to help people understand the unfortunate limitations of reality. Lord willing, maybe one day when the time is right, the rationale right, the full funds available, and the mission of the Holy Christian Church in view, we may be blessed with such an opportunity. However, in the meantime, we will live out our lives together as a worshipping community of saints who confess our faith and live it out in our vocations.

But getting everyone to this understanding was (and still is) a constant challenge. As I attempted to craft a theological strategic plan, I was mindful of those members who were influenced by the idea of "If you build it, they will come." So I wanted to be specific in how the congregation would certainly still be building: not a new worship facility but certainly the kingdom of God. I also wanted to distinguish the reality that the growth of God's kingdom would not be contingent upon attracting people through a new building with bells and whistles, but by going out into the postmodern society and living out our faith in our daily vocations.

Thus, recognizing the possible confusion of many members, as well as the previous mentality that constructing a new building was the key to reaching out to unbelievers, I set out to look at how a "If you build it, they will come" understanding of things would fit into our particular theology of mission. I wanted to assess how effective that approach to mission would be in making new believers into committed disciples. What I found was rather revealing.

CAN'T WE ALL JUST GET ALONG?

If Jesus Christ is really the center of all "Christian" church bodies, are such labels like Roman Catholic, Eastern Orthodox, Lutheran, Presbyterian, Anglican, Baptists, Methodist, Pentecostal, and the nondenominational who says, "I'm just Christian" really necessary or even helpful? Why all the division? In the words of Rodney King, "Can't we all just get along?"

It would be nice. It even sounds rather biblical, doesn't it? But when the Bible is mentioned, there is no shortage of differences. From Augustine, Aquinas, and Anselm to Wesley, Walther, and Warren (Rick), differences have been notably present among those who are called Christian. Today it remains the same. In fact, there is a popular phrase now used by many emergent church members who do not define themselves as Christians, but rather as "disciples who follow in the way of Jesus."[1]

---

1. My first introduction to this was in September 2006 during a doctoral class conversation with emergent church guru Doug Pagitt, pastor of Solomon's Porch in Minneapolis. Their website has changed over the years, but one current line under their Intro tab reads: "Solomon's Porch is a community seeking to live the dreams and love of God in the way of Jesus as a benefit and blessing to the world."

Some even intentionally try not to talk about Christianity.[2] However, it appears that what the "way of Jesus" actually means depends on which emergent church thinker, speaker, or writer is talking.[3] Having no labels has simply ended up creating more. Yet, to be sure, with each confession of faith come inherent standards of orthodoxy (right belief) and orthopraxy (right practice). Deviating from those standards betrays the beliefs associated with them.

The early church was no stranger to this. In fact, as previously noted, this is one of the central reasons why the creeds were first created. The fourth-century heretic Arius had his followers, although they did not formalize into a fellowship. Constantine (the emperor) did not let them. However, the way of Nicaea was also the way of Jesus as "true man" and "true God"—"very God of very God." In other words, parties were formed. Sides were taken. The truth needed to be defended.

The council that convened at Nicaea probably did not originally have in mind developing the Nicene Creed as an outreach tool to seek and save the lost, but it certainly proved helpful against Arius and aided in the furthering of an orthodox faith nonetheless.

In like manner, could an evaluation of the North American church today be of any help? Is there any constructive value to undertaking such a task? Or does the zeal for orthodoxy and orthopraxy only foster power struggles and animosity? What value would there be in such an

2. Donald Miller's book *Blue Like Jazz: Nonreligious Thoughts on Christian Spirituality* expresses it this way: "In a recent radio interview I was sternly asked by the host, who did not consider himself a Christian, to defend Christianity. I told him that I couldn't do it, and moreover, that I didn't want to defend the term. He asked me if I was a Christian, and I told him yes. 'Then why don't you want to defend Christianity?' he asked, confused. I told him I no longer knew what the term meant. Of the hundreds of thousands of people listening to his show that day, some of them had terrible experiences with Christianity; they may have been yelled at by a teacher in a Christian School, abused by a minister, or browbeaten by a Christian parent. To them, the term *Christianity* meant something that no Christian I know would defend. By fortifying the term, I am only making them more and more angry. I won't do it. Stop ten people on the street and ask them what they think of when they hear the word *Christianity*, and they will give you ten different answers. How can I defend a term that means ten different things to tend different people? I told the radio show host that I would rather talk about Jesus and how I came to believe that Jesus exists and that he likes me." 115.

3. Phyllis Tickle notes the differences among the movement, pointing out the reason for the emergent and emerging labels flows out of which leader is speaking. For example, "Emergents, associated with and led by Christians like Brian McLaren, Tony Jones, Doug Pagitt . . . Emerging Christians, whose most visible and influential leaders are Dan Kimball and Erwin McManus." Tickle, *The Great Emergence*, 163.

endeavor? It is a particularly pointed question for my own church body as it has a turbulent recent history over matters of doctrine and practice.[4]

Even so, are Jenson's aforementioned words worth repeating? "First, we must purge our churches themselves of almost-nihilism and abstracted Christianity. Or rather, we must pray God to purge us of them, for we plainly are not going to do it voluntarily. If God is thus merciful, our churches will of course get much smaller than they are."[5] This undoubtedly happened at Nicaea, and no doubt that process was rather painful and messy.

Thus, if we value the tradition and purpose for which the creeds were created, would it not be the responsibility of the church to take an honest assessment and, at the risk of sounding harsh, maybe even prune a few branches if necessary? Didn't even Jesus have something to say about this (John 15:1–8)?

But again, please understand that the aim is not to become vitriolic or inflammatory, but to offer a serious and candid theological assessment of those movements within the North American church that appear to be blurring her vision. Such an endeavor calls for humble honesty and a clear diagnosis—like an eye doctor diagnosing astigmatism, myopia (nearsightedness), or hyperopia (farsightedness).

It is no small task, and I do not claim to be the final authority. But I do desire to create some healthy dialogue. This chapter will take a look at one of the current movements in the North America church: the church growth movement. (Chapter 5 will examine another movement in the church: the emergent/emerging church movement.) The aim will be to note their impact on the North American church. And when it appears the vision of the church is getting blurred, we will take a look at how creedal lenses can help stave off any distorting dangers as well as refocus us on the historic mission of the church.

THE CHURCH GROWTH MOVEMENT

As far as church movements go, the church growth movement is relatively recent in the grand scheme of church history. It began in the 1960s

---

4. For a recent assessment on the nature of power and politics in the Missouri Synod, see historian James C. Burkee's book *Power, Politics, and the Missouri Synod: A Conflict That Changed American Christianity.*

5. Jensen, "What is a Post-Christian?," 29.

and 70s and was founded by Donald McGavran, a third-generation missionary in India.

After over thirty years in India, McGavran ultimately returned to the United States to found the *Institute of Church Growth* based on the observations and questions he wrestled with during his time as a missionary.[6] In what is considered his magnum opus, *Understanding Church Growth* (written in 1970 with two more editions in 1980 and 1990), he established what is believed to be the foundation for growth in the church. This included the use of social theories like the homogenous unit principle as well as the "distinction between discipling and perfecting as two discreet stages of Christianization."[7]

McGavran defined the mission of the church as obedience to the Great Commission, which must be the chief priority over and above any type of social service. The priority was understood to be "an enterprise devoted to proclaiming the Good news of Jesus Christ, and to persuading men to become His disciples and dependable members of His Church."[8]

The idea of persuasion is intentional. MaGavran emphasized the importance of the human action and steps necessary to create the opportunity for a person to make a decision (for Jesus) that would then later be followed by greater teaching of the faith—the "perfecting" step.[9] However, he was also careful, at least in the 1990 edition, to intentionally state, "I cannot consider church growth merely a sociological process: it is that, to be sure; but much more than that, it is what happens when there is faithfulness to God the Father of our Lord Jesus Christ."[10] He is even careful to lift up the understanding of the mission of the church as the *missio Dei,* that it is God's mission, that He is in charge.[11]

6. While in India he was deeply troubled by the apparent lack of success which many missionaries, in spite of their faithful efforts, experienced. He asked: "What *does* make churches grow? More importantly, what makes many churches *stop* growing? How is it possible for Christians to come out of ripe harvest fields empty handed?" *Evangelism and Church Growth: With Special Reference to the Church Growth Movement,* Commission on Theology and Church Relations of The Lutheran Church—Missouri Synod, 25.

7. McGavran, *Understanding Church Growth*, preface to the 1990 edition, x.

8. *Evangelism and Church Growth*, 28.

9. "Church growth is human action: the strong bearing the burdens of the weak and introducing to the hungry the bread by which we humans live." McGavran, *Understanding Church Growth*, 6.

10. Ibid., 7.

11. Ibid., 20.

What began as a reaction to missionary challenges in India was now set forward as a means for growing the church in North America. Distinct attitudes and behaviors of congregations and their pastors were to be adopted if they were to be obedient to the Lord's command and, therefore, have growth to occur. It is, he says, a theologically demanded stance: "Church Growth is basically a theological stance. God requires it. It looks to the Bible for direction as to what God wants done. It holds that belief in Jesus Christ, understood according to the Scriptures, is necessary for salvation. Church growth rises in unshakable theological conviction."[12] Thus, it appears McGavran was attempting to demonstrate the biblical authenticity behind the concept of church growth while laying a corresponding legitimacy for the humanly crafted methods that are employed to attain it. However, according to some, what has happened since the first publication of his book is an explosion and expansion of the social methodologies used to seek and save the lost, coupled with the simultaneous diminishing and decline of the biblical identity and mission of the North American church.

CHURCH GROWTH OR THEOLOGICAL DECLINE

Numerous other books on church growth followed. Each has their own perspectives, additions, and even guarantees of how a congregation can follow certain steps and be sure to grow. The most prominent are from mega-church pastors Bill Hybels and Rick Warren. Hybel's book, *Becoming a Contagious Christian*, provides the secret to their growth with the "fifteen characteristics you'll find in evangelistically effective churches."[13] Warren's *The Purpose Driven Church* claims that "A Great Commitment to the Great Commandment and the Great Commission will grow a great church."[14]

To be sure, it is a movement built on the certainty that modernity seemed to afford. But as postmodernism asserts, perhaps it was a naïve certainty. What became distinctly noticeable in many subsequent books, as well as the movement itself, was the apparent shift from how McGavran attempted to engage in theological discourse and remain mindful of the theological underpinnings and implications of his

---

12. Ibid., 8.

13. Hybels and Mittelberg, *Becoming a Contagious Christian*, 200.

14. Warren, *The Purpose Drive Church*, 103.

assertions to what has now been recognized as an absence of theological discourse and thinking.

Mark Noll begins his 1994 book *The Scandal of the Evangelical Mind* with a piercing diagnosis: "The scandal of the evangelical mind is that there is not much of an evangelical mind . . . Notwithstanding all their other virtues, however, American evangelicals are not exemplary for their thinking, and they have not been so for several generations."[15] Though his endeavor has the intent to survey the broader intellectual landscape of evangelicals, it remains insightful considering the confusing use of the Great Commission and the resulting church growth movement.

One point in particular seems prudent to our conversation. Noll states: "To put it simply, the evangelical ethos is activistic, populist, pragmatic, and utilitarian. It allows little space for broader or deeper intellectual effort because it is dominated by the urgencies of the moment."[16] Consequently, when the urgency of seeking and saving the lost is repeatedly cast as the sole purpose of the church, it seems that healthy theological discernment and discourse is often trumped by that urgency. Unbalanced and unchecked methods, strategies, and tactics that want to "connect people to Jesus" become the preeminent purpose and reason for the church to exist.

But once again, please understand: I am not disparaging the desire to seek and save the lost. Of course we need to do things like this! And certainly the mission of the church obviously includes "calling people by the Gospel" to "connect them to Jesus." (In one instance, I spent more than two years, over $3,000, and countless hours of teaching, praying with and for, and responding to numerous middle-of-the-night phone calls to one troubled, unchurched individual.[17]) My point is that we need to be able to have an honest conversation about the theological integrity of how we seek and save the lost.

15. Noll, *The Scandal of the Evangelical Mind*, 3.

16. Ibid., 12.

17. Sadly, the individual fell back into old ways, stopped attending church, and stopped communicating with me altogether. I grieve for the individual. I pray for the individual. Yet it was a reminder to me that the winning of converts is more complicated than a simple formula of success might indicate.

CHURCH MARKETING

Picking up on McGavran's necessity of persuasion, the primary method and tactic of the church growth movement subsequently developed out of the idea of the marketing done in the business world.

Marketing is "the action or business of promoting and selling products or services, including market research and advertising."[18] It was thought that the same could be done with the church. Consequently, in practical terms, the natural result was that the church became a business, and its product was the Gospel. Would there be any customers?

Consider the following 1988 assessment on using marketing in the church from David Luecke's book *Evangelical Style and Lutheran Substance*:

> For years I taught management in several business schools. I cannot help but look at evangelism as a marketing task. Using that vocabulary, what is the packaging that delivers a church's substantive product most effectively? The answer comes from figuring out the first question: What are the consumers looking for; what are their felt needs? Market research helps identify those needs . . . Good marketers rely heavily on market research. Using their consumer insights, they help shape and package the product offering so that it has a better chance of getting attention and acceptance.[19]

It is important to note that for this church marketing paradigm to work, a distinct shift in the church's identity had to take place. The church as a community of saints had to be changed to the church as a "building with programs, customer service, and staff." This meant that the worship service, along with the congregation, had to be packaged in order to attract the right market share.

The church was previously an organic entity—the community of saints—who would regularly (weekly) gather around the Gospel, given through Word and Sacrament, and then go back out into the world to serve their neighbor and give witness to their faith.[20] But now the

---

18. From Oxford's online dictionary: http://oxforddictionaries.com/view/entry/m _en_gb0500950#m_en_gb0500950

19. Luecke, *Evangelical Style and Lutheran Substance*, 70.

20. In a 1994 essay, LCMS seminary professor Kurt Marquart wrote: "The church as body of Christ gathers round His sacramental body, 1 Cor 10:17. She assembles for worship in response to the instituting mandate and invitation: "This do in remembrance of

community was reduced to a local organization—a local building—that employed workers and housed a product. It needed to be marketed with the hopes of attracting the uninitiated to it by somehow appealing to their felt needs.

If we are being honest, we would have to admit the shift has been colossal. The community of saints, regularly fed and nourished, at work and witnessing through their vocations was traded for a novel, new business idea. The worship service became the primary focal point and would become the chief product to be sold. This meant it had to be packaged in the right way, according to the right felt needs, in order to attract the most buyers. Felt needs trumped essential needs. Thus, put pejoratively, sales were primary, and forgiveness was secondary. Put flippantly, creativity was king, and Jesus was . . . not.

FROM FORGIVING TO IMPACTING

Lee Strobel urged churches to think about it like this: "If unchurched people can somehow be lured back for a service or event, and if the church were to crank up the creativity just a bit, there would be a great potential for positively impacting them."[21] Where the church had unequivocally impacted people by giving the forgiveness of sins, it was now reduced to giving the possibility of a "positive impact," whatever that meant.

The push for this method did not go without question. Os Guinness offered an early and sharp criticism of this methodology: "The present critique focuses primarily on the errors in methodology that result from church-growth's naïve reliance on modernity's 'new ground.' But the even more important theological critique remains to be done. For example, what of megachurches' subordination of worship and discipleship to evangelism, and all three to entertainment, a problem that is already the Achilles' heel of evangelism?"[22] It is a poignant critique that takes

---

Me." The Holy Supper in the New Testament is not an occasional extra. It is the purpose for coming together, Acts 20:7; 1 Cor 11:20–33. This answers the question whether the service is basically for church members or for the unchurched. Obviously, it is for the church—although others may be present, who then must not be given false and weird impressions, 1 Cor 14:23; Col 4:5." "Church Growth as Mission Paradigm." in *Church and Ministry Today: Three Confessional Lutheran Essays*, 119.

21. Strobel, *Inside the Mind of Unchurched Harry and Mary*, 179.

22. Guinness, *Dining with the Devil*, 27.

particular issue with the way in which the worship service has been subjected to methodology rather than theology.

Nonetheless, the argument continued to be made that for the church to be relevant in a changing world, these market-driven business strategies were essential to the vibrancy and life of the church. In my own tradition, congregations were encouraged to know the "business your church is in" because "your business shapes your action."[23] Just as a business like Sears had to have "the flexibility to adapt to a changing world," so must the church. As it was put by one author, "The church is in the midst of constant change. The church must never change its message, but in form, style, communication technique, and delivery systems the church must change if it is to remain a relevant and powerful force in the world."[24] But as things unfolded, we find that there was a tendency for the medium to become the message. As relevancy rules, the Gospel gets lost.

OF SNOW AND THE GOSPEL

For some, even the plain reading of the Scriptures needed to be packaged in just the right way. Again, Strobel encouraged:

> Most services devote a few minutes to have someone read Scripture. But instead of merely reading some verses, why not have the person reflect on the passage during the week so that he can tell a personal anecdote that relates to the verses before he reads them? This can be helpful in illustrating the practical application of that passage in a person's life and also whet the audience's appetite for the upcoming message. Or perhaps props could be used, since the more senses that can be engaged in the listener, the longer he will retain the information. Once the climax to an anecdote I was telling was the fact that snow had started to fall. But rather than me just saying it snowed, at the right moment it actually began to "snow" on the stage behind me. People went home and told their friends, "You'll never guess what happened in church today. It snowed!" Maybe that piqued their curiosity enough that they might check out the church themselves.[25]

---

23. Hunter, *Moving the Church into Action*, 56–57.

24. Ibid., 55.

25. Strobel, *Inside the Mind of Unchurched Harry and Mary*, 186–87.

True, I will readily admit there is something to be said about abundantly engaging hearers with the Gospel proclamation. But this generally assumes the Gospel (Jesus and the forgiveness of sins) will be present and predominate.

A FRANK ASSESSMENT

Permit me a moment of frankness here. If this packaging were truly for the sake of telling others about Jesus and not for entertainment, why not just encourage members actually to tell their friends about Jesus as opposed to telling them that "It snowed"?[26] If we are being honest, it is difficult not to see such props as simple entertainment or attractional measures. I do not doubt people's fervency. However, it makes it seem like the need to sell the service is greater than the proclamation of the Gospel.

Philip Kenneson and James Street have offered a succinct and decidedly negative assessment about using market strategies in the church:

> We believe that placing a marketing orientation at the center of the church's life radically alters the shape and character of the Christian faith by redefining the character and mission of the church in terms of manageable exchanges between producers and consumers. Much that is central to the Christian life will not fit neatly into the management/marketing scheme, and, not surprisingly, these matters are neglected in a marketing paradigm.[27]

This is no small observation. When the confession and worship of the church are changed like this, the Christian faith becomes abstracted and unclear. Gary Giles calls Strobel out.

> What we supposedly learn from marketing study is that the real reason Harry doesn't come to church has little to do with his rebellious, God rejecting nature. Rather it is because church is boring, predictable, irrelevant, money hungry, and does not meet his

---

26. More recently, Sally Morganthaler, rethinking her stance, helps make the point even clearer when she quotes a man who made her begin to rethink worship and evangelism: "If a contemporary worship service is the best witnessing tool in the box, then why give a rip about what goes on outside the worship center? If unbelievers are coming through the doors to check us Christians out, and if they'll fall at Jesus' feet after they listen to us croon worship songs and watch us sway back and forth, well then, a whole lot of churches are just going to say, 'Sign us up!'" "Worship as Evangelism: Sally Morganthaler Rethinks her own Paradigm," 48.

27. Kenneson and Street, *Selling Out the Church*, 62.

needs. The new-paradigm church operates under the credo that Harry is hostile to the church, friendly to Jesus Christ. They have "the misconception that to win the world to Christ we must first win the world's favor. If we can get the world to like us they will embrace our Savior. The expressed design of the user friendly philosophy is to make unconverted sinners feel comfortable with the Christian message." The only way this is possible, I fear, is to change the message. For the Gospel message is not a comfortable one for the unbeliever, and to try to make it so merely deforms it.[28]

Putting it bluntly, a deformed Gospel can only lead to deformed Christians. No parent would willingly give something to their children that would lead to deformity. It makes sense for the church to follow suit.[29]

Probably the most compelling assessment comes from Gregory A. Pritchard. He wrote his doctoral dissertation on the Willow Creek movement, which has been deemed the prototype of all "seeker sensitive" or "seeker-oriented" church-growth-influenced movements.

For over a year, he was given unlimited access and was allowed to sit in on meetings and planning sessions and attend events. He was granted numerous interviews (many with Bill Hybels and Lee Strobel) and regularly attended their worship services. His findings were published in *Willow Creek Seeker Services: Evaluating a New Way of Doing*

---

28. Gilley, *This Little Church Went to Market*, 69.

29. Dietrich Bonhoeffer has some poignant words for us to consider on what he calls communities that spring up from a wish dream: "Innumerable times a whole Christian community has broken down because it has sprung from a wish dream . . . He who loves his dream of a community more than the Christian community itself becomes a destroyer of the later, even though his personal intentions may be ever so honest and earnest and sacrificial. God hates visionary dreaming; it makes the dreamer proud and pretentious. The man who fashions a visionary ideal of community demands that it be realized by God, by others, and by himself. He enters the community of Christians with his demands, sets up his own law, and judges the brethren and God himself accordingly. He stands adamant, a living reproach to all others in the circle of brethren. He acts as if he is the creator of the Christian community, as if his dreams bind men together. When things do not go his way, he calls the effort a failure. When his ideal picture is destroyed, he sees the community going to smash. So he becomes, first an accuser of his brethren, then an accuser of God, and finally the despairing accuser of himself." *Life Together*, 27–28.

Church, which has been called "the definitive study of the most influential church in North America."[30]

His aim, of course, is to be scholarly and objective. So in as neutral a stance as possible, he presents his work in two self-explanatory halves: "Understanding the Willow Creek way of doing church" and "Evaluating the Willow Creek way of doing church." It is in the second half where both affirmations and critical evaluations are made.

Two of his criticisms seem intensely significant for our discussion. First is his evaluation of Willow Creek's use of marketing: "Marketing brings modern tools of communication that are basic elements of America, and increasingly world, culture. Creekers have borrowed these methods in their efforts to reach their unchurched friends and family. Although their intensions are good, the methods have tended to warp the content of the Christian Gospel. As they seek to market the Gospel, the Gospel itself has been distorted."[31] Corrective lenses were needed.

The second, and utterly telling, criticism relates to what Pritchard notes to be Willow Creek's unintentional "accommodation to the psychological worldview." He had observed Hybel's preaching and teaching at the seeker-sensitive services and found then to be regularly framed by "psychological categories."

Pritchard had identified that the average percentage of seekers actually attending these "seeker services" was 10 percent, with the remaining 90 percent identified as Christians. Noting these two factors, here is what he found:

> The psychological categories Hybels teaches, however, become fundamental categories for how Willow Creek Christians view themselves, their relationships, and life in general. Ironically, while Hybels is evangelizing those in the world toward Christianity, he is also evangelizing Christians toward the world. As the unchurched Harrys in the audience (10 percent) move closer to Christianity, the Christians in the audience (90 percent) are often becoming more psychological and worldly.[32]

---

30. Pritchard, *Willow Creek Seeker Services*, inside cover page, no page number. The quote is by Lyle Schaller.

31. Ibid., 257.

32. Ibid., 238.

In the end, marketing was certainly successful at getting people to attend services. However, as we observed in chapter 2, by Willow Creek's own admission, it seems to have been an unsuccessful venture.

PASTOR AS SHEPHERD OR RANCHER

Marketing the church is not the only concerning element of the church growth paradigm. Another significant concern is in the actual organization of the church, along with the type of pastoral care the members of the congregation can expect to receive.

Consider what church growth guru C. Peter Wagner said in *The Everychurch Guide to Growth*: "As I frequently say, the first two axioms to church growth are: (1) the pastor must want the church to grow and be willing to pay the price, and (2) the people must want the church to grow and be willing to pay the price."[33] The price to be paid is how the congregation is to be structured, along with the responsibility of the pastor being distinctly shaped by one sole endeavor. He puts the function of a pastor in no uncertain terms:

> Start the church as a *rancher*, not as a *shepherd* . . . It is hard for some to picture how they can start a brand new church and not shepherd all the people, but they can, as long as there is mutual agreement that this is the way it is done in our church. This mutual agreement requires three basic ingredients: (1) the pastor does not visit the hospital, (2) the pastor does not call on church members in their homes, and (3) the pastor does no personal counseling.[34]

If we are being honest, this is no small irony when the word *pastor* is simply the translation of the Greek word for *shepherd*, not to mention the resurrected Jesus's call for Peter to tend his lambs and feed his sheep. Nonetheless, it can be readily observed that this is the consistent approach used by the church growth paradigm, insisting that the congregation must raise up laymen to do pastoral care and often citing Acts 6 as a rationale for this approach.[35]

33. Towns, Wagner, and Rainer, *The Everychurch Guide to Growth*, 46.

34. Ibid., 63.

35. "The Apostolic twelve made a decision to turn over the ministry of waiting on the widows to seven laymen." Ibid., 107. However, Norman Nagel is rather helpful in clarifying that these seven were no laymen but rather certainly "apostled" or ordained. As Nagel says, "Luke's emphasis on the Word of God as the primary doer in the Acts

However, Kurt Marquart is quick to object: "No! The Lord said not, 'Organize My sheep into work-brigades, to do the real ministry themselves,' but, 'Feed My lambs, feed My sheep!' The shepherds are there precisely to 'do ministry for the sheep,' that is, to preach the Gospel and administer the sacraments to them. The church is not a self-service buffet. The shepherding Gospel ministry is there precisely to 'reproduce' and nourish the sheep."[36] To be sure, the passion, the zeal, and the urgency to reach the lost are entirely desirable, needed, and exemplary. But extreme caution is warranted when it means compromising the actual identity of the church, her confession of Christ, and the mission of God.

FROM CHURCH GROWTH TO EMERGING CHURCH

In the end, it had become clear to me that a strategic plan formed by church growth principles was not desirable. Nonetheless, it was interesting to observe how the church growth movement is decidedly a movement born out of modernity. (Modernity, as we observed in the last chapter, is characterized by the certainty of knowledge and claimed positive progression of life.) It gave birth to the idea that, "If you follow these steps, you are sure to have growth in your church." However, the movement is decidedly a part of what Jenson called "abstracted Christianity."[37] According to him, it was inevitably going to fail. In fact,

---

of the Apostles may help explain why the Seven are not outside the ministry of the Word by their designation 'to serve tables,' any more than the Twelve had been, as is confirmed by what we are later told of Stephen and Philip. Having a Twelve and a Seven is not the final solution. Polity may vary. Constant are the words of the Lord and their delivery as He has mandated. In Acts 6 the number of ministers is augmented with specific allocation of tasks." "The Twelve and the Seven in Acts 6 and the Needy," 119. Thus there is simply a division of responsibility among those in the same office. Titles may vary, tasks may too, but the office is always the same. There is no new office or divvying up of the office into parts so that there is no arguing "which of us is the greatest."

36. Marquart, "Church Growth as Mission Paradigm," *Church and Ministry Today*, 84.

37. "It would be possible to argue that abstracted Christianity was the whole project of modernity. Christianity claimed to tell a universally encompassing story, a 'metanarrative' if you will, and posited as a correlated notion the universal possibility of finding one's place in the narrative. Modernity appropriated the claim and the posit, hoping to maintain the form of the Christian story without telling it about Christ. The universal possibility of finding one's place in the truth was abstracted to become the posit of a formal rationality universally possessed, which was then to discover and construe the universal story." Jenson, "What is a Post-Christian?" *It's a Strange New Word of the Gospel*, 27.

many are pointing out how it has indeed failed, and they are offering a new alternative: the emerging church.

As postmodernism has rebelled against the brazenness of modernity with its incredulity toward such certainty, in a like manner, some in the evangelical church have rebelled against the paradigm of church growth. This is most evident by the counter-movement composed of numerous disenfranchised evangelicals who have undertaken the narrative of postmodernism, rejected the Religious Right, embraced ecumenism, the poor, social justice, and other yet emerging ways of what they call "following Jesus." Collectively they are known as the emergent or emerging church movement. Their desire is to bring a corrective to the church. *Perhaps*, I thought, *this movement would be helpful in shaping a strategic plan*. However, what I found was that in their desire to provide a corrective to the church, an overcorrection was occurring. I will explain how in the next chapter.

Chapter 5

Emerging Confusion

THE BIRTH OF (MY DAUGHTER) TRUTH

THE CONFUSION ABOUT THE importance of new buildings, attracting unbelievers, and cultural relevancy was (and is) not limited to my congregation. It remained a larger issue. In fact, in 2009, it had become a significant issue for the regional district convention of my church body. There was a great amount of confusion regarding a new mission start congregation, their practices, and their beliefs.

Assurances had been given, but skeptics remained. Some wanted to receive the mission start into official membership; others were uncertain. The atmosphere had become political and contentious. I wanted to be there to hear the discussion and plead for collegial and honest dialogue, but my wife was delivering our third baby, a beautiful girl named Aletheia. (Greek scholars will note that her name means "truth").

I had learned from the birth of my second child (Thaddaeus) not to go back to work on the day your child is born! I didn't this time. But the next day I did. I still had a lot to learn. (Have I mentioned my wife is amazing?) Do *not* go back to work on the day your child is born or the day after he or she is born. In fact, take three days off and be with your family! As I was working on this book, our fourth child was born. And I am happy to say I finally learned! Her name is Ekklacia—Greek for "church." When she was born, I finally took multiple days off to be with my bride and family.

While my wife and I named our daughters for He who is "the way, *the truth*, and the life" and He who is "the Lord of *the Church*," the church in North America continues to struggle to agree upon the truth of her mission and the purpose of her being.

As much as the church growth movement has affected the way people think about the mission of the church (my congregation included), a more recent movement is adding some additional confusion in the struggle for truth. It is collectively known as the emergent church movement.

THE EMERGENT CHURCH MOVEMENT

> Too often in recent years, church leaders have acted as if being sensitive to seekers means sliding into a one-size-fits-all, franchise, clone, mimic-*the*-model mentality. Too often, we exchange one set of rigid traditional styles and methods and ways of thinking for equally rigid "contemporary" ones. Too often, we have acted without sufficient reflection, without thinking deeply about the profound relationship between church and culture, between past and present and future, between our methods and our message. And we have been gimmick-prone and thoughtlessly (sometimes desperately) pragmatic, without being as innocent as doves and as wise as serpents (Matt. 10:16).[1]

These are the inflammatory words Brian McLaren offers as part of his forward to Dan Kimball's book *The Emerging Church*. They are, in many respects, a summation of at least one thing that the emerging church movement is doing: thinking.[2]

McLaren has become the most recognized leader of the movement and has provided no shortage of books, articles, and interviews to consider. With each comes his whimsical, distinct, playfully endearing, and

1. Kimball, *The Emerging Church*, 9.

2. John Pless observes, "While the leaders of the Emerging Church are critical of what they describe as the rationalism of modernity, they are not anti-intellectual. The list of theologians most often cited by Emerging Church thinkers include Stanley Grenz, Miroslav Volf, Lesslie Newbigin, Nancy Murphy, James McClendon, John Franke, Robert Webber, N. T. Wright, David Bosch, John Howard Yoder, Stanley Hauerwas, Hans Frei, Clark Pinnock, and Walter Brueggeman. Scholars associated with Fuller Theological Seminary and abroad neo-Evangelicalism, especially those who see themselves as 'postfoundationalists,' figure most prominently in shaping the theology of the movement." "Contemporary Spirituality and the Emerging Church," 350.

yet at times, theologically disturbing, depth of thought. He is well read and has no lack of foundation for his thinking.

Perhaps, in some ways, this foundation is a reaction to Mark Noll's critique about the evangelical mind. Yet on a deeper level, the reason for this thinking and its expression, as demonstrated in his words above, comes as a reaction to what many emergent thinkers feel is so "desperately" wrong with many of the churches in North America. Initially made up of a host of disenfranchised evangelicals fed up with the megachurch madness and the church growth mentality of modernity, the emerging church movement has the venue of postmodernism to voice their discontent and call for change.

As Kimball writes, "Clearly interest is growing in how the church can reach out to emerging generations in what some call a postmodern or post-Christian context . . . Perhaps the Spirit of God is stirring among us, giving us an unsettling feeling that church the way we know it must change."[3] Perhaps. But claiming the movement of the Spirit apart from the clear Word of God can be a rather dubious experiment. There were often claims of the "Spirit" moving among the church growth movement as well.[4] In any case, what will be clear is that the emergent church movement is entirely aware of our cultural condition and is willing to engage it. The question is, "With what theological integrity will they engage it?"

The movement is offering a course correction to the church growth movement and its corresponding mindset toward the church. But as can happen with reactionary movements, it appears they are going to an opposite extreme.

James K. Smith offers a fair warning, which may even hearken back to Noll's critique but with a noted theological emphasis:

> There remains a certain notion that the church needs to "get with" postmodernity such that postmodern culture sets an agenda for the church, rather than postmodernity being a catalyst for the church to recover its own authentic mission. If we hope to be properly postmodern, then we must intentionally resist this correlational model . . . If theology no longer seeks to position,

---

3. Kimball, *The Emerging Church*, 13.

4. The Lutheran understanding of the Holy Spirit remains constant. As the explanation of the third article of the Apostles' Creed reminds us, the Holy Spirit is always present and always at work, regardless of the cultural times, wherever the Gospel is being proclaimed.

qualify or criticize other discourses, then it is inevitable that these discourses will position theology.[5]

This serves as a warning for emergent evangelicals as well as anyone who would let the culture set the agenda for the church. But I think it also serves as permission to celebrate the historic confession of the faith declared by the creeds throughout the centuries. It provides theology the necessary opportunity to determine the position of the cultural impingements on the church. It is not the other way around and not at the expense of the lost, but rather, for the sake of the Gospel.[6] I will say more on this in the next chapter.

THE EMERGENT CONVERSATION

At the moment, the movement is too young to know where it might ultimately land. However, we are beginning to get a fairly good picture. Each year the brushstrokes become finer, offering more details. One of the mantras of the movement is that it is a "conversation."[7] This means there is a prolific amount of literature—books, articles, websites, and blogs—being produced by emergent thinkers. In fact, there is an open invitation for anyone to join the "conversation" at what is called the "Emergent Village."[8]

I, for one, am grateful for their desire to have dialogue. It is, as I have noted, what the church needs to do. And as I continued searching for help in crafting a strategic plan, I thought perhaps this movement would offer some assistance. However, what I found is that the conversations are less about the truth (of the Scriptures and the certainty of the mission of the church) than they are about the conversation itself. To be sure, they are fascinating and whimsical conversationalists, be it

5. Smith, *Who's Afraid of Postmodernism?*, 125.

6. Futurist Leonard Sweet puts it aptly: "Christians should not embrace a postmodern worldview; we must not adapt to postmodernity. Jesus is 'the same yesterday, today, forever' (Heb. 13:8 NKJV). In other words, Jesus is the same in three times zones and two dimensions: the timely (past and present) and the timeless (forever). But we do need to incarnate the timeless in the timely. Postmoderns do need to probe the living-out of our faith in light of the classical Christian tradition." *Postmodern Pilgrims*, xvii.

7. "Thus, when pinned down and forced to answer the question, 'What is emergent or Emerging Church?' most who are will answer, 'A conversation,' which is not only true but which will always be true. The Great Emergence can not 'be,' and be otherwise." Tickle, *The Great Emergence*, 153.

8. http://www.emergentvillage.com/.

online, in person, or through their writings. But they are masterful at avoiding doctrinal precision while simultaneously being certain of their own narrative. Assertive ambiguity and intentional liberality color their language. Ultimately, the desire of the movement is to be generous in both their orthodoxy and their orthopraxy. I will explain below.

Phyllis Tickle is an authority and quasi-spokeswoman for the movement. She is quick to point out that even though "nobody is exactly sure who should and shouldn't be labeled as an 'emergent' or 'emerging,'" she is certain that "by the time the Great Emergence has reached maturity, about 60 percent of practicing Christians will be emergent or some clear variant thereof."[9] She's even bold enough to say that the "emerging church has the potential of being to North American Christianity what Reformation Protestantism was to European Christianity."[10] No small claim!

With such bold predictions, it would serve us well to know what the emergent conversation is about—what they're saying about the church, about the Scriptures, and most certainly, about Jesus.

THE EMERGING/EMERGENT DISCOVERY

Dan Kimball begins this way: "I believe we are at a point in church history when we need to rethink some of our assumptions and reexamine some of our presuppositions about church and ministry . . . [T]he emerging church is emerging in a very quickly changing world. So we need to change how we go about our ministry."[11] If it sounds familiar it is because the claim was made before. It is the same rationale that was used to convince people of the necessity for the church growth model.[12] However, Kimball is sensitive to this, and so he elaborates:

> In recent times, the wave of change came to the church with the seeker-sensitive movement. Another wave of change is now breaking on our shores. This shouldn't surprise us. Time passes, new generations are born, cultures change, so the church must

9. Tickle, *The Great Emergence*, 139.

10. Tickle, from her foreword to Brian McLaren's book *A Generous Orthodoxy*, 12.

11. Kimball, *The Emerging Church*, 27.

12. "The church is in the midst of constant change. The church must never change its message, but in form, style, communication technique, and delivery systems the church must change if it is to remain a relevant and powerful force in the world." Hunter, *Moving the Church into Action*, 55.

> change . . . The type of change I am talking about is not just about
> what happens in the church service, with the music, or with the
> small group strategy. These are only surface issues. It is really a
> revolutionary change that affects almost everything we do—even
> what comes to our minds when we say the word church.[13]

Thus, for Kimball, as with the majority of emergents, a new understanding of church is what is so revolutionary about the movement. For
them, there is a recovery of the church as an authentic and organic body
of believers on a mission, not just a business appealing to the market.

To explain, Kimball shares of a time when he was teaching a Bible
class on the book of Acts. He began by making some provocative statements. First, he said, "There is not one verse in the New Testament that
says they 'went to church.'" Confused looks followed. Then he said,
"According to the Bible it is actually impossible to 'go to church.'" More
confusion.

Finally, to really push their buttons, he said, "If you woke up this
morning and said I'm going to church today, you would actually be
making a theologically incorrect statement." His purpose: "I was trying
to get the point across that the church is not the building, nor is it the
meeting. The church is the people of God who gather together with a
sense of mission (Acts 14:27). We can't *go* to church because *we are* the
church."[14] However, many traditions (my own included) hold they have
retained a distinct understanding of the church as an organic "community of saints." Perhaps, then, the more honest conclusion is that this new
revolutionary understanding of church is more of a parochial, in-house
correction rather than a new discovery.

Even so, Kimball cites the book *The Missional Church* and asserts
that it was actually the first reformers who caused the eventual change in
understanding the church as the "body of believers" to church being the
"place" you go. In fact, the wording he uses might very well be an indictment against creedal church bodies. (Lutherans will note his phrases are
very close to the Augsburg Confession, Article VII):

> The Reformers, in their effort to raise the authority of the Bible
> and ensure sound doctrine, defined the marks of a true church:
> a place where the Gospel is rightly preached, the sacraments
> are rightly administered, and church discipline is exercised.

13. Kimball, *The Emerging Church*, 27–28.
14. Ibid., 91.

However, over time these marks narrowed the definition of the church itself as a "place where" idea instead of a "people who are" reality. The word church became defined as "a place where certain things happen," such as preaching and communion.[15]

For as much truth as there might be in his assessment for present-day creedal congregations and their similar use of the phrase "going to church," it would be shortsighted to claim that this is truly what the first reformers were doing. Yes, some present-day creedal Christians may personally have a similar limited understanding for any number of reasons. When that is the case, Kimball's diagnosis can be appropriately heeded by pastor and parishioner alike. At the same time, we do need to guard against diminishing "preaching and communion" for they do have locatedness, not merely to a building, but to a people. They are significant to the life of the community of saints. And most notably, they have historically been the marks that identify the Holy Christian Church.[16]

We can also read Augsburg Confession Article VII and note that the assertion about the Reformers is not accurate: "It is also taught that at all times there must be and remain one holy, Christian church. It is the assembly of all believers among whom the Gospel is purely preached and the holy sacraments are administered according to the Gospel." Here the church is described as an "assembly of believers." (Using Kimball's words, it is "people who are.") And among other things, this assembly gathers together and receives, marks, and inwardly digests (literally in the Lord's Supper) the Word and Sacraments given for our salvation.

As noted in chapter 1, the third article of the Apostles' Creed readily clarifies what creedal churches believe. The "Holy Christian Church" and the "Community of Saints" is the body of believers where, as Luther's Small Catechism says, "Daily . . . the Holy Spirit abundantly forgives all sins—mine and those of all believers." "Daily" refers to time, not location. And "Holy Spirit" refers to the caller, gatherer, and enlightener, who does His work by nothing other than the Gospel. No building is mentioned. No place is referenced. But certainly they were used, as was

15. Ibid., 93.

16. As Forde says: "[T]he church is not just any assembly that happens to call itself by the name of Jesus for whatever reason or purpose, or where there may be orders calling themselves holy and so on. To counter a current heresy, the church is not just 'people.' That assertion may rightly controvert the idea that church is a building or even an institution, but it too easily forgets that the church is a gathering called and shaped by the Gospel of its Lord, Jesus Christ." *All Theology is for Proclamation*, 186–87.

a tent and a temple in the Old Testament. In the end, Kimball's point can be helpful, but perhaps it is not as revolutionary as he asserts.

THE MISSIONAL EMERGENT CHURCH

Understanding the church as a "people who are" has become the foundation for the emergent church (and the corresponding self-correcting church growth movement) to assess how to be the church. As a result, there has been a welcome renewal in the study of the New Testament church and a fascination with ancient church practices to help guide this revolution.[17] From this study, the transition has been made away from the consumer-oriented seeker services to what is (as we discussed in chapter 2) the *en vogue* "missional churches." As Kimball puts it:

> There is no way a missional church that understands her place in God's story can produce consumer Christians. It would go against its very nature. But becoming a missional church means more than having a mission statement or offering an occasional class. It means "rebirthing" the church from the inside out and maintaining its new psyche. It means constantly resisting the tendency to become consumer-oriented by keeping the mission at the *forefront* of all that we do. How thrilling that we have the opportunity to redefine the church to emerging generations.[18]

Some carry a great sense of optimism about the missional church.[19] Others have called this optimism into question, noting that the idea of being missional has become a label that describes practically everything the church does.[20] Alan Hirsch asks it this way: "As church leaders con-

17. "The emerging church must define the church scripturally again, teaching people how the church fits into the grand story of the Bible." Kimball, *The Emerging Church*, 95.

18. Ibid., 96.

19. "This missional church is not just another phase of church life but a full expression of *who* the church is and *what* it is called to be and do. The missional church builds upon the ideas of church growth and church health but brings the lessons learned from each into full blown missions focus—within their local mission field as well as the ends of the earth." Stetzer and Putnam, *Breaking the Missional Code*, 49.

20. "The team who wrote *Missional Church* introduced the word *missional* as an invitation for people to consider a new way of being the church. It was intended to create a space in which we could get a new imagination for what God wants to do in and through the church. That was over ten years ago, and today there is an extreme problem: *missional church* has become a label used to describe practically everything the church does." Roxburough and Boren, *Introducing the Missional Church*, 31.

tinue to pile onto the missional bandwagon, the true meaning of the word may be getting buried under a pile of assumptions. Is it simply updated nomenclature for being purpose-driven or seeker-sensitive? Is *missional* a new, more mature strain of the emerging church movement?"[21] So the question then remains, is the missional church just another phase?

Since *missional* is now even nomenclature that many creedal church bodies employ, could it be said that it is not just another phase? Or is it the final expression of the church growth movement that needs some renewed validation before it passes away?

Whatever the case, it is part of the conversation, a conversation that, for all intents and purposes, has produced ample dialogue about the church—what it was, what it is, and what it is supposed to be. It is a dialogue that needs to continue. But in my opinion, it needs to continue with a good deal more honest and candid theological considerations. Hopefully, that is beginning here.

ANCIENT EMERGING PRACTICES

Invariably, as it did in the church growth movement, part of this conversation centers on the worship service. However, the conversation has moved to the past, literally, to go beyond the marketing practices of the church growth movement. Now services are filled with a mixed bag of contemporary and cutting-edge, ancient practices, where those practices are meant to pervade all of life and not just the worship service.[22]

To that end, the emergent movement commissioned an eight-book series that sought to explore and lift up these practices. It is aptly called *The Ancient Practices Series*. Each new title was written by "a leading author on spirituality" and is accompanied with an introduction by series

---

21. Hirsch, "Defining Missional," December 12, 2008, www.christianitytoday.com/le/communitylife/evangelism/17.20.html?gclid=CMqdyNHrn6gCFUF95odgUltQw.

22. On ancient practices, Kimball writes: "The senior pastor of the church once said in a staff meeting that my friend and his team were really 'pushing the envelope' and really doing some 'cutting edge' things. 'Crazy things happen in that service,' he said. You may be wondering what was going on in the church. Well my friend told me, 'Dan, we aren't cutting edge at all. All we are doing is praying more in the service. We might get on our knees more. We have times of silence. We read creeds together. This is why my senior pastor says is cutting edge!' How ironic that returning to a raw and ancient form of worship is now seen as new and even cutting edge. We are simply going back to a vintage form of worship which has been around for as long as the church has been in existence." Kimball, *The Emerging Church*, 169.

editor Phyllis Tickle.[23] Brian McLaren wrote the first book, *Finding Our Way Again: The Return of the Ancient Practices*. It acted as a guide for the explanation of the seven spiritual practices detailed in each subsequent book.

The series then proceeded in the following order: *In Constant Prayer* by Robert Benson, *Sabbath* by Dan Allender, *Fasting* by Scot McKnight, *Sacred Meal* by Nora Gallagher, *Sacred Journey* by Diana Butler Bass, *The Liturgical Year* by Joan Chittister, and *Tithing* by Douglas LeBlanc.

McLaren's beginning to the series is intriguing, thought-provoking, playful, and at times quite unsettling. In some ways, it is a foretelling of the highs and lows that would flow out of the series itself and, quite possibly, maybe even the whole emerging church movement. Though an examination of each book is not possible, a brief observation to characterize the highs and lows of the series may suffice before we take a closer look at McLaren's introductory and telling book.

SACRED MEAL SACRED LITURGY

Those church bodies that place a high value on the Lord's Supper would have a keen eye on exploring Nora Gallagher's *Sacred Meal*.[24] On the whole, it serves the emergent conversation with its narrative approach. From a sacramental position, it is a disappointing treatment. Gallagher writes from her emerging Episcopal background, certainly lifting up the meal as sacred but ultimately reducing it, albeit thoughtfully but nonetheless thoroughly, in what it is and what it does. For her, it is a spiritual meal that is open to all and that points to the community. A brief excerpt will demonstrate:

> On the last night of his life, Jesus said, "Do this to remember me" (Luke 22:19 NLT). Many of us think these words, these Last Supper words, mean that we're remembering Jesus when we drink of this cup and eat of this bread. Well, of course, we're remembering Jesus, but that should not be all we're doing. I don't think Jesus was interested in everybody just remembering him.

23. "Religion, wherever it is found, is more than a system of untethered beliefs. Rather, it is an intricate, interlocking lacework of physical laws, intellectual assumptions, and spiritual values that, held in common, are both the faith lived and its perpetuation." Phyllis Tickle, http://news.thomasnelson.com/2007/11/15/thomas-nelson-announces-ground-breaking-series/.

24. With a distinctive "real presence" history, and a practice of close(d) Communion, Lutherans have a watchful eye regarding the theology and practice of the Lord's Supper.

What's the point of that? That puts Jesus in the category with various celebrities who will do anything to get into the media so we'll remember they're still alive. Instead, I think Jesus wanted his disciples and everyone who came after him to remember *what they had together.* What they made together. What it meant to be together. How the things we wanted them to do could not be done alone. How the things he did could not have been done without them.

Instead of thinking of that communion as a ghoulish eating of human flesh, think of those who gather at Communion as the body of Jesus. We are the body given for each other. *This is my body,* he said. *Look around you.*

When we all show up and do our parts, we are the sacrament, the body of Christ. *Do this to remember me. Do this to remember you were with me. Do this to remember who you are.*[25]

It is a dissatisfying treatment, particularly for those church bodies that hold the Sacrament as more than a mere remembrance meal. My own tradition holds that the meal gives the forgiveness of sins precisely because it is the real presence of Jesus Christ in, with, and under the bread and wine. To be sure, we also recognize the body of Christ makes us one in Christ with fellow believers (i.e., the community of saints), but that is the result of the meal and not its only goal.

There was also a high point in the series. *The Liturgical Year* by Joan Chittister is a veritable gem. She is a seasoned Catholic nun who has the ability to let the reader rejoice in the nature of the liturgical year and its accompanying liturgy. True, some traditions will find obvious differences, but she has a beautiful manner of showing that the life of the liturgy is simply the life of Jesus for the life of the believer. Again, an excerpt will demonstrate. It is a bit longer, but it captures the fullness and depth of Chittister's presentation:

Like a great waterwheel, the liturgical year goes on relentlessly irrigating our souls, softening the ground of our hearts, nourishing the soil of our lives until the seed of the Word of God itself begins to grow in us, comes to fruit in us, ripens in us the spiritual journey of a lifetime. So goes the liturgical year through all the days of our lives. It concentrates us on the two great poles of the faith—the birth and death of Jesus of Nazareth. But as Christmas and Easter trace the life of Jesus for us from beginning to end, the

25. Gallagher, *The Sacred Meal,* 23–24.

liturgical year does even more: it also challenges our own life and vision and sense of meaning.

Both a guide to greater spiritual maturity and a path to a deepened spiritual life, the liturgical year leads us through all the great questions of faith as it goes. It rehearses the dimensions of life over and over for us all the years of our days. It leads us back again and again to reflect on the great moments of the life of Jesus and so to apply them to our own . . .

As the liturgical year goes on every day of our lives, every season of every year, tracing the steps of Jesus from Bethlehem to Jerusalem, so does our own life move back and forth between our own beginnings and endings, between our own struggles and triumphs, between the rush of acclamation and the crush of abandonment. It is the link between Jesus and me, between this life and the next, between me and the world around me, that is the gift of the liturgical year.

The meaning and message of the liturgical year is the bedrock on which we strike our own life direction. Rooted in the Resurrection promise of the liturgical year, whatever the weight of our own pressures, we maintain the course. We trust in the future we cannot see and do only know because we have celebrated the death and Resurrection of Jesus year after year. In His life we rest our own.[26]

For her, the life of the liturgy is simply the life of Jesus for the life of the believer. It is a beautiful description that has intrigued members of both liturgical and non-liturgical traditions.[27]

UNSETTLING THOUGHTFULNESS

McLaren's book has similar highs and lows but with an overarching, socially transforming purpose. He begins by recognizing how the church—presumably the one held captive by the church growth movement—has been sorely in need of these practices. But he also notes that these practices have a multi-religious dimension to them.[28] This is not

26. Chittister, *The Liturgical Year*, 209–10.

27. See the numerous reader reviews at www.Amazon.com.

28. "This new focus is an acknowledgement that we have lost the path and are seeking to rediscover our faith as a way of life, shaped and strengthened by ancient practices. Although written by a Christian primarily for Christians, this initial book in the series extends our acknowledgement to unreligious people as well as to adherents of all three Abrahamic faiths: Judaism, Christianity, and Islam. Each of the books following this one in the series will explore in depth and detail one of the seven ancient practices

an uncommon approach for McLaren. Observable in his writings is not only his general appeal to an emergent ecumenism but a distinguishable openness, though perhaps a qualified one, to other faith traditions.[29]

It is a contemplative and thoughtful approach, but one that, despite all his genuineness, has, perhaps intentionally, an unsettling quality about it. For example, in expressing how there are many people today who have a great affinity for Jesus but not for Christianity, he implies the dissolution of church body denominations by asserting that "the 'Jesus thing' should probably be seen less as a religious institution and more as a movement (after all, this is what followers do, they *move* in the direction of their leader)." But then he goes on to expand this view by noting, "The same might be said for the Abraham thing and the Moses thing and the Muhammad thing: they weren't intended to be static repositories of dogma or lists of rules and rituals; they were intended to be movements, each a distinct way of living intended to bring God's shalom or *salaam* into the world."[30]

In other words, he is willing to let other faith practices stand, intentionally avoiding condemning evaluations, and instead engages them as a portal to explore what he considers to be the greater realities of faith itself. As a result, an implication that becomes so unsettling for many is his tacit affirmation of these belief systems, not to mention the possible undermining of normative biblical faith.[31]

---

shared by the Abrahamic faith traditions: fixed-hour prayer, fasting, Sabbath, the sacred meal, pilgrimage, observance of sacred seasons, and giving." McLaren, *Finding Our Way Again*, 6.

29. "More and more of us feel, more and more intensely, the need for a fresh, creative alternative—a fourth alternative, a something beyond militarist scientific secularism, pushy religious fundamentalism, and mushy amorphous spirituality. The alternative, we realize, needs to be creative and new to face the challenges of a new age, a world gone 'post-al'—postmodern, postcolonial, post-Enlightenment, post-Christendom, post-Holocaust, post-9/11. Yet it also needs to derive strength from old religious traditions; it needs to face new-age challenges with age-old wisdom. The challenge of the future will require, we realize, rediscovery and adaptive reuse of resources from the ancient past." McLaren, *Finding Our Way Again*, 5–6.

30. Ibid., 37–38.

31. D.A. Carson, in his detailed critique of the emergent church, offers this: "We have observed that some leaders among the emerging church movement are reluctant to say anything adverse about other religions." He then offers a host of reasons why that is, including "cautious, courteous reticence" as well as the recognition that "there are in fact many good things in other religions." But his aim is to point out that "there is one dominant way in which the Bible describes those who follow other gods, and

In the end, for all of its thoughtfulness, for all of its helpful curiosities, and for all of its ancient insights, McLaren's *Finding Our Way Again* seems to contain what could be called a Gnostic social Gospel.[32] For McLaren, the purpose of these practices ultimately points toward making the world a better place. His final reason why we should "pursue the ancient way in which we learn to practice peace, joy, self-mastery, and justice" is "because the future of the world depends on people like you and me finding it and living it and inviting others to join us."[33]

However, what's curious about his presentation is how the Gospel of Jesus Christ is portrayed. Though he certainly talks of Jesus and even lifts up Jesus' phrase, "the kingdom of heaven," he changes it to be the "harmony of heaven" that can transform society.[34] "The power of the God for the salvation of everyone who believes" (Rom 1:16) is reshaped into a harmony that can reform the world into a better place. Yes, pursuit of justice, care of the poor, and help for the needy do flow out of the Gospel. But those things have not historically been the markers of the church. (Please don't get me wrong. The care of the needy and the pursuit of justice are good things to do! I have sat in multiple courtrooms

---

on this point the writers of the emergent movement with whom I am familiar seem to be strangely silent. The Bible tends to call such people idolaters and their gods idols. When Israel adopts some of these idols into their patterns of worship, the nation is not commended for its openness but condemned for its participation in idolatry." *Becoming Conversant with the Emerging Church*, 200–201.

32. As far as a book on the spiritual practices goes, it is altogether unhelpful from a Lutheran point of view. A suggested alternate comparison, and one much more faithful to the Christian ancient practices, would be John Kleinig's *Grace Upon Grace: Spirituality for Today*. He offers distinct application, identifying the real challenges to the Christian spiritual life (sin and the devil) in the way of the ancient practice of meditation informed by Luther's understanding of "*Oratio* [prayer], *Meditatio* [mediation], *Tentatio* [temptation]" that are all centered upon regularly receiving God grace: "If we have problems in living the life of faith, if we have challenges in the practice of prayer, the solution is not to be found in what we do, our self-appraisal, or our performance. The solution to our problems is found in what we receive from God Himself, in His appraisal of us, and in His gifts to us. Like our physical life and health, our spiritual life is something that is given to us, something that is all a matter of receiving grace upon grace from the fullness of God the Father." Kleinig, *Grace Upon Grace*, 5.

33. McLaren, *Finding Our Way Again*, 201.

34. "What if there is a treasure hidden in the field of our three great monotheisms, long buried but waiting to be rediscovered? And what if that treasure is a way—a way that can train us to stop killing and hating and instead to work together, under God, joining God, to build a better world, a city of peace, a city of God?" McLaren, *Finding Our Way Again*, 202.

alongside of families pursuing justice. Our congregation recently had thirty members make over 5,000 meals for Feed-My-Starving-Children. Our parochial K-8 grade school has waved tuition fees for needy, unchurched families. And more recently, after putting out an e-mail for a community family in need of winter clothes for their six children, we had enough donations for fifteen kids within twenty-four hours. The pile keeps growing! Yes, these behaviors certainly flow out of the Gospel, but my point is that they are not the definitive marks of the Gospel.)

In the end, the series demonstrates how, in many ways, the movement remains highly nuanced and inventive (if not confusing) and that it certainly flows out of multiple past traditions.

EMERGENT HERMENEUTICS

Charting the nascent beginnings of the movement, Phyllis Tickle in *The Great Emergence* has some helpful explanations about the inventiveness of the movement. She is detailed and specific. However, her language is consistent with theologians and scholars indulging in the depths of their field. So, it may start to feel like you are chewing on a mouthful of taffy, wondering if you are ever going to be able to swallow it down. Nonetheless, it is a necessary part of considering the merits of the movement. I will do my best to put things into manageable bites.

To begin, the movement is very aware of the various plights of orthodoxy and orthopraxy within Christendom (i.e., when Christianity became the religion of the empire) and within Christianity (i.e., the various denominations within it). Regardless of where one falls on the spectrum of orthodoxy and orthopraxy, the emergent church tends to gravitate away from the rigidity and unrest that each can individually instigate. Rather, Tickle offers what is not so much a mediating position as much as it is a multifaceted, integrating hermeneutic of sorts. It is here that the language gets technical and detailed, but it is helpful for us to see the development of the movement's thought.

ORTHO . . . WHAT?

In an effort to make the orthodoxy and orthopraxy of the movement as generous as possible, Tickle notes they avoid using the terms altogether. Recognizing the *ortho* of correctness (but not wanting the rigidity of *doxy* or *praxy*), there is added to it the suffix of *nomy* to create *orthonomy*. The *nomy* is understood to be the derivative of the Greek word for *nomos*. According to Tickle, it is "most nearly, the ineffable beauty in that which is divine, especially as it becomes incarnate within space and time."[35] Consequently, *orthonomy*, Tickle asserts, "may be defined as a kind of 'correct harmoniousness' or beauty."[36]

This is why emergent Christians are so confused when arguments of historicity are made. "An emergent, in observing heated debates or impassioned conversations about the factualness of the Virgin birth, for example, can truly be puzzled. For him or her, the whole 'problem' is just not 'there' in any distinguishable or real sense. For the emergent, as he or she will be quick to say, the Virgin birth is so beautiful that it has to be true, whether it happened or not."[37] However, she is well aware of the cries of Keatsian heresy that would accompany such a move.[38] For beauty is relative and, therefore, would be subject to the interpretive filter of human culture. Thus, she offers a careful and inventive explanation. Again, the language is technical but essential for grasping the movement's theory of the church and her mission:

> [T]o counter the tendency toward allowing aesthetic response and/or emotionally or spiritually moving experience to become bases for authority, emergents and emerging on the right of the vertical [her diagram] have reconfigured a word of their own: *theonomy* . . . As a term, it means to say or name the principle that only God can be the source of perfection in action and thought . . . the Bible being the only "source" of authority as well as the one readiest to hand for those who hold with theonomy. As is patently clear, the burden of the argument of theonomy is still the principle of *sola scriptura*, albeit in more modish and culturally attractive clothes, while orthonomy is only a variant of tradition, reason, and inspiration as conduits for safely receiving the holy.[39]

Ultimately, this serves as the basis of the movement's developing and emerging hermeneutic . . . but with a qualification. In what can be described as nothing else than an utterly bold assertion, she states that

35. Tickle, *The Great Emergence*, 149.

36. Tickle adds, "In effect, when it is used as here, it means the employment of aesthetic or harmonic purity as a tool for discerning the truth—and therefore the intent and authority—of anything, be that thing either doctrine or practice." Ibid.

37. Ibid.

38. John Keats made the famous observation that truth is beauty and beauty is truth.

39. Tickle, *The Great Emergence*, 150.

the notion of using "Luther's *sola scriptura* . . . is now seen as hopelessly outmoded or insufficient, even after it is, as here, spruced up and re-couched in more current sensibilities."[40] This is no small claim! Scripture alone is no longer sufficient? What needs to be added? And why? The movement is quick to let us know.

SCRIPTURE + NETWORK THEORY = THE CHURCH?

With such a claim, a new authority base of its own needed to be de-veloped. And so it did. It was derived from the idea of network theory. (Sorry, more technical language.) Tickle describes the resulting un-derstanding of the emerging church in this extended but necessary summary:

> The end result of this dynamic structure is the realization that no one of the member parts or connecting networks has the whole or entire "truth" of anything, either as such and/or when inde-pendent of the others. Each is only a single working piece of what is evolving and is sustainable so long as the interconnectivity of the whole remains intact. No one member parts or their hubs, in other words, has the whole truth as a possession or as its domain. This conceptualization is not just theory. Rather, it has a name: *crowd sourcing*; and crowd sourcing differs from democracy for more substantially than one might at first suspect. It differs in that it employs total egalitarianism, a respect for worth of the hoi polloi that even pure democracy never had and a complete indif-ference to capitalism as a virtue or to individualism as a godly circumstance.
>
> The duty, the challenge, the joy and excitement of the Church and for the Christians who compose her, then, is in discovering what it means to believe that the kingdom of God is within one and in understanding that one is thereby a pulsating, vibrating bit in a much grander network. Neither established human au-thority nor scholarly or priestly discernment alone can lead, be-cause, being human, both are trapped in space/time and thereby prevented from a perspective of total understanding. Rather, it is how the message runs back and forth, over and about, the hubs of the network that is tried and amended and tempered into wis-dom and right action for effecting the Father's will.[41]

40. Ibid., 151.
41. Ibid., 152–53.

To be sure, there is depth of thought and careful articulation in the development of this hermeneutic. And it does afford the distinctive narrative character that is so endearing to the movement. It also provides an open ecumenism to position itself amid the Christian landscape. Perhaps there is even a hint of the creedal tradition within it.

However, from a creedal perspective, the present collective and individual subjective nature of the hermeneutic remains problematic. One wonders who they would have sided with if they had been present during the Arian controversy. Would the logic and tradition of sola Scriptura be insufficient? Would the beauty of Arius's argument win the day? (I am not sure if his argument was considered beautiful by anyone, but for the sake of the dialogue, let us say it was.) How would they have determined the truth of the Scriptures and their testimony about the divinity of Jesus? If it would have been by their network theory, it seems that in all likelihood Arius's claims would still be standing today. If that is the case, we can only surmise that the hermeneutic, though highly nuanced, is flawed at best.

WHAT IT LOOKS LIKE

Prior to Tickle's technical analysis, the best conceptual example of this was exemplified in Brian McLaren's *A Generous Orthodoxy*.[42] And where *A Generous Orthodoxy* provided the best conceptual conversation and framework, McLaren's subsequent work, *Everything Must Change*, provides the best picture of what this would look like.[43]

---

42. "As I've said already, I believe that the kind of generous orthodoxy I am exploring here will pursue a more narrative approach to theology, in the tradition of the great James William McClendon and others. Rather than trying to capture timeless truths in objective statements systematized in analytical outlines and recorded in books and institutionalized in schools and denomination, narrative theology embraces, preserves, and reflects on the stories of people and communities involved in the romance of God— always beginning with and always returning to the treasury of stories in Scripture." McLaren, *A Generous Orthodoxy*, 329.

43. "In searching for a better framing story than we currently proclaim, Christians like myself can discover a fresh vision of our religion's founder and his message, a potentially revolutionary vision that could change everything for us and for the world we inhabit. We can rediscover what it can mean to call Jesus Savior and Lord when we raise the question of what he exactly intended to save us from. (His angry Father? The logical consequences of our actions? Our tendency to act in ways that produce undesirable logical consequences? Global self-destruction?) The popular and domesticated Jesus, who has become little more than a chrome plated hood ornament on the guzzling

Summarizing each would be no short task. Reading the full title of
A Generous Orthodoxy alone is no small activity.[44] McLaren's thought
is detailed and engaging. It is couched in his endearing style, but, as
usual, it has an underlying, unsettling, and unnerving distraction about
it. Jesus and the kingdom of God are central, but they are not centrally
Christological (dealing with Christ and our salvation). The Word of God
is employed, but it is not decidedly normative. Rather, his asserted ethic
of Jesus is normative.

This can then be coupled with the vast ethical description he details
in *Everything Must Change*. In short, it is a picture of what the world
would look like if people put into practice what he (McLaren) preaches—a place that cares for the poor, seeks justice, looks out for oppressed,
strives for peace, respects the environment, loves equally—all as Jesus
did so that the world might be transformed into the kingdom of God.

Boiling it all down, if this were a sermon written from a Lutheran
perspective, it is all law. For all of its beauty, for all of its playfulness,
for all of its care and concern for the poor, for all of its narrative inclu-
sion, Christ as Lord and sinner-Savior is blurred amid clever rhetoric
and emotional appeal, becoming indistinct from the likes of Francis of
Assisi. Using H. Richard Niebuhr's classic divisions in *Christ & Culture*,
this is simply a retread of "Christ the Transformer of Culture."[45]

Hummer of Western civilization, can thus be replaced with a more radical, saving, and
I believe, *real* Jesus. As I worked on this book—grappling to understand our world's top
problems and to see them in relation to the life and message of Jesus—I was struck as
never before with one simple, available, yet surprisingly powerful response called for
by Jesus, a response that can begin to foment a revolution of hope among us, a hope
that can change everything. That hope may happen to you as you read, without even
noting it. If it happens in enough of us, we will face and overcome the global crisis that
threatens us, and we will sow the seeds of a better future." McLaren, *Everything Must
Change*, 6.

44. *A Generous Orthodoxy: Why I am a missional+ evangelical+ post/protestant +
liberal/conservative + mystic/poetic + biblical + charismatic/contemplative + fundamen-
talist/Calvinist + anabaptist/Anglican + Methodist + catholic + green + incarnational +
depressed-yet-hopeful + emergent + unfinished Christian.*

45. "'The kingdom of God begins within, but it is to make itself manifest without…It
is to penetrate the feelings, habits, thoughts, words, acts, of him who is the subject of it.
At last it is to penetrate our whole social existence.' The kingdom of God is transformed
culture, because it is first of all the conversion of the human spirit from faithlessness
and self-service to the knowledge and service of God." Niebuhr quoting F. D. Maurice
and then elaborating, *Christ and Culture*, 228.

For all of its revolutionary claims, the emerging church may not be as novel and radical as its originators hold. Perhaps it is new to our time, but old in what it asks.

FROM CHURCH GROWTH TO EMERGENT CHURCH TO THE HOLY CHRISTIAN CHURCH

John Pless provides an astute evaluation of the emergent church movement:

> Missing Luther's radical move, the Emerging Church begins with life not doctrine, and with ethics not faith. While claiming to be generous, open, and tolerant, McLaren—with his incessant focus on the necessity for authentic discipleship, obedience rather than knowledge, and lives characterized by compassion slips into a rigidity that is unattainable. While the language might sound in- clusive and undiscriminating, it is the language of the law . . . The Emerging Church is not nearly as free from the dreary moralism that they decry. Gerhard Forde has helpfully observed that those who begin with the presupposition of freedom end in bondage. Only a theology that begins with the presupposition that human- ity is in bondage can end in freedom—the freedom of the Spirit.[46]

Luther's explanation to the third article of the Apostles' Creed re- mind us of this bondage: "I believe that I cannot by my own reason or strength . . ."

What began as a counter movement to the antecedent church growth mentality has now seemingly warped into an opposite of sorts coupled with a Gnostic flair. Carl Raske offers a decided solution: "The coming of GloboChristianity under the sovereign rule of the GloboChrist means that this Globo-pseudo Gospel, whether it has a traditional or progressive coloration, must be cast aside in the same way that ancient Gnosticism was cast aside."[47]

---

46. Pless, "Contemporary Spirituality and the Emerging Church," 320.

47. "[T]he collapse of the kingdom-of-God proclamation into social Gospel preoc- cupied with social issues leads to a loss of the sense of majesty and transcendence that infuses both the faith relationship between God and the believer and the relational truth of all relationships, which the Great Commandment and the ideal of *sanctorum communio* necessitate. The reduction of the Great Commission to movement politics preoccupied with school prayer, abortion, and preventing gay marriage is scarcely chal- lenged and critiqued by reducing the Great Commission to movement politics pre- occupied with ending war, increasing funding for the homeless, and legitimizing gay

As well-intentioned as each respective movement may be, a distracting and distorting effect on the clarity and centrality of the Gospel inherent in them has been demonstrated. This is not to disparage the good they may have done. I do not doubt they have touched many lives. However, I believe we need to be honest about the unhealthy side effects inherent to them. I think we need to be honest about the distinct deviation they bring to the historic theology and mission of the church.

Many churches (my own included) continue to feel the influence of the church growth movement in their doctrine and practice. Many have also co-opted the missional adjective and some of its corresponding ambiguous theology from the emergent church movement (again, my own included). Whether we wanted to or not, we have entered into the conversation. But perhaps this is a good thing. It gives us the opportunity to boldly reconsider the church's historic theology and practice. As the creed has preserved the life and faith of the church for centuries, our current dilemma provides a profound means to see again the church's historic doctrine and life in our age. Thus, we will finally take a look at the details of the doctrine and life of the Holy Christian Church through the lens of the Apostles' Creed and the bifocals of Luther's explanation to the third article of the Apostles' Creed. We will also begin to see how it was integral to the development of my congregation's strategic plan.

marriage." Raske, *GloboChrist*, 165–66.

Chapter 6

The Great Confession Part One

"I cannot by my own reason or strength"

NOT BY MY OWN REASON OR STRENGTH

MARTIN LUTHER'S EXPLANATION TO the third article of the Apostles' Creed begins, "I cannot by my own reason or strength . . ." When I arrived at my second congregation, I was trying to do absolutely everything by my own reason and strength. It made me very tired, very lonely, and very desperate to run away and hide. But as I focused more and more on the Apostles' Creed to help shape the congregational strategic plan, this phrase from Luther began to stick with me. The more I reflected on it, the more I simply marveled at how it had followed me through all of life.

I was born in South Dakota. My parents had married young. It was during the Vietnam War. So rather than be drafted, my dad enlisted in the Navy. After a four-year tour on the East Coast and in Guam, they settled in South Dakota to farm. Thus, for the first number of years of my life, I grew up on my dad's dairy farm.

My dad worked hard; being a farmer is not easy. Being the wife of a farmer is no easy chore either, but my parents were faithful and devoted in their vocations.

I didn't know what a vocation was when I was five, but I am thankful my parents lived theirs out so fully. As Christians, they took their family regularly to worship. As a farmer, my dad worked long hours trying to support his family and make a living. As a mother, my mom had three young children to take care of, including one who was plagued by cancer.

My sister Heidi was the oldest, but a Wilms Tumor was ravaging her body. Her favorite song was, "Go Tell It on the Mountain." Even though she was just six years old, she was particular about her songs. She liked the hymns, and if it was not to her liking it got the ax. "Mom, that one just doesn't have enough Jesus in it," she would say, and so out it would go.

By every human reason and by every manner of human strength, they tried to make Heidi get better. They couldn't. While sitting in my mother's lap, her last words were, "Mommy, I know I am going to be with Jesus now." She closed her eyes and then breathed her last. She died in my mother's arms, hair gone, strength gone, and now life gone. Not by her own reason or strength did she go from the arms of her mother into the arms of her Savior. Baptism has a way of doing the impossible.

I was two years younger than Heidi, and my brother Matt was eighteen months younger than me. My brother Josh would not come until three years after Heidi died. Matt and I thought it was cool that Sheriff Roscoe P. Coltrane was leading the funeral procession in his squad car—our favorite show was the Duke's of Hazard.

Not by my own reason or strength could I figure out why they had put Heidi into a box. Not by my own reason or strength could I figure out why they were lowering her into the ground.

I turned to ask my mom. The picture of my dad and mom crumpled in an agonizing embrace, utterly weeping, is forever etched in my mind. Not by their own reason or strength would they be able to bear the burden of seeing their child lowered into the grave. Not by their own reason or strength would they be able to calm the devastating outrage of watching their six-year-old little girl suffer and die.

But their trust was not in their own reason or strength. Their trust was in the One who called them and called Heidi by the Gospel, just as they confessed in the Apostles' Creed that day: "I believe in the Holy Spirit, the Holy Christian Church, the Communion of Saints, *the resurrection of the body*, and the life everlasting." Here, the "Amen" became painfully and expectantly real.

My mom and dad often talked of Jesus, but their vocation was not as missionaries. Their vocation was as parents—diaper-changing, supper-cooking, clothes-folding, cow-milking parents. They told my sister about Jesus, just as they told all of their children about him. They taught each of us the hymns and songs that the church has sung for ages. I am pretty sure Heidi probably sang her favorite song to many of the nurses who cared for her and maybe even told one or two about Jesus, but her vocation was not as a missionary. It was that of a little girl, a daughter who also had the horrid disease called cancer. Yet she was a little girl baptized in the name of the Father, and of the Son, and of the Holy Spirit. She was a daughter, taught by her parents of God's unconditional, irreversible, and resurrecting love promised to her through the water and the Word.

It is no wonder that Luther lifts up the vocation of parents:

> In all the world this is the noblest and most precious work, because to God there can be nothing dearer than the salvation of souls . . . Most certainly father and mother are apostles, bishops, and priests to their children, for it is they who make them acquainted with the Gospel. In short, there is no greater or nobler authority on earth than that of parents over their children, for this authority is both spiritual and temporal.[1]

It should also be no wonder that the latest studies unequivocally show that parents are the most formative influences in the faith life of children.[2] Their vocation is profound. Their vocation is necessary. I am grateful for my parents.

CREEDAL LENSES

As we have noted, narratives form the postmodern mindset. Theology can certainly be proclaimed through narratives. After all, the Gospel is a narrative of God's love for us. And simply because something is in narrative form does not mean it cannot be undergirded by propositional truth or even speak propositional truth.

The Apostles' Creed is this way, particularly the third article. It tells a narrative and speaks a profound propositional truth in the midst

---

1. Luther, *Estate of Marriage*, 1522, AE 45:47.

2. From the largest study of this kind ever done, Christian Smith, in his book *Soul Searching,* now has the research to back up what the Scriptures have said for thousands of years: Parents are the most formative influence in the faith life of their children. "More broadly, one of the most important things that adults who are concerned about how teenagers' religious and spiritual lives are going to turn out can do is to focus attention on strengthening their own and other adults', especially parents', religious and spiritual lives. For in the end, they most likely will get from teens what they as adults themselves are. Like it or not, the message that adults inevitably communicate to youth is 'Become as I am, not (only) as I say.'" Smith, *Soul Searching*, 267.

of it—the forgiveness of sins, the resurrection of the body, and the life everlasting. It mirrors the life of the church. The church is the community of saints gathered around the narrative of the Gospel, receiving the forgiveness of sins, the promise of the resurrection, and the certain hope of life everlasting.

This chapter begins our culminating look at the doctrine and practice of the Holy Christian Church as seen through creedal lenses and third article bifocals. The postmodern North American culture and its corresponding influences have brought significant confusion to the church. Well-intentioned but unorthodox movements have added to the confusion. The vision of the church has become blurred. Corrective lenses are needed. Let's take a look through those lenses.

DOCTRINE AND LIFE: A STRATEGIC PLAN

Since the Holy Christian Church is that which is being examined, the third article provides a natural lens in which to view the doctrine (orthodoxy) and life (orthopraxy) of the North American church. The above narrative serves as a reminder that this doctrine and practice must be considered in the context and culture of real people, real congregations, real pastors, and a real confession of faith.

I was reminded of this as I went through the strategic planning process with my own congregation. It could not be abstract concepts; it had to deal with real life. It could not be ivory tower academics; it had to be life-giving doctrine. It could not be a neat idea; there had to be something historic about the life it gave to the church. Keeping it all balanced was no easy task. Nonetheless, I pressed on, wondering if there might even be a renewed vitality among the congregation by exploring the realities of the Creed in the life of my congregation.

LOOKING THROUGH THE LENS

Exploring the life of the Holy Christian Church through the lens of the third article of the Apostles' Creed was a rewarding experience. It certainly had benefits for my local congregation. I also began to see possibilities for the greater church. Should the broader church pursue it, I contend it will radically celebrate the centrality of the Gospel in the life of the church. It will offer clarity of how the life of the church flows out of the Word and Sacrament worship life of the community of saints. And it will increase the visibility and importance of the Christian's vocational life in the world as integral to the mission of the church.

To that end, pastor and parishioner (called the "royal priesthood" in 1 Peter 2:9), along with their worship and witness, will be examined through the bifocals of the third article of the Apostles' Creed.[3] In so doing, it will also provide us a distinct opportunity to collegially and honestly consider the orthodoxy (doctrine) and the orthopraxy (life) of the church and her mission.

CONSIDERING ORTHODOXY

In a postmodern culture where propositional truth is suspected of illegitimacy, subjected to incredulity, and subverted by relativism, can there be a place for orthodoxy?[4] It is a significant question. At its core, orthodoxy measures truth. Subsequently, it also informs orthopraxy.[5]

---

3. What is meant by *pastors* here is most notably clarified by Augsburg Confession V: "To obtain such faith, God instituted the office of preaching, giving the Gospel and the sacraments. Through these, as through means, he gives the Holy Spirit who produces faith, where and when he wills, in those who hear the Gospel. It teaches that we have a gracious God, not through our merit but through Christ's merit, when we so believe." Kolb & Wengert, AC V, §1–3. And what is meant by *priesthood* here is most notably clarified by 1 Peter 2:9: "But you are a chosen race, a royal priesthood, a holy nation, a people for his own possession, that you may proclaim the excellencies of him who called you out of darkness into his marvelous light." Norman Nagel offers this: "We may prefer to speak with 1 Peter and Luther of the priesthood of the baptized, rather than the priesthood of all believers, for Holy Baptism is what the Lord does. Any starting point other than the Lord and where he is at giving out his gifts with the Means of Grace leads to uncertainty. That is what Luther will have none of in the passage we are considering. We have a Means of Grace doctrine of the Office of the Holy Ministry, and a Means of Grace doctrine of the priestly kingdom, the holy people. Thus connected to and from the Lord they are clear and sure. To get them wrong we would have to disconnect them from him." Nagel, "Luther and the Priesthood of all Believers," 287. I occasional add *vocational* to *priesthood* (i.e., "vocational priesthood,") because it is those vocational stations in life where they exist on a daily basis).

4. The word *orthodoxy*, from the Greek *ortho* ("right" or "correct" and *dox*, meaning "praise" or "opinion") is typically used to refer to the correct observance of religion, as determined by some overseeing body. Orthodoxy is opposed to *heresy* and *schism*. People who deviate from orthodoxy by professing a doctrine considered to be false are called heretics, while those who deviate from orthodoxy by removing themselves from the perceived body of believers (i.e., from full communion) are called schismatics. Not infrequently, these occur together. The distinction in terminology pertains to the subject matter. If one is addressing corporate unity, the emphasis may be on schism. If one is addressing doctrinal coherence, the emphasis may be on heresy.

5. *Orthopraxy* is a term derived from the Greek *orthopraxia*, meaning "correct action/ activity." It has an emphasis on conduct, both ethical and liturgical, as opposed to faith or

Right now the term *orthodoxy* is en vogue, at least as current book titles go. The already-mentioned *A Generous Orthodoxy* by Brian McLaren seeks a postmodern widening of orthodoxy for the church.[6] In a like manner, European emergent thinker Peter Rollins also aimed at widening orthodoxy in *The Orthodox Heretic: And Other Impossible Tales*. His goal is to convey truth by communicating in parables rather than with propositional statements.[7]

James K. Smith goes the opposite way in his book *Introducing Radical Orthodoxy*. One of his stated goals "is to consider parallels between the vision of Radical Orthodoxy and the Reformed tradition, with the correlate goal of signaling the unique contributions to be made by distinctly Reformational thought in our postmodern context."[8] However, perhaps the original by G. K. Chesterton provides a more suitable standard. His century-old book, simply titled *Orthodoxy*, is self-admittedly, "not an ecclesiastical treatise but a sort of slovenly autobiography," but is nonetheless insightful despite his tongue-in-cheek British approach.[9]

For Chesterton, "When the word 'orthodoxy' is used here it means the Apostles' Creed, as understood by everybody calling himself Christian until a very short time ago and the general historic conduct of those who held such a creed."[10] It is another reminder that from age to age the Apostles' Creed is used as a standard to evaluate orthodoxy. Yet if orthodoxy is to be imposed, how rigidly should it be upheld? Is there no wiggle room? Addressing the critic of his day and perhaps anticipating

grace and so on. This contrasts with orthodoxy, which emphasizes correct belief.

6. "For most people, *orthodoxy* means right thinking or right opinions, or in other words, 'what *we* think,' as opposed to 'what they think.' In contrast, orthodoxy in this book may mean something more like 'what God knows, some of which we believe a little, some of which they believe a little, and about which we all have a whole lot to learn.' Or it may mean 'how we search for a kind of truth you can never fully get into your head, so instead you seek to get your head (and heart) into it.'" McLaren, *A Generous Orthodoxy*, 32.

7. "[P]arables represent a model of communicating that cannot be heard without being heeded, in which the only evidence of having 'heard' its message is in the fleshly incarnation of that message. The parable is heard only when it changes one's social standing to the current reality, not one's mere reflection of it . . . [T]he parable facilitates genuine change at the level of action itself. The message is thus hidden in the very words that express it, only to be found by the one who is wholly changed by it." Peter Rollins, *The Orthodox Heretic*, xii–xiii.

8. Smith, *Introducing Radical Orthodoxy*, 26.

9. Chesterton, *Orthodoxy*, 17.

10. Ibid.

the likes of the emerging proposals from today, Chesterton poses a rhetorical question:

> If you see clearly the kernel of common sense in the nut of Christian Orthodoxy, why cannot you simply take the kernel and leave the nut? Why cannot you (to use that cant phrase of the newspapers which I, as a highly scholarly agnostic, am a little ashamed of using), why cannot you simply take what is good in Christianity, what you can define as valuable, what you can comprehend, and leave all the rest, all the absolute dogmas that are in their nature incomprehensible?[11]

Amid his many answers to this question, one seems to hit the mark more poignantly than others: "Orthodoxy," he says, "makes us jump by the sudden brink of hell; it is only afterwards that we realise (sic) that jumping was an athletic exercise beneficial to our health."[12] As we have examined, the church today could use some exercise.

Exercise is good. No one disputes its benefit for the health of our bodies. In fact, doctors endorse it, and athletic trainers demand it. One of the most popular reality TV shows is NBC's *The Biggest Loser*. Entering its thirteenth season, it is a weight loss show that is centered on healthy eating and intense exercising for those afflicted with extreme obesity and unhealthy lifestyles. Viewers of the show see and hear the truth to the often used phrase, "No pain. No gain." The most recent winner, John Rhode, shed over 220 pounds! He started the show at an astounding 445 pounds. To become healthy, he had to confront the truth of his bad health. He had to acknowledge that he was killing himself. To lose the weight and regain his health, he had to exercise right, eat right, and live right. Chesterton's point is that it is like that with orthodoxy. Where the church has indulged and become obese, she needs to jump, to exercise, to lose the fat.

SENSITIVE ORTHODOXY

Speaking in generalities regarding the North American church makes it easy to point out "those guys" who we think need to do some jumping. But if I may be so bold, what about our own church bodies? Could we benefit from some exercising?

---

11. Ibid., 149.
12. Ibid., 164.

Regardless of how one answers, history shows that demands for orthodoxy can create division. In fact, it can create literal, all-out war. The Eastern Orthodox alone remind us of this. However, as I noted in chapter 1, there are necessary approaches to orthodoxy and orthopraxy. My own church body retains them in defining her boundaries.[13] Nonetheless, a short look back into our history also reveals the painful realities of fighting for orthodoxy.

James Burkee, in his recent book *Power, Politics, and the Missouri Synod: A Conflict That Changed American Christianity,* meticulously detailed the tumultuous civil war of the Missouri Synod that ultimately led up to the February 19, 1974, so-called Walkout and resulting church split.[14] The issue at stake was the infallibility of the Word of God and the orthodox teaching of what it declared. However, Burkee's investigation claims that it was more complex than a simple cut-and-dry matter of orthodox or unorthodox teaching about the Bible.[15] For him, it is also about power and politics. Though he readily concedes "that the theological language dominated the conflict as the synod polarized in the postwar years around questions of truth,"[16] his research points to a very sad and ugly reality of how the battle for this truth, as

13. The LCMS has a dogmatics textbook that, though older by some standards, does give significant clarity: "It is God's will and command that in His Church His Word be preached and believed in purity and truth, without adulteration. In God's Church nobody should utter his own, but only God's Word (1 Pet. 4:11). Chaff and wheat do not belong together . . . The distinction between orthodox and heterodox church bodies and congregations is based on this divine order. A congregation or church body which abides by God's order, in which therefore God's Word is taught in its purity and the Sacraments administered according to the divine institution, is properly called an orthodox church (*ecclesia orthodoxa, pura*). But a congregation or church body which, in spite of the divine order, tolerates false doctrine in its midst is properly called a *heterodox church* (*ecclesia heterodoxa, impura*) . . . A church body loses its orthodoxy only when it no longer applies Rom. 16:17, hence does not combat and eventually remove false doctrine, but tolerates it without reproof and thus actually grants it equal right with the truth." Pieper, *Christian Dogmatics Vol. III*, 422–23.

14. "The schism in the Lutheran Church–Missouri Synod was a traumatic and triumphant experience for many of the nearly three million Missouri Synod Lutherans. It tore apart families and church, leaving scars that, in many cases, have never healed." Burkee, *Power, Politics, and the Missouri Synod*, 11.

15. "I argue here what I believe everyone knows but few will confess: the schismatic history of the Lutheran Church–Missouri Synod is about more than just theology." Ibid., 4.

16. Ibid.

important as it is, was fought through slanderous journalism, political maneuvering, bullying, and intimidation.[17]

Sad as this might be, the cyber-tactics employed by members of the broader church today are not all that different. Yes, such tactics aim to protect the truth, but I hold the more honorable way is to offer honest and sincere dialogue that collegially discusses the merits of our theology and practice for the good of the church and for the sake of the Gospel. As I have said before, I realize that not every question can be settled by means of a friendly discussion. I do not hold to the superstitious belief that dialogue is the infallible means to settling everything. I hold to the truth of God's Word, and His word calls us to speak the truth in love and not arrogance (Eph 4:15). That is my aim here.

Thus, I will humbly venture forward. I have no interest in asserting any power plays or political maneuvering. I am deeply sensitive to the wounded nature of my own church body and to the divided nature of the church at large. Nonetheless, fear of disagreement or conflict cannot drive us away from considerations of orthodoxy and orthopraxy within the church. The humility of our Lord Jesus Christ teaches us how this should be done—with patience, charity, compassion, and grace, not doubting, not compromising, not resorting to force or deceit, but rather speaking and confessing the truth in love. That is the nature of the church.

No one is boss but Christ. And the way he went about being boss was by suffering upon the cross. What we have been given to do comes from him. Therefore, we confess the truth clearly, regularly, and openly, not coercing, not legislating, not demanding, but confessing. Orthodoxy is rooted in the Gospel by all means. Those who do not or will not abide in that confession exclude themselves by the nature of their confession. Here a call for repentance would certainly be in order, not as a show of power, not as a means to embarrass, not even as a means to chastise, but as a means of love. Any other use functions as bullying and functions outside the Gospel.

---

17. "This book points to the personalities and ideology that turned disagreement into an all-out war that has not yet ended and whose outcome is still uncertain." Ibid., 11. He notes two key personalities, Jack Preus and Herman Otten, their modes of operation, and their respective followings as significant contributors and instigators of the political power struggles in the Synod.

Thus, it should be decidedly clear that the intention of this chapter is not aimed at the hunting of heretics, but it is aimed at aiding the clarity of our confession[18] and the consistency of our practice with a pastoral heart.[19] As such, I will press forward by using the third article of the Apostles' Creed as a lens to clarify and encourage the historic mission of the church.

THIRD ARTICLE ORTHODOXY

The third article of the Apostles' Creed confesses the belief in the "Holy Spirit, the Holy Christian Church, the communion of saints, the forgiveness of sins, the resurrection of the body, and the life everlasting." In Luther's Small Catechism, we are then reminded of what this means:

> I believe that by my own understanding or strength I cannot believe in Jesus Christ my Lord or come to him, but instead the Holy Spirit has called me through the Gospel, enlightened me with his gifts, and made me holy and kept me in the true faith, just as he calls, gathers, enlightens, and makes holy the whole Christian church on earth and keeps it with Jesus Christ in the one common true faith. Daily in this Christian church the Holy Spirit abundantly forgives all sins—mine and those of all believers. On the Last Day the Holy Spirit will raise me and all the dead and will give to me and all believers in Christ eternal life.[20]

It then ends with an absolute, "This is most certainly true." Admittedly, this is not something that is readily received by our North American postmodern culture. As David Wells has chronicled, it is a condition where "orthodoxies have no place, in which the idea of truth has been abandoned, in which world views have collapsed, in which

18. When speaking of *confession*, the word must be understood with a dual force. As Robert Kolb states, "It is a verbal noun. It denotes not only the content of what is confessed but also the conveying of that content to the appropriate hearers. You cannot have a confession without doing it." Kolb, "Confessing the Faith: Our Lutheran Way of Life," 357.

19. "How do we respond to this cultural interim of our day, this onslaught which has engulfed entire denominations? [N]ot by closing our eyes to facts, not by *pro forma* reaffirmations of old and neglected synodical resolutions which may or may not speak to the issues, but by confession and teaching the whole counsel of God and, like the confessors, bearing in mind always that the Gospel and the salvation of souls are at stake." Robert Preus, "Confessional Lutheranism in Today's World," 112.

20. Kolb and Wengert, SC, Third Article, § 6.

religions and spiritualities jostle side by side with each other, and in which the religious consumer is in the driver's seat."[21] However, what is confessed in the third article is the *truth* that the church—pastors and royal priesthood—speaks confidently to a world inundated with plurality and defined by relativism.

THE RADICAL PROCLAMATION OF THE THIRD ARTICLE

In a world plagued with meaninglessness (nihilism), the Gospel message is to be proclaimed with all boldness. Yes, where Homer Simpson and Jerry Seinfeld amuse us with their emptiness, this message is to be proclaimed. Where Play Station, YouTube, and Facebook have become our reality, this message is to be proclaimed. Even where worldviews have collapsed and purpose is found only in the amusement of the moment, the church is to be audacious in proclaiming the Gospel. Now, as ever, Forde's call echoes in our ears. If the church "is to recover a sense of its identity and mission today, it must begin to consider what it means to preach the Gospel in radical fashion."[22] He leaves no uncertainty about what this means. "The radical Gospel of justification by faith alone does not allow for a middle-of-the-road position. Either one must proclaim it unconditionally as possible . . . or forget it."[23] It applies to the whole church.

Forde contends that this manner of thinking is to pervade all of our theology. Rather than a theology that is side-tracked in slogans, mottos, or new missional meanderings, he unabashedly calls for a clear, simple, central focus that shapes all theology.

> What the church has to offer the modern world is not ancient history but the present-tense unconditional proclamation. The strategy of accommodation and defense has resulted in the sentimentalization and bowdlerization of almost everything. It is time to risk going over to the offense, to recapture the present tense of the Gospel, to speak the unconditional promise and see what happens. To do that it will be necessary to construct a theology that is for proclamation, for going over to the offense, not for defense.[24]

21. Wells, *Above All Earthly Powers*, 90.
22. Forde, "Radical Lutheranism," 11.
23. Ibid.
24. Forde, *Theology is for Proclamation*, 8.

It is with radical confidence, boldness, and audacity that the church must proclaim the Gospel to a postmodern world. As Wells observes, "Whatever merit there is in stressing that postmoderns place great premium on images, on imagination, on relationships, on being part of a community, none of these things can substitute for the fact that the Church has to *proclaim* the truth about Christ, that it cannot do so without using words, and the words are the tools for expressing our thoughts, and our thoughts must correspond to the reality of what God has done in Christ."[25] Even when shows like *Scrubs* tell us it is more about the experience shared than the lesson learned, we cannot stop proclaiming the Gospel. In other words, in a video-screened, Wi-Fi-connected, entertainment-driven, and reality-show-based society, we cannot stop being bold about proclaiming the Gospel.

The distinct nature of the third article not only reaffirms the church in this boldness, but it also offers a paradigm that is readily available for engaging a postmodern world with a word that not only carries meaning and purpose but actually gives meaning and purpose. Luther's declaration of, "I cannot by my own reason or strength" joyfully emphasizes where this boldness, along with this purpose and meaning, come from. They come from nothing other than the Gospel.

THE RADICAL TASK OF THE CHURCH

Putting it simply, the primary task of the church is Gospel proclamation. In fact, in its simplest form, that is the *missio Dei*. Yes, seeking and saving the lost is also central, but that cannot be done without proclaiming the Gospel. Lest a blurring of the mission of God occur, proclaiming the Gospel must lead the church in seeking of the lost. (It was an ordering that I needed to be clear about in my congregation's strategic plan.) It is not the seeking that saves, but the Gospel that saves. The message must precede and process in front of the seeking. As Luther reminds us, "You nor I could ever know anything about Christ, or believe in him and receive him as Lord, unless [the community of saints, the forgiveness of sins, the resurrection of the body, and the life everlasting] were offered to us and bestowed on our hearts through the preaching of the Gospel by the Holy Spirit."[26]

25. Wells, *Above All Earthly Powers*, 229.
26. Kolb and Wengert, LC, The Creed, The Third Article, § 38.

Consequently, carriers of the message cannot actually carry it unless they have received it themselves and are certain of what it is. I wanted my congregation to be certain of what it was. The Reformers wanted us to be certain of what it was. That is why Article VII of the Augsburg Confession simply states: "The Church is the assembly of saints in which the Gospel is taught purely and the sacraments are administered rightly."[27]

Here the "assembly of saints" is identified as the genuine body of believers, not limited to one space or one building, but most easily identified when they have gathered around Word and Sacrament.[28] Each member shares in its blessings and participates in its life. As Luther says, "Of this community I also am a part and a member, a participant and co-partner in all the blessings it possesses. I was brought into it by the Holy Spirit and incorporated into it through the fact that I have heard and still hear God's Word, which is the beginning point for entering it."[29] I wanted my congregation to celebrate in this reality, so our strategic plan needed to reflect this reality. In the end, it would become central to our plan and would be seen in the details of our mission, vision, and strategy as they flowed out of our corporate worship life. But I will say more about this in the conclusion.

KEEP IT SIMPLE

There is great beauty in understanding the church simply. Thom Rainer and Eric Geiger make this especially clear in their book *Simple Church: Returning to God's Process for Making Disciples*: "Many of our churches have become cluttered. So cluttered that people have a difficult time encountering the simple and powerful message of Christ. So cluttered that many people are busy *doing* church instead of *being* the church."[30] It is a

27. Kolb and Wengert, AC VII, § 1.

28. "The word *ecclesia* properly means nothing but an assembly in German. But we are accustomed to using the word *Kirche,* which the common people understand not as an assembled group of people, but as a consecrated house or building. But the house would not be called a church it were not for the single reason that the group of people come together in it. For we who come together choose a special place and give the house its name because of this group. Thus the word 'church' really means nothing else than a common assembly and is not of German but of Greek orign, like the word *ecclesia.*" Ibid, LC, The Creed, The Third Article, § 48.

29. Ibid., § 52.

30. Rainer and Geiger, *Simple Church*, 19.

point that was detailed in the previous two chapters, but one that should make us all the more bold in proclaiming the Gospel and all the more eager to keep the purpose of the church simple and clear.

WORD-DRIVEN CHURCH

On this, Luther speaks plainly: "God be praised, a seven-year-old child knows what the Church is: holy believers and 'little sheep' who hear the voice of their Shepherd."[31] Like my six-year-old sister, if "it doesn't have Jesus," it's out.

Luther's point was that those seven-year-olds (or six-year-olds) who were being raised in the faith would most certainly know this mark of the church. If only this were true for all seven-year-olds, seventeen-year-olds, and seventy-year-olds today. Regardless, what the church has to say remains what it has always said: the Word of Christ.

> The Word in all of its forms (oral, written, sacramental) becomes the divinely instituted marks that identify those who come into contact with the Word and to whom are given the gift of salvation (even if it does not identify those who actually receive that gift by faith). Because the Word creates faith, Word and sacrament are not only the primary marks of the church (according to Ap VII, 7) they are the infallible marks of the church![32]

That seven-year-olds and seventy-year-olds in North America today do not know them only solidifies our desire, with God's desire, to gossip to them the Good News of Jesus Christ.

Thus, for those who desire to take up our cross and follow Jesus Christ, it means we go where He goes, love as He loves, and speak when He speaks. It means we follow Jesus to seven-year-olds and to seventy-year-olds. It means we follow Him to the poor, the rich, the meek, the destitute, the lonely, the happy, the burdened, the sick, to sinners, to the cross, and to the empty tomb, so that we might speak His Word of love and forgiveness, so that we might proclaim the Gospel! (Similar wording found its way into our strategic plan.)

---

31. Kolb and Wengert, Smalcald Articles Part III, Article XII, The Church, § 2.

32. Arand, "A Two dimensional Understanding of the Church for the Twenty-First Century," 149.

CHALLENGES

The challenge facing the North American church today is nothing new. How does the church continue to be the church in the midst of an unbelieving culture? How does it proclaim the Good News in a culture that wants to subvert and subject what it says? How does it avoid letting the culture dictate what and how it should be said? Even greater, how does it proclaim the Gospel to a people who simply want to amuse themselves to death? Postmodernism is pressing hard against the church right now. Marketing remains, and missional is in, so what will the people hear the church say? (My congregation has a clear strategic plan, but there are always pressures to try something new.)

In general, how one shares the Gospel is, indeed, no small matter. Considerable deliberation and care should be given to how such sharing is made to specific individuals as they are set in a specific time and a specific culture. Nonetheless, based on the observations in chapters 4 and 5, I think it is fair to say that the "how" of what is shared should not replace the "what." Said another way, the form cannot be allowed to replace the content. When the form replaces the content, the profound nature of Luther's statement, "I cannot by my own reason or strength believe," is robbed, and so is the power of the words being proclaimed.

When this happens, it's no longer the *Word* being proclaimed. Rather, the medium (the form) that was meant to convey the *Word* causes the *Word* to get lost in distraction, and the medium now becomes the message. In other words, "It snowed at church!" Do not get me wrong. I recognize that forms are indeed important to communicating this Word, but they must remain secondary to the Word and cannot be allowed to dominate it.[33]

COMMUNICATING THE WORD

Here Dale Meyer offers insights to maintaining a proper and healthy balance about communicating the Gospel in understandable words. Though his comments are directed toward preachers, the point could be more broadly applied as well:

33. I do also recognize that the Word is never without the forms of signifiers and the conceptual signified, where these certainly do have a role in Gospel communication. For more on this, see James W. Voelz, *What Does This Mean?*

The sword of the Spirit is the word of God (Eph. 6:17). That's the word of Law and Gospel. This article hasn't been about the sword but about unsheathing the sword. That's our task. Underlying this paper is the assumption that the Word of God does not work *ex opera operato*. The most salvific statements spoken in an unknown foreign language do not work salvation. So also simply getting your doctrinal formulations correct in English isn't enough. When Augsburg Confession V says that the Holy Spirit "works faith, when and where He pleases, in those who hear the Gospel," we understand "hear" to mean that the Gospel is heard with understanding. Scripture is an organ of God, and its entire power consists in its being put into use. Otherwise it would be the same kind of power as in the word that is used by magicians and witches in their incantations . . . The Word of God is effective and the Gospel is the only persuasive power that works salvation. For the Spirit to work through the word you preach, the Word must be heard with understanding.[34]

Note his intent: The Word of God is still central, and his aim is to help proclaimers of this Word be mindful of the specific words they are proclaiming. The point is to foster the hearing *and* understanding of the Word. It is not meant to dumb down but to engage by speaking clearly. Meyer points out that this will no doubt require catechesis (teaching), a term that people may not even know. His point: "To catechize the crowd, use simple words."[35]

I am doing this with the unchurched man that I bailed out of jail (from chapter 2). He does not know church terms. He does not know theological terms. It is not that he will not or cannot grow to learn them. He simply does not know them now. But he does know things like *light* and *darkness*. As it is the Christmas season, we started talking about the lights that decorate the houses. We talked about times when we were

34. Meyer, "PDAs and the Spirits Sword," 176.

35. Ibid., 174. True, keeping it simple can be good. However, I would contend that the need for this simplicity comes not as a result of the masses being uneducated. It is not that we are an illiterate society, but rather, postmodernism has made us become a-literate. In other words, people are smart and they can read, but they don't. Computers, texting, and instant messages have shortened attention spans and decreased the willingness to contemplate sophisticated thoughts and words. Contrast this, then, with the masses of people who love and understand intricate and complex movies. The diagnosis points toward laziness as opposed to lack of education. Hence the renewal in narrative preaching. The art of this, however, is to maintain the reality of Law and Gospel amid the narrative.

little and were scared of the dark. We talked about the comfort of the light and then how light always beat darkness. This led to how Jesus Christ is the light of the world—a light no darkness can overcome—which led to talking about people who love darkness and those who love the light, which led to me reading to him John 3:16–21. His response: "Wow! That makes so much sense. I'm glad you explained it that way. This stuff is all so new to me, and I don't always understand. But this I understand."

Nonetheless, the larger point has been that when culture is the definitive key to making the Gospel effective (which is different than being mindful of the more or less sophisticated words we use to communicate the Gospel), the Word of God is then most certainly being made to take a second seat. The dangers inherent in such a practice were detailed in the previous two chapters.

"I cannot by my own reason or strength believe in Jesus Christ" means that belief comes from outside of a person. As Meyer pointed out, though it is not an *ex opera operato* (i.e., a magical incantation) use of the Word, it is still God's Word, not ours. Thus, the strength to believe most certainly comes from the proclaimed external Word. It is how the Holy Spirit creates faith.[36] Yes, even when spoken at the pedestrian level, where the Word is present, we can trust the Holy Spirit to be present.

This is far better than the winds of the time and far more certain than the ambiance of our culture. This is not a limiting of the Holy Spirit; rather, it is simply celebrating where He has said He would be: in the Gospel! As Luther reminds us, "Where Christ is not preached, there is no Holy Spirit to create, call, and gather the Christian church, apart from which no one can come to the Lord Christ."[37]

NEGLECTING THE WORD

As we observed in the previous chapters, the Word of God continues to be neglected (or at least muddled) by the North American church as she seeks to engage a postmodern society. The church growth movement claims that success is measured quantitatively and not qualitatively. Thus, for them, if the church is losing members, it must mean something

36. This is why Lutherans understand that the Holy Spirit comes no other way than through the external Word, which means that faith comes no other way than through the external Word.

37. Kolb and Wengert, Large Catechism, The Creed, The Third Article, § 45.

is wrong with who we are and what we are doing. This is seen quite regularly when the dwindling numbers of various congregation or church body membership rosters are continually held in front of our eyes.[38]

Identifying the causes of such decline can make some begin to wonder about the power of this Word or the effective nature of those proclaiming it. The temptation is then to go to new methods and strategies to make us more effective in our growing of the church. The thought is that if it is not working, we need to try something new.

Thus, as Detlev Schulz previously noted, when the expansion of Christianity has not "succeeded" in the optimistic terms that were so often predicted, what should the church do?[39] Could it be that Jenson's word about the purging of "abstracted Christianity" is taking place? Could it be, as Chesterton noted, that churches are starting a new exercise routine? Whatever the case, confusion over the Word remains. Focus has been lost. And when focus on the Word is lost, the role of those who administer that Word also tends to go out of focus.

NEGLECTING THE ROLE OF PASTORS

Where the Word of God has been neglected, I contend there is also been a corresponding neglecting of the role of pastors. Many traditions have long understood pastors to be the givers of God's gracious gifts of Word and Sacrament. They have also recognized that pastors have historically had roles of shepherding, feeding, and caring for the souls they have been entrusted with (John 20:19–23; 21:15–17). But over the last number of decades, that role has been increasingly lost. Within the North America church, it has been observed that the role of pastor has morphed from the biblical and historic role of *Seelsorger* and giver of God's gifts to that of a CEO, administrator, and therapist.[40]

As the third article of the Apostles' Creed confesses the "forgiveness of sins," it does the church well to remember that pastors are most assuredly yoked to that task. However, as we have observed, the North American church culture has competing views for what a pastor is to do.

---

38. For the LCMS, consider the March 2010 article from an official LCMS publication written by Mark Blanke: "An 'Educated' Response to Membership Loss," *The Reporter*, 3, 8.

39. Schulz, *Mission from the Cross*, 7.

40. "More Than Leader, Administrator, and Therapist: The Scriptural Substance of the Pastoral Office." In *All Theology is Christology*, 199–213.

"I cannot by my own reason or strength" is turned into "The pastor, by all his reason and strength, runs this place."

In the preface to his Large Catechism, Luther gives a scathing criticism of the pastors of his day regarding what he perceived to be their lack of biblical knowledge and propriety for their role as pastors. His assessment was bolstered by their unwillingness to learn the Small Catechism, the Scriptures, and the prayers of the church as well as to put such learning into practice for the benefit and care of the people they served.

> It is not for trivial reasons that we constantly treat the catechism and exhort and implore others to do the same, for we see that unfortunately many preachers and pastors are very negligent in doing so and thus despise both their office and this teaching . . . Oh these shameful gluttons and servants of their bellies are better suited to be swineherds and keepers of dogs than guardians of souls and pastors. Now that they are free from the useless, bothersome babbling of the seven hours, it would be much better if morning, noon and night they would instead read a page or two from the catechism, the Prayer Book, the New Testament, or some other passage from the Bible, and would pray the Lord's Prayer for themselves and their parishioners. In this way they would once again show honor and respect to the Gospel, through which they have been delivered from so many burdens and troubles, and they might feel a little shame that, like pigs and dogs, they are remembering no more the Gospel than this rotten, pernicious, shameful, carnal liberty. As it is, the common people take the Gospel altogether too lightly, and we accomplish but little, despite all our hard work. What, then, can we expect if we are slothful and lazy[?][41]

Perhaps the current state of the North American church and her pastors could be served by Luther's criticism. Though his tone and condescension may not be so helpful, the urgency and corrective within his criticism are welcome for our time. What it more, it is also my contention that restoring the historic role of pastor will help to clarify the historic mission of the church.

Thus, what has history told us of that role? Historically and biblically, the role of a "minister of the Gospel is eminently a *Seelsorger*, a bishop (overseer), a pastor (shepherd), a watchman, a man who by God

---

41. Kolb and Wengert, LC, Preface, § 1–3.

has been entrusted with the cure (*cura*) of souls, Heb. 13:17; Acts 20:20, 26, 27,31; Ezek. 3:13ff. Such, of course, he is also when in the pulpit, but in addition he is duty-bound to look after the spiritual welfare of each one of his members. Like Paul he is to teach *publicly* and from *house to house* . . . Acts 20:20."[42] But there also remains the desperate need for pastors to remember that "there is no limit to what the savior would do and the patience he exhibited in reclaiming the lost and the erring."[43] To be sure, there is always a careful balancing act, but as of late, many pastors seem to have fallen off the balance beam.

WHAT'S MISSING?

When the mission of the church is in need of a corrective, so, too, is the role of the pastors serving in her midst. Harold Senkbeil notes, "We must admit that something is missing in the life of the church as we know it. We have lost the art of the individual care of souls. Over the generations, great treasures have been allowed to languish dust-covered and untouched in our ecclesiastical attics, while we have been busy using second-hand tools of our own devising."[44] It would serve the church well not only to note the new means of care being used (as we have already chronicled), but also to note those historic means of care that have been abandoned.

Here it seems that Luther's criticism is warranted for North American pastors. Yet Luther's criticism does not stand alone. Echoes of his near five-hundred-year-old criticism can be heard today. Leading the criticisms over the abandonment of the church's historic practices and pastoral care of souls are many prominent pastors and theologians who span multiple traditions.

As we have already observed, one notable critic is Congregationalist minister and distinguished professor David F. Wells. He has written about the good intentions of the North American church but remains an ardent

42 Fritz, *Pastoral Theology*, 172. *Seelsorger* is the German term that refers to the pastor's role as one who gives "care of souls." Included in this would be "the cura animarium—the cure of souls." Here, "Clergy were viewed as 'physicians of the soul' precisely because they were engaged in a healing art. Their work included both diagnosis and treatment, just like physicians of the body. But the work of pastors as spiritual physicians focused on the diagnosis and treatment of ailing souls." Senkbeil, *The Cure of Souls: Good for What Ails You*. Unpublished paper.

43. Mueller and Kraus, eds., *Pastoral Theology*, 179.

44. Senkbeil, "Generation X and the Care of the Soul", in *Mysteria Dei*, 287–304.

critic. "What has not been grasped," he says about the present church growth practices of churches, "is that in the modern world, the means that are available for this task are so effective that we need very little truth in order to have success." He is adamant about the dangers if this is to continue: "Christians risk living unauthorized lives of faith, exercising unauthorized ministries, and proclaiming an unauthorized Gospel."[45]

Likewise, John MacArthur, a well-known, evangelical, community-church pastor and teacher and seminary president sharply criticizes the church and her pastors in his book *The Truth War*: "The church has grown lazy, worldly, and self-satisfied. Church leaders are obsessed with style and methodology, losing interest in the glory of God and becoming grossly apathetic about truth and sound doctrine."[46]

Eugene H. Peterson, Presbyterian scholar and pastor for over thirty years, gives a scathing indictment against pastors, reminiscent of Luther:

> American Pastors are abandoning their posts, left and right, and at an alarming rate. They are not leaving their churches and getting other jobs. Congregations still pay their salaries. Their names remain on the church stationary and they continue to appear in pulpits on Sundays. But they are abandoning their posts, their calling. They have gone whoring after other gods. What they do with their time under the guise of pastoral ministry hasn't the remotest connection with what the churches pastors have done for most of twenty centuries.[47]

William H. Willimon, a bishop in the United Methodist Church in the United States, former Dean of the Chapel at Duke University and considered by some to be one of America's best-known preachers, also has profound insights as well as criticism for the church and her pastors to heed:

> The Gospel is not simply about meeting people's needs. The Gospel is also a critique of our needs, an attempt to give us needs worth having. The Bible appears to have little interest in so many of the needs and desires that consume present-day North Americans. Therefore, Christian pastoral care will be about much more than meeting people's needs. It will also be about indoctrination and inculturation, which is also (from the peculiar viewpoint of the

---

45. Wells, *Above All Earthly Powers*, 307.
46. MacArthur, *The Truth War*, xvii.
47. Peterson, *Working the Angles*, 2.

Gospel) care. Our care must form people into the sort of people who have had their needs rearranged in light of Christ.[48]

And the late, internationally renowned, Catholic theologian, priest, beloved professor, and pastor Henri Nouwen offers a piercing lament:

> Few ministers and priests think theologically. Most of us have been educated in a climate in which the behavioral sciences, such as psychology and sociology, so dominated the educational milieu that little true theology was being learned. Most Christian leaders today raise psychological or sociological questions even though they frame them in scriptural terms. Real theological thinking, which is thinking with the mind of Christ, is hard to find in the practice and the ministry. Without solid theological reflection, future leaders will be little more than pseudo-psychologists, pseudo-sociologists, pseudo-social workers.[49]

The list continues to grow. But it should be clear that where there is a consensus, a corrective is needed. Each of the above authors set out intentionally to demonstrate (some more in depth than others) how the historical heritage of the church and her pastors caring for souls is integral to the mission of the church. In particular, they emphasized how that tradition is exemplary for the contemporary care of souls, the witness of Christ, and the growth of His kingdom.

Willimon proposes a historic corrective for this pastoral malady:

> There is much to be said for the pastor being educated in the *classic forms of Christian ministry*. The Church has much experience as a minority movement. We need to draw from that experience today. In that regard, I predict a recovery of the classical shape of ministry: to teach, to preach, and to evangelize through *the ministries of Word, sacrament, and order*. I sense the end of a proliferation of ministerial duties and a reclamation of the essential classical tasks of Christian ministry.[50]

Where the historic Apostles' Creed serves as a corrective for the mission of the church, so the corresponding historic forms of Christian ministry serve as a corrective for the role of the pastor.

Here, remembering the words, "I cannot by my own reason or strength" becomes essential for the pastor as he begins each day. They

48. Willimon, *Pastor*, 96.

49. Nouwen, *In the Name of Jesus*, 85–87.

50. Willimon, *Pastor*, 70–71.

push him back to the Gospel. They yoke him to Christ. They let the Spirit have His way with him. They locate him in his vocation. They remind him that, as Norman Nagel often told his seminary students, the Office runs the man. The man does not run the Office.[51]

In other words, it is not about the pastor. It is about the Word of Christ that the pastor speaks and the Word the pastor gives in the Sacraments. There is comfort for us here—for pastor and for people. As Luther's words reminds us, "I cannot by my own reason or strength" always point us to Christ and His Word. As I will share in the next chapter, I learned it the hard way. I thought I was in charge. I thought it was about me. I thought I had the strength to handle it on my own. The Lord had to teach me. I had to decrease. He had to increase.

Being humbled is hard. It hurts. There is heartache. There is refining. But when the Lord and His Word are allowed to lead, pastors will walk in His ways, find comfort in His holy calling, and know satisfaction in doing what He has given them to do.

"I cannot by my own reason or strength" points us to "Him who gives us strength" (Phil 4:13) and reminds us that He and His Word are the source of our lives and the life of the Holy Christian Church.

---

51. The Office refers to the Office of the Ministry as that place where the Lord, His Word, and His tasks lead the man forward in his work as a pastor and particularly in his care of souls.

Chapter 7

The Great Confession Part Two

"I cannot by my own reason or strength"

"I CANNOT BY MY own reason or strength . . ." When I arrived at my second congregation, I wanted to show how much I knew. I wanted to show how great a leader I was. I wanted to show that I could lead this congregation to the promise land of a thriving, growing, talked-about church. I did not need anyone else. I was young. I had energy. I was on top of my game. I was full of myself.

As a result, I would endure some of the loneliest times of my life. During my initial visit to the congregation, they did their best to make everything look and sound great. But when I arrived, it was a different story. The congregation was divided over what parcel of land to purchase. There was internal split between supporters of "the church" and supporters of "the school." There were intense staff and personnel strife, accompanied by member suspicion and organizational paranoia. The Lord has a way of humbling those who think too much of themselves. I would learn a hard but needed lesson.

As congregational strife increased, so did the pressure on me. As unrest grew, so did my paranoia. I felt the glare of disapproving eyes. I heard the whispers of gossiping lips. I kept to myself. I tried to tough it out and beat it on my own. Loneliness haunted me. I would be surrounded by hundreds of people and feel utterly alone. But I buried it in the bowels of my intestinal fortitude, only to find my bowels began to stop working properly. There were times when I felt like my only friend was the hot shower I took after my morning workout. No one understood. No one cared. If this is what ministry was going to be, I was not going to last very long.

Sadly (and this tells you just how mentally unhealthy I had become), I would not even eat the candy members gave me at Christmas for fear that it had been poisoned. I am not kidding! I had only shared that with one other person before now. I was not healthy. I had bought into the idea that to make a thriving and growing church, that is what pastors had to do. Take it on the chin, keep it to yourself, put on a smile, and never let them see you are hurting.

I am in a much better place now and so is the congregation. The consolation of a very dear pastor, the direction of the church's historic confession of faith, and the realization that "I cannot by my own reason or strength" do this anymore brought me humbly to confess my sin and my weakness. In turn, the sweet Gospel was proclaimed to my broken heart. And I rejoiced! There is power in the Gospel. Christ was my joy. He was my peace. When I realized it wasn't about me but was instead about Him, things suddenly began getting lighter. I was freed of the outrageous burden I had put on myself. Hope seemed real.

To be sure, it took some time, but the more secure I grew with Christ as my leader, the more confident I grew as a pastor serving His beloved sheep. The more I reflected on His love, His power, and His grace, the more I simply marveled at how it had followed me through all of life. I reflected on how the promise and grace given in Baptism was only the beginning.

I was baptized (as an infant) at Emmanuel, Lutheran Church in Milbank, South Dakota. Though the Lord made use of my uncle Rueben's hands and mouth to baptize me, I was called by the Gospel, not by my own reason or strength, nor by my uncle Rueben's, but through Him who gives us strength. His grace and His strength washed over me through the water and the Word. The Holy Spirit was given, faith was wrought, and God's Word was at work.

Some months after my sister Heidi's funeral, I went out to help my dad round up the heifers from the pasture and bring them into the barn on a rainy day. I loved helping my dad. Most five-year-old farm boys do. Exercising his fatherly vocation, he gave me a job: Stand at the barn door entrance, and make sure the heifers went into the barn. Yes, it was a technical and highly-qualified job, but a kid has to start somewhere.

And as long as that somewhere was with my dad, it was the best job in the world.

So, favorite stick in hand, rubber boots sunk in the mud, and tattered farm hat on my head, I set my face to the rain and became the epitome of a cow doorman. That is, until Nancy came along. Nancy was an ornery heifer. Not by my own reason or strength could I make her go into that barn.

Nancy didn't like me. She decided to head-butt me into the mud. She decided to push me all across the mud-filled, manure-covered pasture. Tormented by an insane heifer and tortured by countless cow pies, I was careened across the mud.

Then, suddenly, I stopped. I turned to see my dad. He was close by. He had traversed the treacherous pasture in seconds and had just launched into the air a massive piece of lumber, ripped from the ground with his muscular hands. I watched in awe as it hit its mark. Not by my own reason or strength could I have done that!

I was a mess: bloody, coated with mud, covered with manure, and missing a rubber boot. My dad did not care. He picked me up with both arms and held me close, my filth smearing all over him.

Tenderness was not always his strong suit, but no one could have cared for me more tenderly than he did then. A hot bath, some clean clothes, and the safety of my father's lap filled me with a lasting comfort still felt some thirty years later.

Not by my own reason or strength was I was washed clean of mud and manure. Not by my own reason or strength was I washed clean of my sins. One was by my earthly father and one was by my Heavenly Father.

My earthly father was fulfilling his vocation given to him by the heavenly Father—not by his own reason or strength but by His. My uncle Rueben was fulfilling his pastoral vocation given to him by the Lord—not by his own reason or strength but by His. It was this grace and this comfort that began freeing me from my burdens. It pointed me away from myself and to the Lord and His Word.

COMFORT IN THE WORD

To be sure, there is great comfort in the Word of God. It is there for children and adults, for pastors and for people (the royal priesthood). Thus, there is great comfort knowing the Word of God has power in itself. It is the great confession of the Holy Christian Church. This chapter will look at the power of that confession.

We can have great assurance that the content of this spoken Word is efficacious. That is, it says what it does and does what it says. There is comfort for both the speaker and the hearer of this Word. Again, this goes for pastors and the royal priesthood. God's Word goes out and accomplishes what it was sent to do.

Putting it academically (you will have to indulge me for a moment), it reassures the proclaimer that something greater than the person speaking is being spoken, that something more powerful than any form is present. Putting it simply, God works powerfully through His Word.

But as Meyer encouraged, this is not meant to minimize the care and compassion with which we speak the Word, nor the context in which we (pastor and royal priesthood) speak it. Rather, it simply lifts up the power inherent in God's Word. Through it, faith is born. Trust is created. Hope is given. We are invited to live it. We are invited to share it in our vocations. There is comfort in God's Word!

PULPIT PROCLAMATION

This comfort is especially relevant for pastors as they exercise their vocation of preacher. True, the church as a whole confesses and proclaims the Gospel. But pastors have a distinct and privileged responsibility in this regard. Historically, pastors have carried a vocation distinct from but in service to and flowing out of the royal priesthood.

The Augsburg Confession, Article V makes it clear: "To obtain such faith, God instituted the office of preaching, giving the Gospel and the sacraments. Through these, as through means, he gives the Holy Spirit who produces faith, where and when he wills, in those who hear the Gospel. It teaches that we have a gracious God, not through our merit but through Christ's merit, when we so believe."[1] This (along with the last chapter) makes clear the role of the pastor. However, what about the composition of his preaching? If the church has been suffering, as Forde notes, from a crisis of Gospel proclamation, what is it that pastors have been preaching?

---

1. Kolb and Wengert, AC V, §1–3.

LAW AND GOSPEL

In the Lutheran tradition, the hallmark for preaching has long been the presence and proper distinction of Law and Gospel. The first president of The Lutheran Church—Missouri Synod, C. F. W. Walther, made this abundantly clear in his nineteenth-century classic *Law and Gospel*.[2] However, if the crisis facing the North American church is a lack of Gospel proclamation, those of us who are preachers would do well to shudder for the alternative to preaching the Gospel is to preach the Law (or, at best, mere empty distraction).

Could the lack of Gospel proclamation be a symptom of our preoccupation with success? Could it be that we have become so obsessed with forms, style, and relevancy that the Gospel gets left out?[3] Could the demand to be missional overlook the gift of the Gospel? When the Gospel gets lost, our hearers are then tragically left to work things out for themselves. As Walther notes, "Law is anything that refers to what we are to do."[4] This means that imperatives, commands, demands, and orders to be obeyed flow out of the Law. But they are not the way of salvation. And that is not how the church is to preach salvation.

Tullian Tchividjan (cha-vi-jin), the grandson of Billy Graham, and senior pastor of the renowned Coral Ridge Presbyterian Church in Fort Lauderdale, Florida, agrees. Commenting on the unhealthy obsession North American preachers have with the Law, he clarifies:

2. "Every sermon must contain both doctrines. As soon as one of them is missing, the other is wrong. For any sermon is wrong that does not present all that is necessary for a person's salvation." Walther, *Law and Gospel*, 29.

3. Consider *The Crossing Church* in Elk River and Zimmerman, Minnesota. During Easter 2010, they gave away three cars to first-time, non-churched guests in order to attract more people to their Easter service. They were featured on Fox 9 news during Holy Week as well as written up in the "Star News" of Elk River: www.erstarnews.com/content/view/11798/26/. Consider also what Carl Raschke says: "The Word 'relevant,' as veterans of the 1960s counterculture like myself are old enough to remember, is a well-worn mantra that has been taken up again as a watchword by emerging Christians, yet with little historical consciousness of what went on a generation or more ago. But within twenty years the Christian counterculture had basically given up on allowing the power of the Gospel to transform personal lives as well as entirely new cultures and circumstances . . . The mainline churches became liberal. They were preoccupied with social issues rather than with questions of the heart. When those social issues seemed less compelling or relevant, the mainline churches rapidly faded from the picture." Raschke, *GloboChrist*, 51.

4. Walther, *Law and Gospel*, 23.

> [W]hile the law guides, it does not give. It has the power to reveal sin but not the power to remove sin. It simply cannot engender what it commands. The law shows us what godliness is, but it cannot make us godly like the Gospel can. The law shows us what a sanctified life looks like, but it does not have sanctifying power as the Gospel does. So, apart from the Gospel, the law crushes. The law shows us what to do. The Gospel announces what God has done. The law directs us, but only the Gospel can drive us. It's very important to keep these distinctions in mind.[5]

It is a refreshing voice that reclaims the Gospel, calls for theological correction, and urges faithful preaching.[6]

Walther also relished making the Gospel clear. He notes, "[T]he Gospel, or the Creed, is any doctrine or word of God that does not require works from us and does not command us to do something but bids us simply to accept as a gift the gracious forgiveness of sins and the everlasting bliss offered us."[7] The Apostles' Creed is Gospel because it simply invites us to believe what God has done for us. And as both Luther and Walther make clear, the Gospel must always predominate. Thus, for a church culture obsessed with the Law, Walther's reference to the creed is yet another reason to use this ancient confession of faith as corrective lenses for the North American church.

THE GOSPEL MAKES NO DEMANDS

Luther was unequivocal about the Gospel: "The Gospel, however, is a blessed word; it makes no demands on us but only proclaims everything that is good, namely, that God has given His only Son for us poor sinners. This good news also includes that He is to be our Shepherd, seeking us starving and scattered sheep, giving His life for us, redeeming

---

5. Tchividjan, *Jesus + Nothing = Everything*, 188.

6. David Peter also offers the following critique about contemporary preaching: "There exists a demonstrable trend in contemporary preaching toward flattening out a sermon so that the human aspect dominates and the divine aspect is diminished. More and more preaching is characterized by a horizontal, anthropocentric focus, rather than a vertical theocentric one. Three contemporary forces contribute significantly to this trend: sermons that conform to a relativistic epistemology (hearer based), sermons that conform to a consumer ethos (felt needs), and self-help sermons that present stepped directions for self-improvement (solution based)." Peter, "Reaching Out Without Losing Our Balance," 263.

7. Walther, *Law and Gospel*, 23.

us from sin, everlasting death, and the power of the devil."[8] The Gospel makes no demands! Too many preachers continue to confuse Law and Gospel, telling people they have to do something, and then saying, "This is the Gospel of our Lord." It is, as David Wells has said, an "unauthorized" message.

The Gospel makes no demands! Rather, the Gospel frees. It does not coerce. It does not force. It does not insist. The Law says, "You shall do this" and "You shall not do that." The Law demands. The Law commands. The Law says you must obey. But the Gospel makes no demands whatsoever! It is all gift. It is all love. It utterly frees.

The Gospel frees us from our sins. It frees us to love others not because we have to, not because we get to, but simply because that is what Christ's love for us and in us does to us. That is the proclamation of the Gospel.[9] That is what preachers are to do.

THEOLOGY IS FOR PROCLAMATION

To be sure, the freedom of the Gospel permits us not to love others, but then we must deal with the Law. For here is the right work of the Law: It convicts us for our lack of love and drives us to repentance, back into the gift of the Gospel. Yes, the Law also shows us what God desires of us, but that is not the Gospel.

It is a high art to rightly preach Law and Gospel where the Gospel always predominates. But this is what preachers are called to do. If the growth of the church is dependent upon the Gospel, then we must preach the Gospel! Forde's challenge is worth repeating, "It is time to risk going over to the offense, to recapture the present tense of the Gospel, to speak the unconditional promise and see what happens. To do that it will be necessary to construct a theology that is for proclamation, for going over to the offense, not for defense."[10]

8. Cited by Walther, ibid., 30.

9. David Peter puts it this way, "Historically, Christian preachers have preached *from*—from the text of Scripture. That has been their beginning point. Today, however, increasing numbers of preachers are preaching *to*—to the felt needs of the people. Lutherans highlight another preposition: *of*. Lutheran preaching should be a proclamation *of* the Gospel (objective genitive)." Peter, "Reaching Out Without Losing Our Balance," 259.

10. Forde, *Theology is for Proclamation*, 8.

This draws out a profound implication for us. In short, it is a bold clarification of the opening claim that "Mission is what theology is *for*."[11] For Forde, the proclamation of theology is the mission! In other words, proclaiming the Gospel is the mission. Seeking and saving the lost flows out of this proclamation. It does not organize it or oversee it, but it is a natural result of it. Perhaps it is a subtle difference at first glance, but it is one that is essential for understanding the mission of the church. When it is reversed, we have seen how it impairs the vision of the church.

THE ENGAGING WORD

To "believe in the Holy Spirit, the Holy Christian Church, the communion of saints, the forgiveness of sins, the resurrection of the body, and the life everlasting" is to recognize and confess the power of the external Word. It means that one engages the people of the world with this belief through the only way in which this belief is made possible—by preaching, teaching, proclaiming, confessing, and sharing the truth of the Word in their lives where they are and out of love for them.

It is recognized that a postmodern world may readily discard, ignore, marginalize, or even pluralistically embrace this Word, but that does not indicate a lack of power or a failure of this Word. This Word is not void (Is 55:11). It is powerful (Rom 1:16). It enters into the empty void of postmodernism with a piercing, pervading, and prevailing absolute called "the way, the truth, and the life" (John 14:6). There it speaks and acts right in the midst of a world that would call it irrelevant.

Where postmodernism says that there is "no final purpose, no ultimate meaning that is considered in the pursuit of life [and] the empty Void within is pushed from view by substituting in its place a multitude of activities and much consumption,"[12] even here the word of Christ comes and does indeed have something relevant to say. As the apostle Paul reminds us, "I am not ashamed of the Gospel, for it is the power of God" (Rom 1:16). However, for this power to be enacted, there must be one who intentionally speaks and intentionally teaches this Word, to incarnate the Word in the lives of people.

Unless one proclaims and teaches the Word, there can be no piercing of meaninglessness, no pervading of relevant truth, and no

11. Schumacher, "Theology or Mission?," 117.
12. Wells, *Above All Earthly Powers*, 189.

prevailing of purposeful living. Again, as Paul reminds, "How, then, can they call on the one they have not believed in? And how can they believe in the one of whom they have not heard? And how can they hear without someone preaching to them?" (Rom 10:14). Thus, the mission becomes clear: to proclaim!

To preach and teach Christ crucified and risen is to pierce an empty and dead world with the resurrection and the life. To proclaim Christ is to let his reconciling truth pervade what was once meaningless. To speak the Word is to bring hope and purpose to lives filled with empty entertainment, disguised despair, and aimless drifting. Sooner or later, *The Simpsons, Seinfeld,* and *Scrubs* will lose their ability to distract wondering minds and sustain wandering hearts. But even with the TV blaring, the Word of Christ is still strong enough to speak through the empty and fading amusement.

When the church (pastors and royal priesthood) are unwavering in the proclaiming and teaching of His Word, the Lord is unwavering in His promises of grace. And those promises are readily confessed in the third article of the Apostles' Creed—the forgiveness of sins, the resurrection of the body, and the life everlasting.

THE INCARNATIONAL WORD

When the Word is proclaimed and taught, there the Spirit stands ready to act. And where the Spirit comes to reside, faith in Christ resides, and where such faith resides, there comes with it membership into the community of saints, the forgiveness of sins, the resurrection of the body, and the life everlasting.

For those who have "pointed to the emptiness of life" and "the absence of meaning," there is now relevance and meaning found through the Word of Christ enacted in and by the community of saints. To those who are "left to drift in the flow of melting reality,"[13] direction is given by the promises of Christ celebrated in the community of saints. For those who have been "diverting, concealing, or distracting themselves of their inner corrosion,"[14] there is newness and rejuvenation through Christ, His Word, and the people gathered around it.

13. Ibid., 193.
14. Ibid., 192.

The connection to postmodern people comes through the incarnation of Christ and our authentic embodiment (incarnation) of Christ as the community of saints. Postmodern people hear the life of Christ through our authentic teaching, confessing, and worshiping words; they will see the life of Christ through our loving, caring, and genuine deeds.[15]

The incarnational Christian who lives his life in the midst of his vocation is thus always pointing to the incarnate Christ, who, as a man Himself, entered into the human predicament. He shared the very real humanity in which postmodern people find themselves. Christ shared in human suffering. He cried, hungered, faced enemies, and experienced all that was a part of the seeming void of life, and He came through it. Yet He came through it with something greater than having lived for the moment (or being distracted from it) and something bigger than superficial self-gratification. He was resurrected! As the community of saints, we gather around this truth, order our lives by it, share it with others, and invite them to be a part of it.

FILLING THE VOID

At the cross, Christ triumphed over His enemies. "In that triumph lie human freedom and meaning."[16] Here the meaning of the resurrection pierces the postmodern mind, not because life loses its emptiness since there is life beyond the grave, but rather, "What has made life empty is destroyed by Christ's death and resurrection."[17] This means that *Seinfeld* is stricken, *The Simpsons* are smitten, and *Scrubs* is afflicted by the

15. Carl Rascke notes, "To be a Christ-follower and a disciple implies that we are manifesting Christ's fullness in a fully relational sense in all our thought and deeds. At the conclusion of the treatise *The Freedom of a Christian,* the little book that became the manifesto of the Protestant Reformation of the sixteenth century, Martin Luther espoused the radical meaning of incarnational Christianity when he declared that as Christians we must be 'Christs to each other.' We are to each other, and the other is to us, what Luther calls a *larva,* a 'mask' of the holy. Luther's insight anticipates by four centuries the postmodern philosopher Emmanuel Levinas's notion that the face of the Other is the portal to the holy. As Christ, who was God, became one of us, so his infinite love flows through us in our self-giving relation to the Other. In Luther's words, 'As our Heavenly Father has in Christ freely come to our aid, we also ought freely to help our neighbor through our body and its works, and each one should become as it were a Christ to the other that we may be *Christs to one another* and Christ may be the same in all, that is, that we may be truly Christians." Rascke, *GloboChrist,* 65.

16. Wells, *Above All Earthly Powers,* 198.

17. Ibid.

resurrection of Jesus Christ. All the empty entertainment of postmodernism is destroyed by the life, death, and resurrection of Jesus Christ.

The channel is changed. The movie is re-made. Meaningless amusement is ended. Empty living is filled. New life has begun! And the nature by which Christ did it is a narrative and incarnational mystery that postmodern people are prone to see as no threat, but rather as one that creates a comfortable realness.[18]

Here the promises of grace rush to fill the void of a meaningless existence. They offer eternal purpose and permanent significance. Life is now seen through the newness of the resurrection and the life to come, all because the church (pastor and royal priesthood) cared enough to love in Christ's name and speak in His name!

VOCATION AND PROCLAMATION

Very often, the most natural and easy way this proclamation occurs on a daily basis is when the community of saints go out into their earthly vocations. Not everyone is called to be a missionary. Not everyone is called

---

18.   Wells has two different quotes that are profound in what they say and bring home this point even further. One is from Emil Brunner and his work *The Mediator:* "Hence the Cross, conceived as the expiatory penal sacrifice of the Son of God, is the fulfillment of the scriptural revelation of God, in its most paradoxical incomprehensible guise. It is precisely in His revelation that the God of the Bible is incomprehensible, because in His nearness He reveals His distance, in His mercy His Holiness, in His grace His judgment, in His personality His absoluteness; because in His revelation His glory and the salvation of man, His own will and His love for men, His majesty and His 'homeliness' cannot be separated from one another. It is thus that He is God, the One who comes, the one who comes to us in reality: who comes in the likeness of sinful flesh, the one who Himself pays the price, Himself bears the penalty, Himself overcomes all that separates us from Him—*really* overcomes it, does not merely declare that it does not exist. The real event is His real coming, and therefore it is both the revelation of that which *we* are and that which *He* is." Wells, 225. The other is from Luther: "Thus the sweetest names Christ is called my Law, my sin, and my death, in opposition to the Law, sin and death, even though in fact He is nothing but sheer liberty, righteousness, life, and eternal salvation, therefore, He became Law to the Law, sin to sin, and death to death, in order that He might redeem me from the curse of the Law, justify me, and make me alive. And so Christ is both: While He is the Law, He is liberty; while He is sin, He is righteousness; and while He is death, He is life. For by the very fact that He permitted the Law to accuse Him, sin to damn Him, and death to devour Him He abrogated the Law, damned sin, destroyed death, and justified and saved me. Thus Christ is a poison against the Law, sin, and death, and simultaneously a remedy to regain liberty, righteousness, and eternal life" (*Luther's Works* AE Vol. 26, p. 163). Wells, *Above All Earthly Powers*, 227.

to be a pastor. (Ordinarily, according to the Scriptures, these vocations are specifically trained, intensely taught, and accompanied by a regular call and ordination—the laying on of hands [1 Tim 4:14; 5:22; 2 Tim 1:6; Acts 6:6; 8:17].)

Nonetheless, each person has a distinct vocation. It is just as valid as a missionary or pastor, but it is, nonetheless, uniquely arranged for that believer and his life of service.[19] Thus, whether parent, postman, pastor, painter, or paralegal, each vocation brings us into contact with others around us to serve them according to that vocation, and where possible, during the natural course of interactions, and with intentionality, proclaim the good news of Christ as appropriate to the opportunity and situation.

As most of us know, sharing the faith with unbelievers (or new believers) is very often most effectively done through personal, trusted relationships.[20] No, it will not happen every time an interaction occurs. But the joy of life in our vocation is that it is God-pleasing independent of our Gospel-sharing. "As Luther and the Lutheran Confessions understand vocation, it is not a call of the Spirit out of the world but the calling of the Spirit to live within the mundane estates of congregation, family, and government. Luther spoke of these orders as the most fundamental forms of human existence."[21] Thus, as we noted in chapter 1, people are freed to see the divine value and worth of the service they give in their vocation. This frees them from feeling unimportant or insignificant in God's eyes. But it also makes them mindful of the relationships they create through their vocations and the opportunity to share the faith in those vocations.

19. Norman Nagle puts it like this: "The Holy Spirit is alive and at work through his gifts in every Christian, who then 'offers Spiritual sacrifices acceptable to God through Jesus Christ.' Christians are both the temple and the royal priesthood and the sacrifice: all of them, all of their lives, bodily (Romans 12). What follows there, as in 1 Peter 2, is *Haustafel—paranesis*—which recognizes, indeed rejoices in, the diversity of the way the same gifts, which are given by the Spirit as confessed in the Third Article, work out in the particularity of each Christian life. Here there is no bondage of 'all men are equal.' Each is unique." Nagel, "Luther and the Priesthood of All Believers," 293.

20. For more on this, including practices for passing on the faith in our home and through our homes in the way of the Small Catechism, see *Frogs without Legs Can't Hear: Nurturing Disciples in home and Congregation* by David W. Anderson and Paul Hill. See also *From the Great Omission to Vibrant Faith: The Role of the Home in Renewing the Church* by David W. Anderson.

21. Pless, "Contemporary Spirituality and the Emerging Church," 363.

VOCATION VS. CHURCH ORGANIZATION

Unfortunately, this profound understanding of vocation is often undermined when the church service and church programs are elevated as the primary modes of outreach. This is also the case when the organizational structure of the church is geared toward "making disciples who make disciples" rather than proclaiming the Word and administering the Sacraments to the disciples so that sinners can be forgiven and freed, renewed and refreshed, discipled and dispersed back out into their vocations.

Harold Senkbeil provides a good reminder: "[T]he key to Christian living is the real presence of Christ with his church through His Holy Word and Sacrament. The best way to tell you what to do as a Christian is to tell you who you are in Christ. He will do the rest."[22] In short, when the value of the mundane estates of everyday life are trivialized and dismissed as unimportant by the church in the name of what is claimed to be a more important missional way of life—whatever that means—a great loss is suffered and an undue burden begins to afflict the believer.

For example, a Christian mother and her four young children go to the grocery store and meet a fellow shopper, but because she needs to tend to her children and do the grocery shopping for her family, she does not evangelize to the fellow shopper. Does this mean that she is not a missional person or, worse, that she is sinning? What about the college student who is tending to his studies instead of formally evangelizing the students on campus? Does he lack a missional attitude? Is he sinning? Or is he simply living his vocation as a student?

I am by no means saying they cannot or should not share the faith. Rather, my point is that demands to be missional can often evoke guilt or even the illegitimate abandonment of a God-given vocation. And again, to be clear, this is by no means meant to discourage witnessing to others. It is simply meant to celebrate and intentionally recognize, as Wingren demonstrated, that the mission of God encompasses the greater whole of life. Therefore, if we are being honest, perhaps we should consider whether or not a missional pressure to abandon one's vocation is not actually a disservice to the church.[23]

22. Senkbeil, *Dying to Live*, 163.

23. Consider the radical abandonment of such vocations that popular evangelical megachurch pastor David Platt seems to call for in his book *Radical: Taking Back Your Faith From the American Dream*. He does have some thoughtful things to say about

Yes, there is always a balancing act. But I believe we need to be careful. Demands to be missional flow out of the Law. They have a tendency to make the Gospel into a burden. And when this happens, joy is lost, Good News is gone, and love becomes an obligation rather than a genuine manifestation of the Gospel.

THE WHEEL THAT MOVES THE CHURCH

When the saints assemble around Word and Sacrament, they do so to be ritually forgiven and freed, renewed and refreshed, discipled and dispersed out into the vocations of their daily lives. In worship, the royal priesthood is served by God. He loves us. He feeds us. He nourishes us. In turn, we are then sent out into the vocations of our lives to serve and love our neighbors. Thus, it is my contention that worship is the wheel that moves the church out into the world. And, as I will demonstrate in the conclusion, the formal worship service moves the church *out* into the world rather than trying to attract people *in* to it.

Consider this proposition: The more God-centered (Father, Son, and Holy Spirit) we are in life, the more active we will become in our faith. Being regularly discipled makes regular disciples. We become more and more cognizant that through Baptism and the Holy Spirit we are Christ-bearers and Kingdom-bringers to those around us. As Senkbeil

---

the church's indulgence of American materialism. However, in the end, he turns the Gospel into a Law to obey rather than a message to be proclaimed: "You need to *commit to obey* what you have heard. The Gospel does not prompt you to mere reflection; the Gospel requires a response. In the process of hearing Jesus, you are compelled to take an honest look at your life, your family, and your church and not just ask, 'What is he saying?' but also ask, 'What shall I do,'" 20–21 (italics added). Although he has sold many copies of the book, many people have also given negative reviews expressing the guilt and struggle they have with what he says true disciples must give up and give away. You can see many of the reviews at www.amazon.com, but consider what noted Reformed pastor Kevin DeYoung had to say in his formal review of the book posted on his website on May 25, 2010: "I worry that some young Christians reading his book might walk away wondering if a life spent working as a loan officer, tithing to their church, praying for their kids, learning to love Christ more, and serving in the Sunday school could possibly be pleasing to God. We need to find a way to attack the American dream while still allowing for differing vocations and that sort of ordinary Christian life that can plod along for fifty years. I imagine David wants this same thing. I'm just not sure this came through consistently in the book." http://theGospelcoalition.org/blogs/kevindeyoung/2010/05/25/getting-to-the-root-of-radical/.

reminds us, "Faith toward God and love toward the neighbor find common nourishment in forgiveness through Jesus Christ our Lord."[24]

In those traditions that confess the creed in worship, they also often pray the Lord's Prayer. As the third article of the Apostle's Creed confesses the work of the Holy Spirit, so also the second petition of the Lord's Prayer reminds us of it.[25] In it, we pray to the Lord, "Thy (Your) Kingdom come." Luther's explanation of this petition in his Small Catechism brings us deeper into our prayer. "God's kingdom comes when our Heavenly Father gives us His Holy Spirit, so that by His grace we believe His holy Word and lead godly lives here in time and there in eternity."

Note the profound connection between what the Holy Spirit gives to us (faith and the kingdom of God) and where the Holy Spirit places us (in the world to live a godly, vocational life). "The same Spirit who calls us to faith through the externality of his word also calls us to life in creation."[26] Consequently, the more active we are in the faith (i.e., the more discipled we are through Word and Sacrament), the more prone (and prepared) we are to share the faith through the vocations of our life as we go out into the world.

If the church would begin to focus more intentionally upon the doctrine of vocation—celebrating the vibrant work of the Holy Spirit in us amid the mundane and ordinariness of our lives—rather than focusing upon the empty aesthetics of abstracted Christianity and law-oriented demands to be missional, there would be, I contend, a discipled growth within the church. But I will say more on this in the conclusion.

In the end, the purpose of the church is beginning to come clear. The church (pastor and royal priesthood) go out into the world in the places where the Lord has put them, doing what the Lord has given them to do: proclaiming the Gospel in their vocations. But they do so, "not by their own reason or strength," but "through Him who gives us strength" (Phil 4:13). They do so by ritually gathering around the Word of Christ, which gives them the words to say and the actions to do. "I cannot by my own reason or strength" reminds us that Christ and His Word are the source of our lives and the life of the Holy Christian Church.

24. Senkbeil, *Dying to Live*, 163.

25. I am thankful to Harold Senkbeil for personally drawing my attention to this profound connection.

26. Pless, "Contemporary Spirituality and the Emerging Church," 362.

The conclusion details what this looks like. It examines the worship life of the Holy Christian Church and the witness that flows from it. It is what would become the definitive element used to shape our strategic plan.

Conclusion

The Great Confession of the Worshipping Church

"I CANNOT BY MY own reason or strength . . ." This phrase continues to follow me around today. My vocations abound—child of God, a son of my parents, a brother, a husband, a father of four, a pastor, author, and neighbor. Time is always short. There's much to do.

Living in a fallen and broken world isn't easy. My sins afflict me. Satan assails me. Life burdens me. And tragedies test me. Not by my own reason or strength do I stay whole, healthy or hopeful. In fact, left to oneself, life can beat all the hope and all the strength right out of a person.

I used to think I was pretty strong. I played football in college. I had a 350 pound bench press, a 550 pound squat, and I ate quarterbacks for lunch.

In fact, my younger brother Matt and I played college ball together, racing each other to see who would get to the quarterback first. I was All Conference. Matt was All American.

From little on we played football, baseball, and basketball together. We hunted, fished, ate, and fought together. Only 18 months apart, we did everything together. He was my best man in my wedding, I preached at his. We even gave our parents their first grandkids on the same day, both girls—Maddie and Isabella. His wife (Lora) was late; mine (Becca) was early.

Then came December 30, 2004. Christmas was at our house. I was serving First Immanuel in Cedarburg, Wisconsin at the time. My mom and dad were driving over from Minnesota. My youngest brother, Joshua, now a proud United States Marine, was coming from North Carolina. Matt and Lora (pregnant with their second child), and one-year-old Maddie, were driving over from Minnesota. This day was also their four year wedding anniversary.

I had taken the day off. Becca had taken Bella to get some groceries. I was home alone. The phone rang. It was Lora's mom. "There was an accident." Maddie was O.K. Lora was badly broken up and loosing the baby. "Matt, didn't make it . . ."

The highway was covered in ice. They spun out. The car crossed the median. They had time to say, "I love you . . . Goodbye . . ." Then Matt intentionally turned the car so he would take the direct hit from the oncoming car. He died instantly.

Not by my own reason or strength could I bear up under the absolute devastation and utter outrage. Bench presses and squats didn't mean a thing. They gave no comfort. They offered no strength. Tough guys don't cry. I wept bitterly. Despair set in. Not by my own reason or strength did I have any hope.

Our home pastor did—not by his own reason or strength, but by the Lord's. He proclaimed it boldly at the funeral. Family and friends gathered to listen and be "enlightened" by the Holy Spirit. I have listened, read, and reread that sermon countless times:

> When you and I realize that no human words will suffice, we turn to the Word. We turn to the Word of God on the page before us. We turn to the Word made flesh, Jesus Christ. In the psalms, God lets us know that we don't have to use any words at all: "Be still and know that I am God." And we know that the only way we can get through this is to turn to that Word, that solid rock, that sure foundation, our King of Kings and Lord of Lords. And we must. If Matt Woodford had one thing written upon his heart, it was this, his favorite verse: "I can do everything through him who gives me strength" (Philippians 4:13).[1]

This man is a preacher of the Gospel! He proclaimed there was hope even in the midst of this misery and death. He was clear. This

1. Rev. Steven Bielenberg, Funeral sermon, *For the family and friends of Matthew Woodford.* "Through Him Who Gives Me Strength" Philippians 4:13, January 5, 2005, 1.

hope came through Christ. In Him there is strength, in Him there is the resurrection:

> With Paul we proclaim, *"I have been crucified with Christ and I no longer live, but Christ lives in me."* This is our treasure: Jesus Christ lived and died and rose from the dead and now he lives in each of us. Because of this, *"I can do everything through him who gives me strength."* And we will need his strength as long as we live. We just sang about the difference between the saints above and the saints here below:
>
> *Oh, blest communion, fellowship divine,*
> *We feebly struggle, they in glory shine;*
> *Yet all are one within your great design. Alleluia! Alleluia!*
> *And when the strife is fierce, the warfare long,*
> *Steals on the ear the distant triumph song,*
> *And hearts are brave again and arms are strong. Alleluia!*
> *Alleluia!*
>
> *Through him who gives us strength,* we will get through this battle of life, be it one day, one hour, one minute, one breath at a time. *Through him who gives us strength,* we will discard these jars of clay that the treasure of Jesus Christ may be seen in all its glory. *Through him who gives us strength,* we will be reunited with all the saints who have gone before us and sing praise to the Lamb of our salvation. *Through him who gives us strength,* our tears will be wiped away, by the loving hand of God, and by his hand alone. Until then, we must lean on *him who gives us strength.* Amen.[2]

Not by my own reason or strength could I bear up under such sorrow and grief. The vocation of my pastor gave me a living hope. He spoke solace into my ears, and into all those listening—including my parents, who were burying a second child far too young.

It was not by my pastor's own reason or strength, but "Through Him who gives us strength." The Spirit of Christ brought comfort to our lives, just as He brought my brother Matt to the comfort of eternal life and promises him, and all believers, the resurrection of the body.

The Holy Spirit "calls, gathers, and enlightens" by the Gospel, so that we can boldly believe and boldly confess, *I believe in the Holy Spirit, the Holy Christian Church, the Communion of Saints, the forgiveness of sins, and the resurrection of the body,* here in time, and on into eternity.

With the Gospel there is always comfort, even in the face of great loss. The Word of Christ brings hope. His Word brings life. The

2. Ibid., 7–8.

community of saints gather around this Word, in worship, throughout life, especially in death, and then, when death is destroyed, for all eternity. Until then, the Holy Christian continues to be fed and nourished by this Word in her worship and led by this Word in her witness to the world.

This concluding chapter takes a look at the profound nature of how the worship and witness of the church goes hand in hand. It unpacks how it would become the definitive element that shaped our strategic plan, and how it gives clarity to the mission of the Holy Christian Church.

FINDING UNITY

Crafting and implementing a theologically shaped strategic plan was a taxing, yet very rewarding experience. Presently, I continue serving the saints of Zion Lutheran Church and School as their Senior Pastor. The congregation is in a good place. I am in a good place. Yes, challenges remain. What congregation doesn't have them? What family doesn't have them?

However, there is much to rejoice about. At this writing, the new strategic plan has been in place for nearly three years. It's been well received. Members value their daily vocations. Members confess their faith in their vocations. The congregation continues to grow in discipleship and, not that it matters, numerically (for those who like to keep track). And on the whole, it is united. In fact, by the testimony of one lay leader and lifelong member of over 50 years, "We are in as good a place as we have ever been."

But before reaching this point, the definitive element of the strategic plan had yet to be put in place. Interestingly enough, it would came through the most regular and frequent part of the congregation's corporate life—worship.

As the saints at Zion gather for worship (Lutherans call it the Divine Service) they come to be served with God's gifts of grace—His Word and His sacraments. It's the formal gathering of the community of saints, week in and week out, year after year. And it was here that the definitive piece for a new strategic plan fell into place. I was struck with the realization that as we are ritually served with God' gifts of grace, we are forgiven and freed, renewed and refreshed, discipled and dispersed to go out and serve others in the name of Christ. And it was this realization that became the central thrust for the strategic plan.[3]

WHY DO YOU DO WHAT YOU DO?

Understanding why we worship the way we worship, the rhyme and the reason for it, its connection to the historic Holy Christian Church, and its importance for our daily living, was a natural and obvious connection to make. It's what brought us together. It's a part of our weekly life. It was familiar.

Working through the historic understanding of Word and sacrament worship proved to be a grand adventure for all of us. We were challenged. We asked questions. Sometimes we disagreed. But we talked. We discussed. We searched the Scriptures. We studied our theology. We studied church history. And then we talked some more.

As the historic confession of the Apostles' Creed solidified our faith, so the historic elements of the liturgy solidified our worship. They would both serve our strategic plan. In the end, we came to an agreement. We wanted to share hope by teaching Christ through Word and sacrament liturgical living.[4] And as it all came together, a realization occurred that this would not only help our congregation, but it could help serve the dialogue of the greater church.

In a time that is full of spiritual confusion, and a church culture accosted by worship wars, we need to talk. We need to dialogue. We need to search the Scriptures, study our theology, and revisit our history. It will help bring clarity. It will help us work toward consensus. It will help us recognize that the corporate worship life of a congregation is essential to the witness of the Holy Christian Church.

It was the definitive piece for our strategic plan. But I believe it's also the defining piece in our dialogue about the mission of the Holy Christian Church; one that will hopefully drive us toward greater unity. So let's have at it. Let's search the Scriptures. Let's study our theology. Let's examine church history. Let's see what we discover.

---

3. For a more detailed view of what the actual plan looked like you can take a look at Appendix 1 and 2, or for even greater detail, see Part II of my dissertation: "*Shaping a Congregational Strategic Plan through The Third Article of the Apostles' Creed: Practical Considerations.*" It can be found through Concordia Theological Seminary, Fort Wayne, IN.

4. This wording found its way into our mission statement.

WORSHIP, WITNESS, AND THE GOSPEL

As we've noted, when the Holy Spirit "calls, gathers, and enlightens the whole Christian church on earth," He does so by the Gospel in all its forms, (i.e., Word and sacramental forms). By these means the Holy Spirit brings into existence a believing people—a church, a community of saints—and by these means He gathers them to worship the One who brought them to faith.

So the means by which the Holy Spirit "calls" the church into being are also the means by which He regularly "gathers" them. It's a fascinating cycle, present even in the early New Testament church (Acts 2:42–47). This is why the Augsburg Confession, Article VII says what it does: "The Church is the assembly of saints in which the Gospel is taught purely and the sacraments are administered rightly."

I believe it's a framing statement that not only gives direction to the mission of the church, but to the worship of the church. There's an integral connection between the two. Word and sacrament are essential to the mission of the church and they're also essential to the church as she worships.

LITURGICAL BAGGAGE

Throughout the ages, Word and sacrament worship has been given expression by "the historic liturgy that has been used by countless Christians for almost fourteen hundred years, perhaps even longer."[5] I recognize that in our church culture the word "liturgy" has a lot of negative baggage. However, I think that's not so much the fault of the liturgy itself as it is the failure of pastors to teach and parishioners to learn what the liturgy is and what it does. Thus, for the moment, let's set the negative baggage aside and unpack what it's all about. Then we'll return to unpack that baggage.

LITURGY AS NARRATIVE

The nature of the liturgy becomes significant, not because it's what we have always done, though I suppose that could be a part of it, but because it's the story that forms us. Much more than a mere mundane order of a formal worship service, it's the narrative that tells our story, or rather, the

5. Just, *Heaven on Earth*, 13.

story of Christ which, by faith, is now our story. And what has become so provocative in our time is the recognition that the narrative nature of the liturgy is now indispensible to the postmodern church. That is, with postmodernism so incredulous toward metanarratives, people now emerge in a world where they do not know the story of the world. It's not a narratable world for them, and so they are left with many questions. "Who am I? Where am I going? How do I make sense of this chaotic world?"

Here the church need not answer with arrogant certainties, but with a simple confession of faith, telling her story, though her vocational witness, but also, and especially, through her liturgy. As Jenson notes, "The church has in fact had great experience in this role. One of the many analogies between postmodernity and dying antiquity—in which the church lived for her most creative period—is that the late antique world also insisted on being a meaningless chaos, and that the church had to save her converts by offering herself as the narratable world within which life could be lived with dramatic coherence . . .The church so constituted herself in her *liturgy.*"[6] In other words, the liturgy told her story. The liturgy shaped her people. It informed and it formed who they were and whose they were. Arthur Just explains it this way:

> This is how the Church has survived persecution, heresy, wars, famine, and plague. It had a place to retreat and to engage in a confident expression of the story of the world. When it seemed as if the World might be coming to an end, or even worse, as if the world was losing its story, the Church regrouped to the measured cadences of the biblical story told through the historic liturgy. When things looked as if they could not get much worse, the Church entered into the safe haven of the historic liturgy, where through Kyrie and Gloria, through Sanctus and Agnus Dei, it proclaimed to a world in chaos the story of God's redeeming love.[7]

Liturgy was more than a stuffy, old fashioned way of doing church. It told the church's story and confessed the faith all at once. In fact, as we have noted, there has been a tremendous call for the postmodern church to make an intentional return to the ancient liturgy precisely because of the narrative that it is. James K. Smith is adamant: "I will argue that

6. Jenson, "How the World Lost Its Story," 5 of 9.
7. Just, *Heaven on Earth*, 13.

the postmodern church could do nothing better than be ancient, that the most powerful way to reach a postmodern world is by recovering tradition, and that the most effective means of discipleship is found in liturgy."[8] In other words, it tells the story of Christ and it brings us into His story to live as a part of His story.

RITUAL LITURGY

The ancient rituals associated with the liturgy enliven the heart, mind, body, and soul of worshippers by imbuing them with the body and blood of Christ and his comforting words of life. It's intriguing that this call is not simply by liturgical traditionalists or preservationists, but, as already explored, by the emergent church as well. The return to the "ancient" liturgy has enlivened the emergent church in new ways, while simultaneously testifying to the timeless appeal of this ritual-filled narrative.[9]

John Kleinig is resolute in affirming the powerful role of such narrative-driven, liturgical rituals. "[R]ituals do not just embody the basic values of a community; they constitute and maintain its common life. The Lutheran Confessions acknowledge this function when they insist that rites and ceremonies are necessary for 'the good order' and 'well being' of the Church. Rituals are not just dramatic performances which celebrate what people have in common; they are performative actions which do what they mean."[10] In fact, the ritual of worship has been thoroughly demonstrated to assimilate converts into the faith:

> E. Bryon Anderson summarizes a growing body of material from theology, religious education and anthropology, concluding that ritual is the primary way one learns faith, for in ritual one is most fully engaged in the religious message. Anderson asserts that "liturgical practice is intrinsically formational and transformational. It is a means by which we come to know ourselves as people

8. Smith, *Who's Afraid of Postmodernism*, 25.

9. "Liturgy is a designed, time-tested set and order of communal spiritual practices that must be adapted as needed for the times and communities in which it is employed." McLaren. *Finding Our Way Again*, 102. Also consider the following: "The liturgical year is not a matter of recollection and ritual. It is the eternally spiritual dynamic. It is the movement through calendar time of Jesus and the development of Christian community. It is also, then, the growing bond between master and disciple, the gradual adherence of the neophyte soul with the Spirit that drives it." "The Ancient Practices Series," Chittister, *The Liturgical Year*, 211.

10. Kleinig, "Witting or Unwitting Ritualist," 13–22 electronic copy.

of faith and to know the God whom we worship." Supporting John Westerhoff's argument, Anderson asserts that rituals are the most important influence in shaping faith, character, and consciousness. Succinctly put, it is through ritual that we learn how to be a Christian.[11]

Thus, through the liturgy we are a story formed, ritualized people of the Gospel, who, as a community of saints, assemble around the narrative of Word and sacrament. We do so in order to be ritually forgiven and freed, renewed and refreshed, and discipled and dispersed into the vocations of our daily lives.

Senkbeil draws it all together: "There is no separating the liturgical life of the church from the mission of the church; they are organically one piece. The two find common nourishment in the incarnate flesh of Jesus Christ, who is our life. As the Father has sent Him, so He sends His church, cleansing her by the water and the Spirit to be His Holy Bride. And so, for as long as she is in this dying world, the church proclaims her heavenly Husband's life-giving invitation."[12] The picture of a wedding brings out the beauty of God's love for his people. It's how the Scriptures speak. It's how we are invited to see ourselves—as the Holy Christian Church—the bride of Christ.

Even the Apostles' Creed, an element of the liturgy itself, confesses the narrative of the Christian faith. And as we have amply explored, the third article of this creed reminds us that we are a "community of saints" who have a story to tell, a Gospel to proclaim, and neighbors to serve. But, as we have also explored, confusion remains and disagreement is present. In fact, intense and at times volatile opinions about worship continue to confuse the church today.

UNPACKING THE BAGGAGE OF WORSHIP WARS

The controversy over the liturgy spans multiple traditions. However, in terms of the history of the church it's a rather recent event. Nonetheless, they are named "worship wars" for a reason. "Traditional" versus "contemporary" gets people worked up. "Right worship" and "user friendly worship" causes blood pressures to rise. (Maybe yours is right now.)

---

11. Johnson, "Truth Decay: Rethinking Evangelism in the New Century," in *The Strange New Word of the Gospel: Re-Evangelizing in the Postmodern World*, 129.

12. Senkbeil, *Dying to Live*, 135.

Families are divided over the issue. Congregations are split by it. Church bodies are consumed with it.

However, if we are being honest, and this is not meant as a disingenuous jab, but an objective assessment, "contemporary" worship styles are the result of the church growth influence. Objectively speaking, they seek to accommodate the worship service to the sensibilities of the culture. Contemporary worship desires to be relevant and attractive to the participants in the hopes that it might draw them in rather than scare them away by what some call the drabness and irrelevancy of traditional worship. Perhaps this makes you angry. Perhaps you're applauding. My aim is not to incite irritation or invoke approval, but to have an honest and candid conversation.

The truth is, "contemporary" forms of worship are just that, contemporary. They have recently been introduced into church traditions (like my own) that had formerly never had them as a part of their worship life. Perhaps they were well meaning. I understand the design is to reach the masses, the disinterested, and the wandering. But as was chronicled, the meaning of worship, along with the purpose of the church, is being blurred through these forms—well intentioned as they are.

Jesus tells the woman at the well that worship of God is done in spirit and truth (John 4:23). No, not every element of contemporary worship has lost sight of this truth. But many have. And yes, some contemporary songs and hymns have profound and truthful things to say. But many don't. In fact, right now, blogs are loaded with discussions of what "contemporary" style churches are calling the "new worship" forms. Ironically, such forms include a return to the old hymns. My point is that considerations need to be given to the nature of worship as "truth" versus worship as entertainment or emotional appeal. On the whole, the church remains confused about worship.

Consequently, countless congregations and numerous church bodies continue to have intense divides, not only over preferred styles of worship (which, in the end, often simply have to do with musical tastes), but over the actual purpose of the worship service.[13] Is it for outreach

13. Lutheran Worship has room for use of multiple different instruments. However, music, whatever the instrument, is always meant to be in service to the liturgy and is to never displace or surpass in prominence the means of grace given in the Divine Service. Thus the following description remains helpful for any musical use in the worship setting: "Music in the Lutheran tradition is noted by the following adjectives: *doxological* (it focuses on praising the Trinity), *scriptural* (the texts are rooted in God's

or discipling? Is it human centered or God centered? Is it for attracting sheep or feeding sheep?

FINDING OUR WAY

With the above said, the worship wars have produced some thoughtful considerations. However, they have also intensified battle lines. James Alan Waddell offers a critique about my own tradition: "The conversation about worship in the Lutheran Church has taken a bad turn. Battle lines have been drawn, and the warfare has been engaged for some time now. For the sake of the Gospel in the church, for the sake of the church's mission and her ministry, it is time for us to move beyond the worship wars. It is time for us to reconsider the ways that we think about worship, and the ways that we speak to each other about worship. This is the direction in which we need to go, for the sake of the church and for the sake of the Gospel in the church."[14] No doubt these are welcome words for the broader church as well.

To that end, Waddell offers a very thoughtful approach. (Again, it's specific to my church body, but the approach is helpful for fostering honest and collegial dialogue.) He considers the adiaphora (things neither commanded, nor forbidden) of worship, but carefully remains faithful to the norming means of worship.

He clearly identifies those norms to be the "Gospel," the "Scripture," the "creeds," and the "Lutheran Confessions." Simultaneously, he is careful to honor the local congregation's "confessional authority and freedom to order its own rites and ceremonies in worship."[15] Thus, he notes that uniformity in worship is salutary but it cannot be made to be mandatory. In plain terms, variety within reason and faithfulness is acceptable. Some will find his assessment too rigid. Others, no doubt, will think it too lenient. I like it because it's defined and yet reasonable.

Word), *liturgical* (it fits into the ordered Divine Service within the pattern of the Church Year), *proclamational* (it communicates the Gospel of Jesus Christ), *participatory* (the congregation actively sings), *pedagogical* (it teaches the truth of God's love and forgiveness in Christ), *traditional* (it is built on the best of the past), *eclectic* (it employs styles and practices from various sources that aid the Gospel), *creative* (it eagerly explores new expressions), and it aspires to *excellence* (it desires and seeks to give God the best). Maschke, *Gathered Guests*, 265.

14. Waddel, *A Simplified Guide to Worshipping as Lutherans*, 11.

15. Ibid., 77, 79.

WHICH LITURGY?

However, before we go any further, there's a recognition that needs to be made. What's being discussed is the word "liturgy." In the context of the Lutheran "worship wars" the word has positive and negative associations with it.[16] Some esteem it and some despise it, pastors and parishioners alike.

Further, each person may have a different connotation of what the word "liturgy" actually means, particularly as it pertains to Lutheran liturgy. To be sure, Word and sacrament need to be at the center, but what each person specifically understands "liturgy" to imply can vary unless specified.

For many, the word liturgy means a stuffy, outdated, formalized, impersonal, organ-music way of having a church service. (Some of you are nodding your heads). For them, it detracts from worship because they feel the form gets in the way of the expression of worship they wish to give to God. In other words, they have a particular definition of worship. However, Lutherans have historically had a very distinct understanding of worship:

> Worship is God speaking. It is our listening. Worship begins with God's Word. He is the content. Evangelical Lutheran worship begins with God giving us his Word. It comes to us and we respond in faith and devotion. It is God's action, not ours. He is the mover, the doer. Faith comes as the gift from God, not from our own doing or action. Such an understanding of worship is quite different from the dictionary definition of the word. It is for that reason

16. What I found while doing research and interviews of my own members for this project, at least with those congregational members who do not have an affinity for the word "liturgy," and the liturgy itself, was a two-fold assessment. First, there was, for them, the belief that the word "liturgy" was simply a dated and foreign word that denoted an "old" way of "doing" church. However, there was the admission that they really did not actually know what "liturgy" meant. In the words of one member: "I had never been taught what it was before you taught on it." The second assessment was that those who did not like the practice of the traditional liturgy attributed that dislike to a previous bad experience with what was expressed to be a condescending and rigid pastor, who they perceived to love the liturgy more than his people. But after some conversation they came to realize this was not the fault of the liturgy itself. Thus the lesson learned for pastors: Be sure your people know you love them more than the liturgy and be regular in lovingly teaching them the meaning of the liturgy. For lectionary-based sermon examples, bible study examples, and new member class examples of teaching the liturgy, as well as using the liturgy as a means for shaping the mission, vision, and strategy of a congregation, see the Appendices.

that the Evangelical Lutheran Church has shown a preference for the word *service*. The chief gathering of Christians on Sunday morning is called the divine service. In the Divine Service, God serves us. He gives us his Word and sacraments. Only after we have received the Word and the gifts that he offers do we respond in our sacrifice of thanksgiving and praise.[17]

To be sure, the liturgy frames this back-and-forth, ensuring that God's gifts are given, and that we have the opportunity to respond in thanks and praise, all within the divine Gospel narrative the liturgy proclaims. Nonetheless, Word and sacrament liturgy has also historically had different orders of the various elements in it. Waddel draws this out:

> What does it mean that the sacraments are to be given in accordance with God's Word? Is this an implied reference to "the liturgy that the Lutheran confessions *assume*," as some have said? Or do they refer to 'the meaning and the intention of the Lutheran Confessions' comments about worship,' with the preconceived conclusion that the Confessions are referring to a specific liturgical form. Here I would simply ask of those who say this, which liturgy is that? Would it be Luther's *Latin Mass* (1523) or Luther's *German Mass* (1526)?[18]

The point is that the specific contents and order may not be common reference points with a generalized use of the word "liturgy." The word can be used to refer to a general framework, but also to a specific prescribed order. As such, given our "worship wars" context, care should be taken when speaking about liturgy, so that our assumptions do not make out of us, what we tell our children they will.

EVALUATING THE LITURGY

Waddell goes on to offer a thoughtful evaluation of the liturgy. He does so in terms of its "essence"—which is specifically the Gospel;

17. Pittelko, "Corporate Worship of the Church: Worship and the Community of Faith." In *Lutheran Worship: History and Practice*, 45.

18. Waddell, *A Simplified Guide to Worshipping as Lutherans*, 27.

"form"—which also entails structure[19] and "style"[20] and "function."[21] His aim is to help the Lutheran church have an honest dialogue about worship in terms of what their own confessions actually confess, and what the integrity of Lutheran worship looks like, all within the historic understanding and practice of the liturgy.

As such, (and this is sure to raise the dander of a few folks) both the "Liturgical-Repristination"[22] and the church growth[23] imperatives on the worship service of the church are objectively evaluated in light of the Lutheran confessions. He considers them both illegitimate based upon the scriptural and confessional standards adhered to by our church body.

Summing it up, there is flexibility, within limits, where uniformity cannot be legislatively imposed, but where there are indeed non-negotiables (both theological and structural) to Lutheran liturgy. In short, Waddell puts it this way, "Lutheran theology for Lutheran Worship."[24] It is specific to my tradition, but it's helpful to our greater dialogue because of the emphasis on the theological thoughtfulness that is significant for the church and her worship to consider.

19. "Here the most basic service of the Word and Sacrament consists of these elements: Scripture readings, sermon, Creed, prayer of the church, words of institution, and distribution of the body and blood of Christ. These elements, including the Sacrament of Holy Baptism, are non-negotiable. They are non-negotiable because they reflect the basic requirements for the unity and the orthodoxy of the church according to Article VII of the *Augsburg Confession*." Waddell, *A Simplified Guide to Worshipping as Lutherans*, 93.

20. Which is "an issue of aesthetics, or the art form," and which, he notes, should certainly be done with "excellence." Ibid., 94.

21. According to the Lutheran confessions the function of liturgy involves five specific things: delivery of the Gospel, decorum or good order in the church, catechesis (or teaching), edification in the Gospel, and the avoidance of frivolity and offense." Ibid., 95.

22. "The 'Litugical-Repristination' point of view insists that we may use only historic liturgical forms. It is characterized by slogans like, *"Litourgia divina adiaphora nonest,"* a Latin phrase that means "The Divine liturgy is not adiaphora." This point of view follows a model of confession that seeks to correct an error by confessing (or promoting) the error's opposite." Ibid., 13.

23. "It is also inappropriate for anyone to insist that, if we want the church to grow, a congregation must adopt contemporary forms of worship. This argument is based on the flawed premise that external forms, rather than the Holy Spirit working through the Gospel and the sacraments, are what makes the church grow." Ibid., 80–81.

24. Ibid., 117.

NEW TESTAMENT WORSHIP AND WITNESS

Thus, the liturgy, regardless of the variable forms it takes, it's still the story of the church. As the third article reminds us, it's about the "community of saints" gathered around the Gospel of Jesus Christ for *"the forgiveness of sins, the resurrection of the body, and the life everlasting."* It's the same story that the first disciples gathered around, the same message they taught, and the same Gospel they proclaimed.

As such, it's important to note the worship practice of the early New Testament church. First, as a means to demonstrate the origination of the liturgical framework, and second, to show that the worship service, rather than being used as something to attract people *in* to the church, is actually the wheel that moves the church *out* into the world.

Accordingly, study of the New Testament church quickly reveals that worship and witness had a distinct and intimate relationship in the life of the early church. In fact, this relationship was integral to the formation of the first New Testament church. This is most notably seen in Acts 2:42–47.

> 42And they devoted themselves to the apostles' teaching and the fellowship, to the breaking of bread and the prayers. 43And awe came upon every soul, and many wonders and signs were being done through the apostles. 44And all who believed were together and had all things in common. 45And they were selling their possessions and belongings and distributing the proceeds to all, as any had need. 46And day by day, attending the temple together and breaking bread in their homes, they received their food with glad and generous hearts, 47praising God and having favor with all the people. And the Lord added to their number day by day those who were being saved. (ESV)

From the start of the New Testament church there is worship. God is speaking (through the Apostles' teaching) and believers are listening. God is giving his gifts (through the breaking of the bread) and believers are receiving gifts. Said another way, the believers are gathered around Word and sacrament. They have gathered around "the apostle's teaching," and "the breaking of bread" (as well as baptism, see Acts 2:38–41), corporate "fellowship," and "the prayers." God comes to them and they respond with faith and devotion, not to mention a little bit of "awe" and service to those in "need." From the start we see there was worship, witness, and service to their neighbors.

But there's something else very intriguing about this worship. It appears that it facilitated the incorporation of new believers into the community of saints. And even more, implicit in this worship was the presence of the outreach going on among the "fellowship" of believers. When *"the Lord added to their number day by day those who were being saved,"* it implies that those who were *"added to their number"* were added through nothing other than the means which the believers had devoted themselves to—*"the apostles' teaching . . . the fellowship . . . the breaking of bread and . . . the prayers."*

ACTS 1:8 TO 8:1

In addition to the Great Commission, Acts 1:8 is also often held up as the key "missional" verse for the New Testament church: *"But you will receive power when the Holy Spirit comes on you; and you will be my witnesses in Jerusalem, and in all Judea and Samaria, and to the ends of the earth."* If this is so, then Acts 2:42–47 shows how this was done.

It's a disciple-making process that's inherent in the worship of New Testament believers. Whether in their homes or at the temple, Christ was present and among them in this worship just as he promised, not only "to the ends of the earth" (Acts 1:8) but "to the end of the age" (Matthew 28:20). And it was through this worship that believers were dispersed out into the world through their various vocations to serve their neighbors and tell the Good News.

It is a pattern for the life of the church that is sorely underemphasized. Unbelievers are "called" by the Gospel and thus converted, and then "gathered," again by the Gospel, only to be dispersed out into the service of their vocations, where, in the natural course of those vocational relationships, and as opportunity arises, they share the Good News.

This calling and gathering, we are reminded, did not happen dislocatedly, that is, apart from the Holy Spirit making use of people's mouths. (I know, "dislocatedly" isn't technically a word, but it does express my point. And besides, theologians are notorious for making up helpful words like that. So I'm just joining the fun.)

The Word of Christ went out for ears to hear and hearts to believe. The Apostles' mouths were used most clearly, but we can only conclude that due to the "daily" additions of believers to the church in Jerusalem, there was also some vocational witnessing happening: Parents telling children, the blacksmith telling his apprentice, the tent maker telling the merchant? Gossiping of the Gospel was happening.

Consider what Acts records. At first there were the 120 gathered believers, including the Apostles from Acts 1:15. Then there was the approximate "three thousands souls" added after Peter's sermon in Acts 2:41. Then come those who were "added day by day" in Acts 2:47, which also described their regular pattern of Word and Sacrament worship. This is followed by the "multitudes of men and women" added in Acts 5:14. Perhaps wives told husbands and husbands told wives? Then, the "disciples multiplying greatly" in Acts 6:7.

To be sure, pastors (those "apostled") were always present, as was Word and sacrament worship. And most assuredly, though perhaps quietly spoken, were the variously vocationed people of Jerusalem.

This does not make "everyone a minister," nor does it make "everyone a missionary." Not in the proper sense of the words. Rather this simply recognizes and affirms everyone would have exercised their vocations—affirming what the third article confesses—"The same Spirit who calls us to faith through the externality of his word also calls us to life in creation."[25]

Thus, whether a parent, apostle, physician (i.e., Luke) or fishermen (i.e., Peter, Andrew, James, and John), each vocation brought them into contact with others around them, first to serve them according to that vocation, and then, where possible, during the natural course of interactions, to intentionally proclaim the good news of Christ as appropriate to the opportunity and situation.

No, this is not meant to give the excuse to hide behind one's vocation and not share the Gospel. Rather it affirms that it is the Lord who is hiding behind each vocation, ensuring that His creatures are cared for, and that people are specifically put into relationships so that they can in fact share the Gospel.

This is the pattern that first moved the church out into Jerusalem. It was no doubt the same after the dispersion in Acts 8:1. Word and Sacrament worship was the wheel that moved the church out "to the ends of the earth" as it was foretold in (note the inverse numbers) Acts 1:8.

25. Pless, "Contemporary Spirituality and the Emerging Church," 362.

GATHERING *IN* AND SENDING *OUT*

The pattern is cyclical. At the center of this wheel is Christ and His Gospel, who "calls" and "gathers" disciples around Him through Word and Sacrament, where believers are ritually forgiven and freed, renewed and refreshed, discipled and dispersed into their vocations to serve their neighbor and gossip the Gospel. Here others are then called by that Gospel, and so they too are gathered (discipled) into the community of saints through Word and sacrament. The pattern repeats itself, daily and weekly, as confessed in Luther's explanation to the third article of the Apostles' Creed.[26] It's the wheel that moves the church *out* into the world, while bringing people *in* to the faith.

It's a sorely underemphasized theology. But if it would be celebrated and championed by the church there would be, I contend, an increased vibrancy to the daily life of the church and an increased fidelity to the mission of God. Thus, it would be helpful to see how this would look in the church today.

WORSHIP AND WITNESS IN THE NORTH AMERICAN CHURCH TODAY

There's an adage that is useful toward understanding how outreach and assimilation flow out of worship. The maxim of Prosper of Aquitaine states, "The law of worshiping founds the law of believing."[27] Put simply, the way we worship rules and express what we believe.

Throughout the history of God's people, this has been the primary manner by which the people of God have come to understand and know who He is and what he has done for us. In fact, James K. Smith is quick to point out that the "people of God called out (*ek-klēsia*) to be the church were worshipping long before they got all their doctrines in order or articulated the elements of Christian worldview; and they were engaged in and developing worship practices long before what we now

---

26. Kolb and Wengert, Small Catechism, Third Article, § 6, ". . . the Holy Spirit has called me through the Gospel, enlightened me with his gifts, and made me holy and kept me in the true faith, just as he calls, gathers, enlightens, and makes holy the whole Christian church on earth and keeps it with Jesus Christ in the one common true faith. *Daily in this Christian church* the Holy Spirit abundantly forgives all sins – mine and those of all believers." Emphasis added.

27. Just, "Liturgical Renewal in the Parish," in *Lutheran Worship: History and Practice*, 25.

call our *Bible* emerged and was solidified, so to speak."[28] If this is true, it would only follow that assimilation (the incorporation of unbelievers) and outreach flow out of worship.

God's gifts of grace are given in Word and sacrament worship. Here, faith is given, strengthened, and sustained. Here instruction, teaching, and discipling occur. Here lives are formed for daily living. Here believers also respond in faith, with devotion, prayer, thanksgiving, and praise. And then, at the end, believers are also dispersed in the name of Christ, with His blessing, to be "a light to the Gentiles" and to serve their neighbor as they have been served by Christ.

The New Testament believers of Acts 2 ritually worshipped and regularly brought unbelievers with them to worship. At the temple or the home, we are told the Lord added *"to their number day by day those who were being saved."* Likewise, the New Testament believers of today are called to ritually worship and regularly bring unbelievers with them, so that they too, like the believers of Acts 2, might have the Lord add to *"their number day by day those who were being saved."*

DISCIPLING WORSHIP

However, this isn't meant to make the worship service the primary mode of outreach. Rather, as it has been expressed, it's quite the opposite. What's being examined here is the discipling nature of the worship service. As it was used as such for the believers in Acts 2, so I believe it is to be used today. Not as an attractional outreach tool, but as the evangelizing and discipling means of grace. Arthur Just put it this way:

> Here is where evangelism and missions are properly placed, not as the essence of the Church, but as what the Church does. Our greatest act of love to our unbelieving neighbors is to bring them into the liturgical assembly to receive the gifts of salvation. The Great Commission is an act of love, inspired by faith that receives the gifts in the liturgy, to go out to the highways and byways and bring our lost neighbors into the liturgy so they may behold the presence of Jesus Christ and receive the gifts of the Gospel proclaimed in the Service of the Word.[29]

28. Smith, *Desiring the Kingdom,* 135.
29. Just, *Heaven on Earth,* 25.

To be sure, pastors and priesthood would need to use their mouths (at the appropriate times) to explain what such a service is about to an unbeliever, particularly the why and what of the liturgy. As Dale Meyer pointed out, we will need to use appropriate words and understandable language. But this doesn't mean the liturgy is too complicated. It means that, like any good story teller, we need to use a clear voice to tell and teach what the liturgy is all about—its rituals, its traditions, and its story.

As James K. Smith notes, "The Liturgy is a 'hearts and minds' strategy, a pedagogy that trains us as disciples precisely by putting our bodies through a regimen of repeated practices that get hold of our heart and 'aim' our love toward the kingdom of God."[30] It's the same for the child being brought up in the faith, the unbeliever being introduced to the faith, and the lifelong Christian. Worship forms and informs faith. It shapes and molds believers into the community of saints who serve their neighbors.

In general, long before one can provide a comprehensively detailed or intensely systematic presentation of the faith, worship served to build the foundations of faith. Again, as Smith puts it, "Before we articulate a worldview, we worship. Before we put into words the lineaments of an ontology or an epistemology, we pray for God's healing and illumination. Before we theorize the nature of God, we sing his praises. Before we express moral principles, we receive forgiveness. Before we codify the doctrine of Christ's two natures, we receive the body of Christ in the Eucharist. Before we think, we pray."[31] Worship forms and informs us. It molds us and it makes us to be God's holy creatures. Like the young toddler who doesn't yet know her father's full formal name, but knows that he is her "daddy," the Holy Christian Church prays "Our Father" and trusts in His goodness long before every member knows all of His names.

WORSHIP THAT GIVES GRACE

Yet, as we have observed, there remains a current trend among some North American congregations to, in the name of outreach, disassemble and reshape the historic worship of the church. Here the worship setting is no longer seen primarily as the time and place where God gives

30. Smith, *Desiring the Kingdom*, 33.
31. Ibid., 33–34.

his gifts of Word and sacrament and disciples the community of saints (and any visiting unbeliever). Rather it's seen as the place where people are offering praise to God and the primary place where outreach should occur.

Once again, though perhaps well intentioned, and while aiming to be culturally sensitive and relevant, this practice seems to be antithetical to the understanding of worship demonstrated in Acts 2.[32] True, there might be things *about* God in it, but it nonetheless ends up lacking in the actual ritual discipling and the *giving* of God's abundant gifts of grace.

In fact, while aiming to be "accessible" and "relevant" I contend there is often a distancing effect.[33] It reduces the real presence of God and His grace to that of an abstract exercise of merely thinking *about* God. Making an observation regarding the handicapped in worship, Smith captures it well:

> While we have worries about elevators and barriers, too many Protestant churches continue to offer a (very modern) style of worship that is dominated by quite abstract, heady forms, center-ing on a sermon that communicates only a cognitive level (often difficult even for those without college degrees)—rather than adopting historic forms of Christian liturgy that enact the whole person and thus reach those without such cognitive capacities with the story of the Gospel.[34]

32. Arthur Just offers a timely critique of the "cultural relevancy" movement to replace liturgical forms of worship with "contemporary" or free-form worship styles: "Perhaps what is wrong is not the liturgy but those who do the liturgy. The targets of liturgical renewal are the clergy and the congregation. The problems are less liturgical and more theological, centering more in our anthropology and ecclesiology than our liturgiology. What is wrong is not the liturgy but the culture, and thus instead of con-stantly asking 'What's wrong with the liturgy?' we should be asking 'What's wrong with the culture?' concentrating our attention on the renewal of the culture through liturgy, not vice versa. The goal of good liturgy is always to transform the lives of people [the transforming of culture] by the Gospel of Jesus Christ. This is hardly accomplished if the liturgy is subjected to the whimsies of culture." Just, *Heaven on Earth*, 21–22.

33. Carl Raschke remains adamant about what must be done when this is the case: "We need to turn over the tables and throw out not only the money changers—the growth gurus who both run and ruin the evangelical churches—but also the traders in conceptual currency who transform God's *ekklesia* into a brothel of philosophical and cultural fashions rather than a genuine house of prayer; we need to open our hearts and minds into authentic relationship with the Lord." Raschke, *GloboChrist*, 158.

34. Smith, *Desiring the Kingdom*, 136, footnote 7.

In short, there remains an essential need for the liturgy in the church today. As such, a collegial and pastoral call for the renewal of the historic worship forms of the church seems entirely appropriate.

RENEWING THE WORSHIP AND WITNESS OF THE CHURCH

What's being lost today are pastors and congregations who understand, teach, and pass on what it is that the liturgy frames, gives, rehearses, and celebrates. The irony is that in the attempt to speak to a world that has lost its story, such churches, as we have observed, wind up losing their own story—the Gospel!

Robert Jenson remains adamant about how the mission and the message of the church ring out through the liturgy, especially to a postmodern world.

> For the ancient Church, the walls of the place of Eucharist, whether these were the walls of a basement or of Hagia Sophia or of an imaginary circle in the desert, enclosed a world. And the great drama of the Eucharist was the narrative life of that world. Nor was this a fictive world, for its drama is precisely the 'real' presence of all realty's true author, elsewhere denied. The classic liturgical action of the church was not about anything else at all; it was itself the reality about which truth could be told. In the postmodern world, if a congregation or churchly agency wants to be 'relevant,' here is the first step: it must recover the classic liturgy of the church, in all its dramatic density, sensual actuality, and brutal realism, and make this the one exclusive center of its life. In the postmodern world, all else must at best be decoration and more likely, distraction.[35]

In the end, as it did for the New Testament believers of Acts 2, the liturgy as the narrative of Christ, has the power to speak and ritualize the church's story in the midst of all cultures, and all times, and be efficacious and effective to those gathered around it. It forms and informs. It shapes and molds. It tells the narrative of salvation. It draws us into the story of Christ. Not merely in and of itself, but also insofar as there are pastors and the royal priesthood who regularly celebrate it, teach it, and live it.[36]

---

35. Jenson, "How the World Lost Its Story," 5.

36. This dual approach (Word/sacrament worship and vocation) naturally ensures that there are no tendencies to, as David Peter suggests, have vertical or horizontal

Harold Senkbeil has some definitive words on the benefits of the liturgy for the 21st century North American church: "The liturgy is filled with the life of Jesus Christ in His Word and Sacrament. Therefore the liturgy is both the foundation and the pattern of the Christian life. It is not only the source of the church's life in Christ, but also the shape of the church's life in Christ. It is the place where she draws life and where she gives it back again. It is where she inhales the life-giving power of the Spirit and where she exhales in the power of the Spirit."[37] Thus, it can be said that to live by the liturgy is nothing other than to be called by the Gospel, gathered around Christ's Word, served by His sacraments, and dispersed into our vocations to serve our neighbor and give witness to our Savior.[38] It is the mission of the church.

---

dimension reduction regarding outreach. As Peter notes, "vertical reductionism occurs when the practice of evangelism is understood as purely God's action (the vertical) with a negating of the human role (the horizontal)." Horizontal reductionism would mean placing all the emphasis on the human evangelism effort or program. Peter, "A Framework for the Practice of Evangelism and Congregational Outreach," 210–12.

37. Senkbeil, *Dying to Live*, 123.

38. This is the framework for my congregation's Mission, Vision and Strategy. See the Appendices for more details.

Epilogue

Life in my household remains eventful. It's probably not much different from many young households in our country. We have four young children—an infant, a two-year-old, a five-year-old, and an eight-year-old. There are not too many dull moments. My wife and I aren't worried about getting bored. It also made writing this book no small endeavor.

Parenting is no half time job. It's a keep the older two from fighting, get the two-year-old a snack, nurse the baby, help with homework, change the poopy diaper, cook the supper, good manner teaching, kiss the boo-boo, Jesus loving, find the nuk, potty training, bad dream comforter, child hugging, no sleep getting, full time, nonstop job.

That's where my life is at right now. Sure I get tired. Yes, I get cranky. (Just ask my bride.) Not by our own reason or strength can we make it through. But through Him who gives us strength do we tackle each day. But that's my life and I'm thankful for it. I have no desire to wish away the busyness, or to wish my children older. As one wise mother told me: "Little kids, little problems, bigger kids, bigger problems." The Lord has put me in this vocation at this time and I'm rejoicing in it, even if it is rather messy. (And believe me, the poopy diapers going on at my house have been messy!)

Yes, I do also have another full time job as a pastor. As I've already shared, that has its own challenges and burdens too. But it is through Him who gives me strength that I bear up under it and, yes, even find joy in it.

"I cannot by my own reason or strength . . ." The bifocals of the third article of the Apostles' Creed keep us focused on the Lord and His Word. They keep us focused on His work in us, His work among us, and His work through us. The Holy Christian Church "called, gathered and enlightened" by the Holy Spirit, is alive and vibrant because the Holy Spirit, through Word and sacrament, makes her to be so.

It is not about numbers—"my church is growing more than yours." It is not about the culture—"my church is more relevant that yours." It is about the Word. "I cannot by my own reason or strength," points us to the Word of Christ, which tells us what He has done and for whom he has done it.

This word declares that as "the grass withers and the flower falls," so "all men" will wither and fall (1 Peter 1:25). It means that postmodernism will wither and fall. "But," as Peter reminds, "the word of the Lord remains forever. And this word is the good news that was preached to you" (1 Peter 1:25).

This Word of Christ is a word of life—the abundant life—to be lived by believers in the kingdom of God, here in time, and there in eternity. While here "in time," this living goes on through each person's vocation. And while here in time, the church's mission, through all of time, through every culture, and to every person, is to proclaim this Good News!

So take heart. The Good News is the Gospel by which the Holy Spirit calls me, and calls you dear reader. Where the Word is, there the Holy Spirit is, making believers, gathering worshipers, and enlightening the whole Christian church on earth. This is the *missio Dei*—the mission of God.

Pastor and the royal priesthood do what they have been given to do. Pastors preach the Word and administer the sacraments. The royal priesthood serves their neighbors and proclaim the Gospel.

"I cannot by my own reason or strength . . ." frames the daily life of believers in the world as they assemble as the "community of saints" and as they disperse as the Holy Christian Church. I challenge the North American church to reclaim the radical nature of this Gospel proclamation, trusting that the Word is powerful and effective. I challenge the North American church to rejoice in the royal priesthood. If it does, perhaps we'll be privileged to witness the distinct growth of God's kingdom here in time, and then, when time has ended, in all of its fullness there in eternity.

Zion Lutheran

Sharing *hope*, *teaching* *Christ*

Appendix 1

Congregational Mission, Vision, and Strategy

OUR MINISTRY AT ZION LUTHERAN

Our Mission

Sharing Hope Teaching Christ through Word and Sacrament *liturgical living.*

Our Vision

Being disciples by *following Jesus* Christ to the poor . . . the meek . . . the destitute . . . the lonely . . . the burdened . . . the sick . . . to sinners . . . to the cross . . . and to the empty tomb!

Our Strategy

Be the Royal Priesthood (1 Peter 2:9) by sharing what we have been given to share through *cradle to grave Christian education* by using: Caring Conversations, Rituals & Traditions, Devotions, Service

The Wheel that Moves the Church

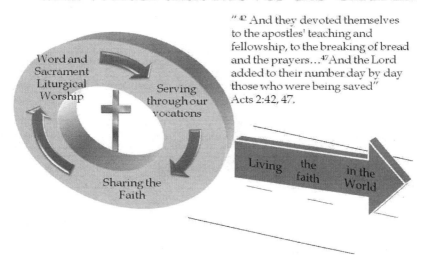

" ⁴² And they devoted themselves to the apostles' teaching and fellowship, to the breaking of bread and the prayers...⁴⁷And the Lord added to their number day by day those who were being saved" Acts 2:42, 47.

Word and Sacrament Liturgical Worship

Serving through our vocations

Sharing the Faith

Living the faith in the World

Appendix 2

Lectionary Based Sermons and Bible Study Examples of Teaching the Liturgy

LECTIONARY BASED SERMONS

"Divine Service" Mark 9:30–37, Series B, Proper 20

The school year is now back under way. This year was a big step in my family. Our daughter Isabella started Kindergarten. It's a big change for her. For three days a week she will be at school for the whole day. (It's also a big change for her "mama" and little brother.) Nonetheless, things are going great.

However, the days leading up to that first day of school found my daughter with a mix of emotions. She was excited to go to school all day. She couldn't wait to eat lunch at school. She had been dreaming about riding the bus home. And she was filled with eager anticipation for her turn to be the line leader.

However, I found out she was discouraged about her last name. She remembered from pre-school that line leaders were selected based on the alphabetical order of last names. And knowing her alphabet quite well, she recognized the curse of her name. *"I'm a Woodford! It's going to take forever to get to be the line leader."*

Nonetheless, the first day of school came. When I saw her in the hallway, low and behold who was at the front of the line! *"Daddy, daddy! Mrs. Aurich started at the end of the Alphabet! I get to be the first line leader!"* That girl was floating on cloud nine all day long. It gave perspective to Jesus' words from the Gospel lesson: *"If anyone wants to be first, he must be last . . ."*

Bella was last in the alphabet but was made first by her teacher. It was fun for Bella. But it's not exactly what Jesus was referring to when he spoke to the disciples in the Gospel reading.

Take a closer look at what Jesus says, *35 "If anyone wants to be first, he must be last and servant of all."* This is different than our kindergarten—or adult—impulse of wanting to be the first one in line and the first one served.

Jesus illustrates, rather poignantly, what he means when he takes a child and places him in their midst. We aren't certain of the exact age of the child. But the text lends us to believe that the child is probably anywhere from an infant to an older toddler: *36 "And he took a child and put him in the midst of them, and taking him in his arms, he said to them, 37 "Whoever receives one such child in my name receives me, and whoever receives me, receives not me but him who sent me."*

That Jesus uses a child is no small thing. Every parent understands how infants and young children are entirely dependent upon their parents. A parent's life is that of food maker and care taker. They are the providers, the nurturers, and the protectors. Until thier child goes out on his or her own, it's a life of service for parents.

Thus, when Jesus says, *37 "Whoever receives one such child in my name receives me . . ."* there is a twofold meaning. First, to receive a child is to willingly enter into a life of service. His point is that whether infant, adult, or elderly, those received by us in Jesus' name, are those who we willingly and gladly serve. As Jesus said, *35 "If anyone wants to be first, he must be last and servant of all."*

Second, Jesus' love and grace is meant for all people, irrespective of age or ability. It's *his* grace after all. He can give it as he chooses. And he chooses that infants, adults, and the elderly should all equally receive it. That's why Lutherans are glad to baptize infants and happy to baptize adults—young or old—recognizing that in each case baptism is always God's gift of grace and love.

37 "Whoever receives one such child in my name receives me, and whoever receives me, receives not me but him who sent me." Do you see how the Heavenly Father ordered it? God does not come demanding our service. He first sent his Son Jesus Christ to serve us.

The service Jesus gives was put this way in the Gospel: 31 *"The Son of Man is going to be delivered into the hands of men, and they will kill him. And, after three days he will rise."* Jesus comes not to be served, but to serve and give his life as a ransom for many. As such, our service to God is only out of response to his divine service to us.

In fact, the way Lutherans worship reflects this relationship. The liturgical structure that shapes Lutheran worship is distinct in its emphasis on God serving us and our response to that service. This is why Lutherans call our manner of worship the *Divine Service*.

Look at the order of our worship service. It starts with God coming to us through his word: *"In the name of the Father and of the Son and of the Holy Spirit"* (Matthew 28:19). The *Invocation* not only invokes God to be present, but it is a reminder of how we have been baptized in the name of the triune God and served with his grace.

As God is called upon and comes to us, we then respond with the *confession of our sins*. God in turn graciously responds with *absolution (forgiveness)*. We then respond in *prayer and praise*.

Our worship continues with God serving us through his Word in the *Scripture readings*. We respond by confessing him as our living God in the *Apostles' or Nicene Creed*. God comes to us through his Word as we focus on it in the *sermon*. We respond with *offerings and prayers*. Then Christ himself comes to us in the *Lord's Supper*, and we respond with *thanks and praise*. Finally, God sends us on our way with his *Blessing*.

Did you notice the service begins and ends with God coming to us? However, it is important to note that the "service" (our service to God) does not end when the worship service ends. When the Divine Service comes to an end, believers who had gathered around the liturgy go out into the world and bear witness in our words and lives to the Christ who serves us and invites us to serve others.

There is something significant about the *Blessing* that comes at the end of the liturgy. Some may think that the blessing means, *"Whew! The service is finally over and we can get home to the game!"* (This was me during every football season throughout high school and college).

However, in the blessing God gives his affirmation and final words of comfort before we go back into the world and into our vocations. Though the weekly worship service may have ended, our life of service is once again just beginning.

This is Jesus' point in the Gospel lesson. *"35If anyone wants to be first, he must be last and servant of all."* Every Sunday we are served by God. His Word breathes life back into broken spirits. His sacrament brings healing to weary bodies and forgiveness to burdened consciences. His blessing speaks hope into our hearts and sends us into service of one another.

Jesus said, *37"Whoever receives one such child in my name receives me . . ."* In other words, the way we "serve" God is seen through our care of those we receive in Jesus' name.

But you ask, *"Who are those we receive in Jesus name?"* Look at those in your life. Look at your spouse. Look at your children. Look across the street. Look at the cubicle next to you. Look at the car driver in front of you.

We have been divinely served so that we might serve in the name of Jesus. Whether at home, at work, or in the community, we live lives of service—to our spouses . . . our children . . . our neighbors . . . the woman with the flat tire on the side of the road . . . the coworker going through the divorce . . . the struggling mother of five . . . the elderly shut-in desperate for some companionship.

To be sure, our acts of service will not all look the same. We each have different stations in life. The mother who cares for her children is not the same as the mailman delivering our mail. A father is not the same as a nurse. The dairy farmer is not the same as the volunteer fire-fighter. The food shelf volunteer is not the same as the carpenter donating his time.

The way we serve may not always look the same, but when we serve in the name of Jesus, it is divinely pleasing and divinely ordered. It is the liturgy lived in everyday life.

35"If anyone wants to be first, he must be last and servant of all." Jesus can back this up. As the creator of all, he was first in line in Heaven. As the servant of all, he was last in line on earth. His life was given for our sins. His death was given for our salvation. The empty tomb was given for our resurrection!

Having been served by Jesus, we are freed to serve in his name. It is the divine service of God. Amen.

"INCREASE OUR FAITH! WHY WE WORSHIP"

Luke 17:1–10, Series C, Proper 22

What is faith? My haunch is that you are here this morning for one of two reasons. Either someone made you come here—mom, dad, wife or husband—or, you are here because you say you have faith in Jesus Christ.

But what is faith? Boiling it down to its simplest understanding, what is faith? Where does it come from? How do you get it? What's it all about? Is it something we create within ourselves, or is it something that is given to us?

How we answer this impacts the way that we worship. It is impacts the way that we witness. It impacts the way that we live—which is especially important when we live in what's now a non-Christian (or Post-Christian society).

I want you to think about this today. I want you to think about this all this week. The Gospel lesson for today is all about faith. In fact, we find the disciples emphatically asking Jesus to *"Increase our faith!"*

As the mission here at Zion is to share this faith, this is a great text for us to study. Not only for our own personal faith growth, but also as a basis for understanding how faith impacts our worship, our witness, and our way of life.

At the start, Jesus goes to the core of faith when he talks about temptation, sin, repentance, and forgiveness. To be sure, there are a number of elements to understand about faith, but faith does have a core.

Just like a car has a number of important parts, there are still the absolute essentials. Without the engine, it doesn't matter whether you have power windows, a CD player, air conditioning or a heater. With no engine, the car isn't going to work.

Likewise, the core elements of faith (the engine of faith) come in knowing about temptation, sin, repentance, and forgiveness in Christ. Take a look at what Jesus says:

"1 Temptations to sin are sure to come, but woe to the one through whom they come! 2 It would be better for him if a millstone were hung around his neck and he were cast into the sea than that he should cause one of these little ones to sin. 3 Pay attention to yourselves! If your brother sins, rebuke him, and if he repents, forgive him, 4 and if he sins against you seven times in the day, and turns to you seven times, saying, 'I repent,' you must forgive him." (Luke 17:1–4)

I don't know if Jesus can put the gravity of sin any more clear, particularly for those who cause others to sin. Jesus is talking to the disciples at this point, so there is an extra strong emphasis for pastors who teach about the faith.

However, the warning also goes for any person who tempts others to sin: *2 It would be better for him if a millstone were hung around his neck and he were cast into the sea than that he should cause one of these little ones to sin.* Just in case you are wondering what he means, try swimming with a 500 pound rock tied to your neck.

The disciples pick up on this warning. They recognize that as teachers of the faith they have a great responsibility to live and teach the truth of this faith. So what do they do? *5 The apostles said to the Lord, "Increase our faith!"*

Have you ever felt this way? Have you ever felt your faith isn't strong enough? Not good enough? Not full enough? The disciples did. So they asked Jesus to increase their faith. And how does Jesus respond? *"6If you had faith like a grain of mustard seed, you could say to this mulberry tree, 'Be uprooted and planted in the sea,' and it would obey you."*

Sounds impossible, doesn't it? I know we have plenty of faith-filled believers here this morning. However, I am not so sure many of us would *feel* we had the ability to talk to trees and actually have a tree obey.

So, because we don't feel this way, does this then mean we don't have faith? As he was doing for the disciples, he does for us. By these words, Jesus points us to the object of faith. When we *feel* we lack faith, it's not that we don't have faith; it's that we are focusing too much on ourselves rather than on the object of our faith.

In other words, it brings us back to the question, "What is faith?" Where does it come from? How do you get it? Again, how we answer these questions impacts the way that we worship, the way that we witness, and the way that we live.

So here is a congregational question for you. Is faith something we create in ourselves or is it something given to us?

I'll put it to you this way. Faith is all gift! The disciples didn't get it on their own. Jesus gave it to them. And since he is the giver of faith, the disciples know where to go to receive an increase of faith. They go to Jesus and they cry out, *"Increase our faith!"*

Every time we come to worship, this is what we're asking. When we recognize faith is a gift—something that we receive—it changes how we understand worship. Most people think worship is simply something that we do to God. But when faith is understood as a gift, you see worship as the place where God gives his gifts of grace—the manner in which God gives and increases faith.

This is why Lutherans call our worship the *Divine Service*. It recognizes that worship is about God increasing your faith by *serving* you with his gifts of grace. *"But pastor, what if I don't feel it? What if it's not fun? What if the service just doesn't float my boat?"* Did you notice the disciples' request to Jesus? *"Increase our faith!"*

They didn't ask to have Jesus change their feelings. They didn't ask him to make his teachings easier. They didn't say, *"Hey Jesus, can you make this disciple business a little more fun."* They said, *"Increase our faith!"*

This can be a challenge as fallen human beings, but belief in Christ is a matter of faith. It's not a matter of simple feelings. *"Whoa . . . Wait a minute here pastor! What did you say?"*

Belief in Christ is a matter of faith. It's not primarily a matter of feelings. In other words, you are not so much to *feel* faith as you are to *believe* it! I know, this may raise an eyebrow or two, but listen closely.

There is so much confusion today that makes faith to be all about feelings, rather than about believing. But you will not find a verse saying that you need to "feel" faith. The Bible talks about believing faith. (Yes, the bible does say we are to trust God, and trust is an emotion. But that does not then make faith to be all *feeling*.)

Consider this. What happens when you don't *feel* God's judgment? What happens when you don't *feel* that what you did was a sin? Does this mean if you don't feel it, then it is not a sin? Or what happens when you don't *feel* Jesus loves you? *"How could he love me? I am such a failure, how could he love me?"* What happens when you don't *feel* Jesus' forgiveness? *"He couldn't forgive me. What I did was too terrible."* If you can't feel it, does that mean that he really doesn't love you. Does that mean he doesn't forgive you?

Do you see the perils of making faith only a matter of feelings? To be sure, trust is involved. And so we balance that trust with the content of faith. And thus faith is believed—when we confess our sins, when we lose our jobs, when depression sets in, when marriages fail, when the diagnosis is given, when loved ones die—faith is believed. Feelings come and go, but faith is believed because God can be trusted!

Every week you come to the Divine Service so that your sins might be forgiven and your faith might be increased. You come so that you can receive God's gifts of grace and respond in faith. The Divine Service reflects this. Look at the liturgy of the worship service for a moment.

It starts with God coming to you. The Invocation (God's Word) not only invokes God to be present but it's a reminder of how you have been baptized in that name. And as God comes to you, you respond in faith with the confession of your sins. God graciously responds with absolution (forgiveness). You then respond in prayer and praise, not because God needs your worship, but because this is simply faith in action.

God responds through his Word, coming to us through the Scripture readings. Then we respond by confessing Him as our living God in the Apostles' or Nicene Creed. God comes to you through his Word as we focus on it in the sermon. You respond with offerings and prayers.

Then Christ himself comes to us in the Lord's Supper, and we respond with thanks and praise. And finally, God then sends you on your way with his Blessing. Worship is all about God giving us his gifts of grace, to forgive your sins, and to increase your faith.

So regardless of how you *felt* during the service, whether or not you liked the music, thought the service was fun, or if you *felt* it moved you—you were still being served by God's gifts of grace. Now, sure, if you are here simply for a show and could care less about Jesus, then, no, faith will not be increased because faith is not present in you to receive these gifts of grace.

Thus, worship is not as much about your feelings as it is about your faith. To be sure, feelings come into play—we are human after all—and our emotions are God created wonders of our personalities. And yes, the emotion of *trust* is a part of faith. But feelings alone are not what determine worship. Thus, with the disciples, we cry, "*Lord, increase our faith!*"

The way that we understand faith not only impacts the way that we worship, it also impacts the way that we live and the witness that we give. Zion is all about passing on the faith. It is what our mission, vision, and strategy are all about: *Sharing Hope teaching Christ through Word and Sacrament liturgical living.*

Faith and worship are centerpieces of this Mission. Why? Because faith and worship were the centerpieces of the New Testament Church. Look at the NT reading for today.

The believers gathered together for "fellowship" (Acts 2:42). They surrounded themselves with the Word of God, at that time called "the apostles' teaching (v.42)," as well as the sacraments – "baptism" (v.38) and "the breaking of bread" (v.42) along with devotion to "the prayers" (v.42).

Notice anything familiar? God comes to them with gifts of grace and they respond with faith and devotion. From the start of the New Testament Church there was the Divine Service.

But there is also something else very profound about this worship. It facilitated the gathering in and the discipling of those who were previously unbelievers. Even more, implicit in this worship was the presence of the outreach to unbelievers that was going on among the "fellowship" of believers: "*47And the Lord added to their number day by day those who were being saved.*"

This biblical account recognizes that those who were "added to their number" were added through nothing other than the means to which the believers had devoted themselves—*"the apostles' teaching... the fellowship... the breaking of bread and... the prayers."* It testifies to the regular manner in which these believers worshipped *and* reached out to unbelievers.

If faith is the engine of the church, then worship (the Divine Service) is the *wheel* that moves the Church. It moves the Church forward in faith and forgiveness, and forward out into the world, to reach out to unbelievers.

In the Divine Service Christ gives his gifts of faith and forgiveness. You take these gifts into your daily life, into your vocations as workers, as spouses, as parents, and as neighbors, where you share them throughout out the week, and then come back to the Divine Service to be given them all over again—to increase your faith! This is the Christian life and so this is the Mission of our congregation. Amen.

"THE *INVOCATION* AND THE *KYRIE* IN OUR LIVES EVERYDAY"

Luke 17:11–19, Series C, Proper 23

When you meet someone new for the first time, what is one of the standard introductory rituals that you do? Does this sound and look familiar? You stick your hand out, say, *"Hello. My name's Lucas. It's nice to meet you,"* as you grab hold of their hand and shake it.

But have you ever wondered why do we shake hands? I mean, why hands? Why not touch elbows, or big toes, give a hip check, or maybe rub noses? Why do we shake hands?

It is kind of an odd ritual. But, I guess, so are a lot of other greetings out there. The French kiss hello. Italians hug. The Japanese bow. Dogs sniff one another. And emperor penguins bellow with a head dance. But we shake hands. In our culture it is our ritual custom.

The fact is our lives, and our culture, are filled with all kinds of rituals. Whether we realize it or not, we are a ritualized people.

From noon meals, to birthday parties; from the exchange of wedding rings, to the male bonding of hunting seasons; from the pledge of allegiance, to the answering of our phone with "hello," we are a society full of rituals.

Rituals don't just embody the basic values of a community; they constitute and maintain our common life. Whether you know it or not, you are a ritualized people. From your bedtime routine, to the way that you worship, you are witting or unwitting ritualists.

Rituals have meaning. They teach us. They feed us. They shape us. Rituals are full of significance. This is especially true for the way that we worship. The way that we worship is filled with powerful ritual.

Our liturgy is not there for mere empty repetition. It has meaning. Just like a hand shake has meaning and significance, the liturgy has profound meaning and significance. It ritually ensures God's gifts of grace get delivered. And it ritually ensures that we have the opportunity to give thanks and praise.

Consider the Gospel lesson for today. Ten lepers come to Jesus and cry out, *"13Jesus, Master, [Lord] have Mercy on us."* Leprosy is not a pretty disease. Though it's not always deadly, it disfigures and discolors skin, plugs the mucus membranes, gnaws on internal nerves, and ostracizes the afflicted.

Not only were these ten men covered by disease, they were detached from society. So they come to Jesus and cry out, *"Lord have mercy!"*

Sound familiar? They are the ritualized words of the Kyrie in our liturgy. "Kyrie" is simply the Greek word for "Lord." *Kyrie Eleison* —"Lord have mercy!"

It's what the lepers were crying out to Jesus. It's what you and I cry out to Jesus. Not just here in the Liturgy, but anytime, and any day. When the bills keep adding up, when sickness sets in, when the kids are too much, when our kids make us worry, when our bodies grow old, when marriages struggle, when depression makes us feel hopeless, when the sinful choice makes a mess of our lives. *"Lord have mercy!"*

The lepers cry out to Jesus. And what does Jesus do? *"14 When he saw them he said to them, "Go and show yourselves to the priests . . ."* Curiously, he sends them on to the priests.

And without hesitation, they go on their way. Why? It was the ritual in Jesus' day. In order for lepers to be cleansed, this was standard operating procedure. In fact, Leviticus 14 (of which Jesus would be very familiar with and why he would direct them to the priests) prescribes a very specific and very elaborate ritual to be followed for those who desired cleansing from leprosy.

What follows is just a small portion of the ritual: *"1 The LORD spoke to Moses, saying, 2 "This shall be the law of the leprous person for the day of his cleansing. He shall be brought to the priest . . . 12 And the priest shall take one of the male lambs and offer it for a guilt offering, along with the log of oil, and wave them for a wave offering before the LORD . . . 14 The priest shall take some of the blood of the guilt offering, and the priest shall put it on the lobe of the right ear of him who is to be cleansed and on the thumb of his right hand and on the big toe of his right foot"* (Leviticus 14).

From our perspective it is a bit of an odd ritual. But this certainly explains why the lepers would have gone on their way to the priests. No doubt, they may have already tried this, but, by faith, they listen to the voice of Jesus and head for the priest. *"14 . . . And as they went they were cleansed."*

They cry out, "Lord have mercy!" And mercy is given. Every week in the words of our liturgy we cry out, "Lord have mercy." Yes, it's ritualized. Yes, it's routine. But it's not empty. It's not meaningless! We sing out with the lepers and all those who gone before us, crying out to Jesus asking him to have mercy on us!

We sing it here together, but we take it with us every day of the week. The liturgy is meant to be lived and not just simply performed. When the ritual of the liturgy seems like it's becoming mundane, boring, or irrelevant, it is not the fault of the liturgy. Rather it's because the fullness of the liturgy is not being taught and not being lived.

Think about this for a moment. When you and I shake hands with someone we know what it means. We know what is symbolizes. Typically what hand do you shake with? Your right hand, correct? What if someone would shake hands with you using their left hand? What would you do?

In some countries of Africa or the Middle East, if you offer your left hand as a greeting, you would be giving great offense. In fact, in America, it would be similar to greeting someone with the obscene gesture of the middle finger.

Why? Well, let me put it this way. In America we use toilet paper and in some countries, well . . . they don't. They use the left hand. Hence it's considered unclean and an insult to use the left hand to shake hands.

Ritual has meaning. But if it isn't taught we lose its meaning and the opportunity to live being shaped by its meaning.

Liturgy has meaning. So it must be taught, just like the seventh inning stretch of a pro baseball game; placing your hand on your heart during the national anthem; or your college's fight song. If it's not taught, ritual can lose its purposeful practice, but not its meaning or value.

Thus, unbelievers are taught the truth of the Scriptures, and new Christians need to be taught the rituals of Christianity. Otherwise, just like shaking with your left hand in Africa, we risk giving offense by something that it unclean or unknown.

Unclean. Like lepers who were covered by disease. Like you and me, covered with sin. But Jesus has mercy upon those lepers and made them clean. Jesus has mercy upon you and me and makes us clean.

Baptized in the name of the Father and the Son and the Holy Spirit, we are washed clean, named and claimed as God's very own.

Every week the words of the Invocation not only invoke God's presence in our worship, but they remind us that we live by his name, washed clean and forgiven. By grace, these words (*In the name of the Father Son and Holy Spirit*) were imprinted upon you in baptism. And so, by grace, they are spoken at the start of worship as a powerful reminder that God has had mercy upon on you and continues to have mercy on you.

When Jesus had mercy on the lepers what happened? *"15 Then one of them, when he saw that he was healed, turned back, praising God with a loud voice; 16 and he fell on his face at Jesus' feet, giving him thanks. Now he was a Samaritan. 17 Then Jesus answered, 'Were not ten cleansed? Where are the nine? 18 Was no one found to return and give praise to God except this foreigner?' 19 And he said to him, 'Rise and go your way; your faith has made you well.'"*

Realizing his cry for mercy had been answered, the Samaritan returns, *"praising God with a loud voice"* and *"giving thanks"* to Jesus. But Jesus asks, *"Where are the nine? 18Was no one found to return and give praise to God except this foreigner?"*

Was Jesus angry because the other nine did not come and give to *him* the proper praise and thanks due him for the mercy he granted? I don't think that was quite it. Jesus was upset because only one returned to be affirmed in his faith.

Jesus did not *need* thanks and praise. In fact, he does not need *our* thanks and praise. God is God, regardless of our thanks and praise. However, our thanks and praise are important because they make us all the more mindful of God's love and mercy.

You see, we are intended to be praise singers and thanks givers because doing so makes us all the more aware of the gifts of grace that we have been given by God. By being praise singers and thanks givers—like the Samaritan leper—you increase your receptivity to God's gifts of grace.

If you are a grouch and nothing good ever happens to you, being a thanks giver and a praise singer is tough for you, isn't it? It also makes it more difficult to be receptive to God's gifts of grace. (But it certainly won't stop God from loving you.)

Being a thanks giver and praise singer allows you to exercise your faith in Christ and creates an increased capacity for enjoyment in life. Giving thanks and singing praise, comes only as a result of receiving an incredible gift. When someone gives you a gift, what is the ritual that we are taught? We are taught to say, "Thank you."

Every week the liturgy provides us the opportunity to once again be thanks givers, and praise singers, for the mercy and forgiveness given to us through Jesus Christ.

With the Samaritan leper, and all those who have gone before us, we praise and we thank Christ, not because he needs it, but because it makes us grow in confidence and hopefulness of God's continual gift of mercy. We take it with us, we live it— like the leper.

The liturgy comes from the Scriptures. It is full of life and full of meaning. This is why the liturgy is meant to be lived and not just performed.

When you live the liturgy there is witness to Christ in the way that you live. Thanks givers and praise singers proclaim what Christ has done and so give witness to him by their praise and through their thanks.

Your very lives become a witness to Christ because you live being those forgiven, mercy filled, thanks givers and praise singers. Liturgical living is nothing other than taking the truth and gifts of our weekly worship with you as you go on your way, where you live it, and by living it, you share it. Amen.

"THE SALUTATION AND THE BLESSING GIVEN FOR OUR POSSESSING"

Genesis 32:22–30, Series C, Proper 24

Growing up I played a lot of sports. In fact, for a good amount of time during my younger years, I lived and breathed sports. Football, basketball, track, and baseball—grade school, junior high, and high school—they were all filled with sports. College was no different.

Throughout my years as an athlete, I heard a common phrase being regularly used before each game or event. Can you guess what it may have been? *"Good luck!"*

It's still a phrase I hear quite often today. In fact, I hear it at more than just a sports event. I've heard it said to kids about to take a test. I've heard it said to people looking for a job. I've heard it said to others who are going in for surgery.

"Good luck!" I know what is meant by the phrase. People are simply wishing someone well—whether that be a sporting event, a test, a job or surgery. The desire is to express encouragement. *"Good Luck!"*

But have you ever wondered, what is luck? I mean, what is it, really? When we say *"Good luck"* to someone, are we confessing a belief in some unseen power, where, by some chance, a random occurrence of good fortune will hopefully fall upon that person?

What is luck? If you think about it, the idea of luck is actually quite the opposite of your Christian faith. As people who believe in a triune God as the Creator, Redeemer, and Sanctifier of your lives, you confess a sure and certain belief in the Lord of all that there is, and who is always in control.

Yes, we do believe in the supernatural, but it is a very specific supernatural. As we confess in the creeds, we believe in the power of Jesus

Christ who was crucified and died for our sins, but rose from the dead and who now sends us his Holy Spirit to lead us in our lives of worship and witness.

So the idea of some unknown force that we call "luck," is really rather contrary to our belief in the Almighty God. So then what *is* luck?

The best definition that I have ever heard on luck was from my college football coach. The notion of luck came up one day at practice. So I asked what he thought about luck. He said that luck was, "when preparation meets opportunity."

In other words—and this matched his coaching style—if I, as a defensive lineman, was *prepared*—meaning that I was in shape, well conditioned, alert to the game—and the ball happened to be fumbled out in front of me, I would be ready for the *opportunity* to pick up the ball and run it back for a touchdown.

For Coach O'Brien, this was luck. And I would have to agree. "When preparation meets opportunity" is the best definition of luck I've ever heard. It recognizes that there's no such thing as an unknown special force out there.

But that still begs the question. If, as Christians, you do not believe in luck, but rather you believe in the triune God, why would you wish someone luck?

As a Christian, is there something more profound and more powerful that you have to offer or give? You bet there is. It's called a blessing.

When Christians say, "Good luck" the desire is to wish someone well. So why not wish someone well in the name of the Lord?

Blessing is powerful. Blessing enacts (carries out) the word of God in peoples' lives. This is why we have it in the liturgy. In fact, blessing is an important mission tool.

Imagine how people might be affected, if before a game, before a test, before a job interview, or before surgery, you would say, *"God bless you"* or *"The Lord be with you."*

As baptized and redeemed Christians, you are Christ-bearers to the people you interact with and to the community that you are in. You have the incredible privilege to bless others in the name of the Lord and to enact God's word in their lives—family members, friends, neighbors, or coworkers.

Blessing is powerful. The Old Testament lesson gives an example about the power of God's blessing. In fact, you might say this blessing comes in the midst of a sort of quasi-sports event. In this portion of Scripture Jacob wrestles with God.

I love this section of Scripture because it gives a powerful image. First, because it gives a fantastic image of what it is to wrestle with God. And second, because it gives an image of what it is to be blessed by God.

Think of it like this. Have you ever wrestled with God about something in life? Have you ever questioned his wisdom, struggled with circumstances, or asked him, "Why?" Have you ever been upset with the Lord, wondered why he allowed something to happen, and in your anger, just really wanted to pin him down?

No matter how bad you're struggling with God or asking him questions—no matter how much you are wrestling with him—this image reminds you that in your struggle, God has a hold on you. He won't let go of you, no matter what your doubts or distress, your anxieties or afflictions. To wrestle with God is also to be held by God. It's an awesome image.

In Jacob's case, he physically wrestled with God and then asked for God's blessing. You are invited to do the same in your spiritual life. God's blessing is profound and powerful, especially in the midst of struggles.

Blessing is more than a mere ritual. It's the delivery of God's gifts. This is reflected in our worship. It is reflected in our liturgy.

Take a closer look at the Old Testament lesson for today. I have to admit that the text itself is rather odd. As a reader, we are tracking along, learning about Jacob, and then all of a sudden Jacob is now, of all things, *wrestling* with someone.

Who is it? Where does this person come from? Why is he there? And of all things, why are they wrestling?

If you're like me, perhaps you've taken to the high, sophisticated art of wondering what kind of wrestling this was. Was it free style or Greco-Roman? Was it like Wrestlemania, Smackdown, or Raw on WWE? Was it mixed martial arts? Was it Sumo? What was it?

We aren't told. We're simply told that they were "wrestling." But apparently this was a marathon wrestling match, because they wrestled all through the night, all the way until day break.

I don't know about you, but I find this whole wrestling match rather curious. Was Jacob really that strong? What kind of moves did the guy have that he could wrestle with God and hold his own? Did he put him in the sleeper, the full nelson, or the figure four leg lock? Whatever he did, it is was pretty successful and caused the man who he was wrestling (God) to resort to some other tactics:

"*25 When the man saw that he did not prevail against Jacob, he touched his hip socket, and Jacob's hip was put out of joint as he wrestled with him.*" But even then Jacob wouldn't stop: *26 Then he [God] said, "Let me go, for the day has broken." But Jacob said, "I will not let you go unless you bless me."*

Jacob had figured it out. He knew who he was wrestling, and he wasn't going to stop until he received the Lord's blessing. He knew the power of blessing. After all, he was the one who had tricked his father Isaac into giving him the blessing meant for his twin brother Esau.

The blessing God gave here was no small thing. Jacob was given a new name with the blessing: "*28 Then he [God] said, "Your name shall no longer be called Jacob, but Israel, for you have striven with God and with men, and have prevailed."* Jacob's wrestle with the Lord encapsulated his struggles with his own family.

First, Jacob steals a birthright from Esau. Then he takes Esau's blessing from his father. Now he and his family were crossing the ford at Jabbok (v.22), to set things straight with Esau. Walking in repentance, Jacob wrestles with God and is blessed.

This is the life you and I live. By faith in Christ we walk in repentance and we receive the forgiveness of sins and the incredible blessing of God almighty. Blessing is powerful. And there is no more powerful blessing than one given by the Lord Almighty.

Our liturgy picks up on this and ritualizes the giving of God's blessing in a couple of places. In the *Salutation* there is the blessing of the Lord's presence spoken by the pastor and a blessing spoken back to the pastor by the people. And then in the Benediction (the last element in the liturgy) God sends us on our way with his divine blessing.

The *Salutation* is the ritual expression and giving of Christ's presence to be with those with whom we are speaking: The pastor says, "*The Lord be with you.*" The people respond, "*And also with you.*"

We speak this as a blessing that actually conveys the Lord's presence, not because we thought it a neat sound alike line from Star Wars. (By the way, you know you are watching Star Wars with a bunch of Lutherans when you hear the phrase, "*May the force be with you*" and you instinctively respond with "*And also with you.*")

But the *Salutation* is much more than mere meaningless ritual or empty performance. It is an actual giving of the crucified and risen Lord Jesus Christ. In the liturgy it usually comes before the prayer of the day, noting that since the Lord himself has now been shared with one another (i.e. "*The Lord be with you*"), we will now go to him with our prayers and petitions.

We go to him with those very prayers that, as Jesus reminded his disciples in the Gospel reading, he promises to hear (v.1,8). Thus, as he did for the disciples, he does for you. He invites you to *always to pray and not lose heart.* He is with you. He hears your cries for mercy.

Both the *Salutation* and the *Benediction* (final Blessing of the liturgy) are ritualized in our liturgy as the actual giving of the Lord. They are for comfort, for peace, and for strength. They also serve as the reminder that as baptized Christ bearers we go out into our daily lives, and daily vocations, and as opportunity affords, we share Christ with those in our daily lives.

Think about this for a moment. When the challenges of life come your way, which is more powerful and comforting; telling someone, "*Good Luck,*" or saying "*The Lord be with you?*"

When someone is enduring a hardship, is suffering, frightened, or hurting, what is more powerful and comforting; saying, "*Hey, I hope you feel better*" or "*The Lord bless you and keep you*" or "*The Lord be with you*"?

There is tremendous power in blessing because of who the blessing is rooted in. Blessing comes from the Lord. It enacts his word—it makes it present, it gives peace and provides comfort.

Therefore to bless family members, friends, coworkers, or strangers in this way, is a wonderful exercising of faith. In fact, it is a wonderful and powerful tool for evangelism.

Try it. Bless the clerk at the store, "*God bless your day*" or "*The Lord be with you*" as you leave with your groceries. Tell your neighbor who is going in for surgery or looking for a new job, "*The Lord be with you*" and see what happens.

This is what we mean by liturgical living. By giving a blessing we *share hope.* By giving blessings in the name of Christ, we *teach Christ.*

The liturgy is meant to be lived and shared, not just performed. It is the Christian life. It is the mission of our congregation. Amen.

"SALVATION, CONGREGATION, VOCATION: LIFE THROUGH THE DIVINE SERVICE"

Luke 23:27–43, Series C, Proper 29

Have you heard the big news? It was all over the media this past week. Every tabloid, talk show, and TV reporter was talking about. What is it?

If you haven't heard, its official, Prince William, the future King of England, is now engaged. His bride to be is 28 year old Kate Middleton.

Apparently this is not just back page news. It's front page, block buster news! This is particularly so for the citizens of Great Britain.

As Americans, it is hard for us to really understand all the fuss. We don't have a royal family. We've never lived under a monarchy. We don't know what it's like to have a King or a Queen. So we're thinking, what's the big deal?

However, if you happened to catch any of the interviews or talk shows you'd think that this was our salvation and our best hope in the midst of this recession. For some, it's the next best thing to world peace.

Listen to what Piers Morgan (talk show host taking over for Larry King and judge from *America's Got Talent*) had to say on NBC's *Today* show: "*What is great for Britain, and for the world, is that we are in this terrible recession, everyone is suffering and people are losing their jobs, and along comes a good old fashioned British royal wedding. And it is going to be the biggest event, not just of the century, but of the millennium.*"

That is no small boast. I guess we will have to wait and see just how big or world changing event this will be.

As this is the last Sunday of the Church year, it's an event that is marked as *Christ the King* Sunday. Here we're reminded of the life changing and world changing event that happened when Jesus Christ was nailed to the cross of Calvary for the sins of the whole world.

Above his head there was the written notice, "*This is the King of the Jews.*" However, being beaten by fists, mocked by mouths, whipped by weapons, and crucified on a cross, was anything but royal treatment.

The salvation of this world is not found in royal weddings or the fame and fortune of any royal family unless it comes from the divine royalty of the crucified Jesus Christ who is the King of all Kings, and Lord of all Lords.

But oh, how easy it is to put hope in things of this world. Recessions and depressions bring hardships and heartaches. Difficult times bring desperate desires. When hope seems lost, the lost are prone to hope in anything—a famous wedding, a wealthy friend, or a friendly liar.

American or English, Asian or African, it works just the same. Sin is seductive. But the hope that it offers is only a veiled lie. Addictions only hide our ailments. Fame forces out faith. Love for money replaces love for the Lord. The true promise of salvation is traded for the fleeting lies of damnation.

Whether Prince William or Queen Elizabeth, whether Queen Latiffa or the artist formerly known as Prince (now just Prince again), true hope cannot be found in such personalities.

Salvation cannot be found in such people. True hope and true salvation comes through one King only—the one nailed to the cross, the once called the *King of the Jews.*

Curiously, this King of the Jews willingly gave up all the royal treatment of heaven to come down to this earth and be treated as a criminal. He did it just so that he might make you and me into royalty. The Son of God did not come to be served, but to serve, and give his life as a ransom for many.

Day in and day out, even in a world full of despair, there is a place where hope and salvation are found. In fact, week in and week out, even in a society oppressed by a recession, there is a place where hope and salvation are spoken into your ear holes and fed into your mouths. It's called the *Divine Service.* It is the foundation of our congregation.

Our liturgy, our hymns, and our sermons all breathe the hope and the salvation that comes through the word and Sacraments given by Jesus Christ. This is why congregations exist.

This is what the mission, vision, and strategy of our congregation are all about: *Sharing Hope teaching Christ through Word and Sacrament liturgical living.*

The last number of weeks we have been exploring the biblical truths about the mission, vision, and strategy of our congregation. We have heard how integral our worship life is to our witness life and even how the worship life of the New Testament Church shaped the growth of Church.

As worship was the wheel that moved the Church out into the world, we recognize it continues to be so today. When those New Testament believers gathered around "the apostles teaching," the "fellowship" (Acts 2:42), "baptism" (v.38) and "the breaking of bread" and "the prayers" (v.42), the Bible says that *"47the Lord added to their number day by day those who were being saved."*

We continue to follow those New Testament believers today. The *Divine Service* continues to be the sure and steady place that gives hope to a hurting world.

The Divine Service is the *wheel* that moves the Church. It moves the Church forward *in* faith and forgiveness and forward *out* into the world to reach out to unbelievers. And by God's grace, he continues to add to our number day by day, those who are being saved.

Where recessions and obsessions throw us into chaos and confusion and lead us into selfishness and sin, the steady voice of the Gospel is proclaimed week in and week out through the *Divine Service*.

Where the anxiety of uncertainty and the darkness of depression leave us crippled and hopeless, the word of God speaks comfort and hope. Paul said it this way in our Epistle lesson:

"13 [God] has delivered us from the domain of darkness and transferred us to the kingdom of his beloved Son, 14in whom we have redemption, the forgiveness of sins . . . 17 And he is before all things, and in him all things hold together. 18 And he is the head of the body, the church" (Col.1:13).

Did you catch that? Jesus is the head of the Church, which means he is the head of this congregation. Anything that puts him second is not legitimate. In case you forgot, Jesus is King.

Therefore everything that this congregation does must be about the message of Jesus Christ. If Christ is not King, then our purpose is without importance. The life of this congregation comes from the life of Jesus Christ. And we're given this life every time we gather for worship.

In the *Divine Service* Christ gives his gifts of faith and forgiveness. You then take these gifts into your daily life, into our vocations as workers, as spouses, as parents, and as neighbors, where you pass them on throughout out the week and then come back to the Divine Service to be given them all over again.

As you are served by Christ in the *Divine Service*, we go out into the world and serve others. You see, as Jesus is the source of our *salvation*, and the basis of our *congregation*, he is also at the core of our *vocation*.

Every day you and I go about our daily lives, wearing different hats, having different jobs, living different stations in life—from farmer to firefighter, teacher to a truck driver, parent to pastor, neighbor to nurse.

No, you may not have the status or job of a Prince William or a Queen Elizabeth, but your work is no less important.

The service you give to others through your Christian vocation is actually an expression of God's action through you. The service you give through your vocation is profound. It flows out of the Divine Service—the place where God serves you with his gifts of grace.

Without farmers we wouldn't have milk and we wouldn't have bread. Without shoemakers we wouldn't have shoes for our feet. Without mechanics we wouldn't have cars that work. Without doctors we wouldn't have health care. Without lawyers . . . well we wouldn't have headaches. (Just kidding! I suppose it could be said that without pastors we wouldn't have long winded sermons.)

Every vocation that seeks to serve our neighbor is a God pleasing and God ordained activity. Not one is more important than the other.

When you think of it is this way, your Christian vocation is not another burdened placed on you—something else that you can fail at, bog you down, or make you feel bad—but a realm in which you can experience God's love and grace. You can experience this both in the blessings you receive from others and in the way God is working through you despite your failures.

The service you give through your Christian vocation is a face of God. Husbands who serve their wives, wives who love their husbands, mothers that change diapers, fathers that wipe noses, neighbors that cook meals, Christians who pray for one another—all are God at work, all are God in action.

This means you don't need to go looking for something to do in order to fulfill you or find value in who you are or what you do.

This means you don't have to serve on a church committee to be doing God's work. You can simply look where you have been called to right now, whatever it is, parent, grandparent, neighbor or worker, and know that God is working through you as you love and serve others in Christ's name!

In the end, it is all about Christ—His divine service to you and through you. He is your *salvation*. He is your King and the head of our *congregation*. He works through us in our *vocation*. Amen.

THE CHURCH, THE LITURGY, AND LITURGICAL LIVING: LECTURE OUTLINE

1. Understanding the nature of ritual: Ritual is:
    a. of or relating to rites or a ritual: ceremonial, like a ritual dance or initiation ritual.
    b. according to religious law: ritual purity.
    c. done in accordance with social custom or normal protocol: handshakes or greetings.
2. Worship is:
    a. reverence offered a divine being or supernatural power; an act of expressing such reverence.
    b. a form of religious practice with its creed and ritual.
3. The Divine Service – what is it? What's important in Worship?

4. Liturgy – What is it?
5. Contemporary vs. Traditional worship: How are they different as does it matter?
6. Liturgical Living—The art of living in God's Grace
    a. The *Invocation* and the *Kyrie* in our lives every day:
    b. The *Salutation* and the *Blessing* given for our possessing

LITURGICAL LIVING: THE *INVOCATION* AND THE *KYRIE* IN OUR LIVES EVERYDAY

The Invocation

Read Matthew 28:18–20

The Kyrie

Read Mark 10:46–52, especially verse 47.

LITURGICAL LIVING: THE *SALUTATION* AND THE *BLESSING* GIVEN FOR OUR POSSESSING

The Salutation: 2 Timothy 4:22

The Lord be with you.

And also with you.

"The Salutation is a special greeting between the congregation and its pastor. The Salutation announces the Lord's coming to us in the readings that follow and makes us aware that important things are about to happen." (From *Worshiping with the Angels and Archangels*, p.18)

The Blessing: Numbers 6:24–26; 2 Corinthians 13:14

The Lord Bless you and keep you. The Lord make his face shine upon you and be gracious to you. The Lord look upon you with favor and give you His peace. *Num. 6:24–26*

The Grace of our Lord Jesus Christ and the love of God and the communion of the Holy Spirit be with you all. *2 Corinthians 13:14*

Bibliography

Allen, Roland. *Missionary Methods: St. Paul's or Ours?* Grand Rapids: Eerdmans, 1962.

Allender, Dan B. *Sabbath.* Nashville: Thomas Nelson, 2009.

Anderson, David W. *From the Great Omission to Vibrant Faith: The Role of the Home in Renewing the Church.* Vibrant Faith Publishing, 2009.

———, and Paul Hill. *Frogs without Legs Can't Hear: Nurturing Discipleship in Home and Congregation.* Minneapolis: Augsburg, 2003.

Arand, Charles P. "Not All Adiaphora Are Created Equal." *Concordia Journal* 30:3 (July 2004):156–64.

———. "A Two Dimensional Understanding of the Church for the Twenty-First Century." *Concordia Journal* 33:2 (April 2007):146–65.

———. "He Walks with Me and Talks with Me: Today's New Creeds." *Concordia Journal* 22:4 (October 1996): 370–77.

———. "The Ministry of the Church in Light of the Two Kinds of Righteousness." *Concordia Journal* 33:4 (October 2007): 344–56.

Baker, Robert. ed. *Lutheran Spirituality: Life as God's Child.* St. Louis: Concordia, 2010.

Barry, Alvin L. "Doctrine and Evangelism." *Concordia Theological Quarterly* 65:1 (January 2001): 3–13.

Bartelt, Andrew H. "Keeping Our Balance: Maintaining Unity in a World (and Church!) of Diversity." *Concordia Journal* 30:3 (July 2004): 137–55.

Baue, Frederic W., *The Spiritual Society: What Lurks Beyond Postmodernism.* (Wheaton, IL: Crossway, 2001).

Bliese, Richard, and Craig Van Gelrder, eds. *The Evangelizing Church: A Lutheran Contribution.* Minneapolis: Augsburg Fortress, 2005.

Bonhoeffer, Dietrich. *Life Together: A Discussion of Christian Fellowship.* Translated by John W. Doberstien. San Francisco: Harper, 1954.

Borden, Paul D. *Direct Hit: Aiming Leaders at the Mission Field.* Nashville: Abingdon, 2006.

Bosch, David J. *Transforming Mission: Paradigm Shifts in Theology of Mission.* New York: Orbis, 1991.

Braaten, Carl E. and Robert Jenson eds. *The Strange New World of the Gospel: Re-Evangelizing in the Postmodern World.* Grand Rapids: Eerdmans, 2002.

Bunkowske, Eugene W. "A Hand of Life Giving Love" *The Lutheran Witness* 127:1 (January 2008) 26–28.

Burkee, James C. *Power, Politics and the Missouri Synod: A Conflict that Changed American Christianity.* Minneapolis: Fortress, 2011.

Caputo, John D. *What Would Jesus Deconstruct: The Good News of Postmodernism for the Church.* Church and Postmodern Culture Series, editor James K.A. Smith. Grand Rapids: Baker, 2007.

Carson, D.A. *Becoming Conversant with the Emerging Church: Understanding a Movement and Its Implications.* Grand Rapids: Zondervan, 2005.

Chesterton, G. K. *Orthodoxy.* San Francisco: Ignatius Press, 1995, 1908.

Chittister, Joan. *The Liturgical Year: The Spiraling Adventure of the Spiritual Life.* Nashville: Thomas Nelson, 2009.

Colson, Charles. "The Postmodern Crackup: From Soccer Moms to College Campuses, Signs of the End," *Christianity Today,* December 2003.

Downing, Crystal L. *How Postmodernism Serves (my) Faith: Questioning, Truth in Language, Philosophy and Art.* Downers Grove: InterVarsity, 2006.

Englebrecht, Edward E. ed. *The Lutheran Difference: An Explanation & Comparison of Christian Beliefs.* St. Louis: Concordia, 2010.

Evangelism and Church Growth: With Special Reference to the Church Growth, A Report of the Commission on Theology and Church Relations of The Lutheran Church—Missouri Synod. September, 1987.

Eyer, Richard C. *They Will See His Face: Worship and Healing.* St. Louis: Concordia, 2002.

For the Sake of Christ's Commission: The Report of the Church Growth Study Committee of the Lutheran Church–Missouri Synod. St. Louis: The Lutheran Church—Missouri Synod, 2001.

Forde, Gerhard O. *Justification by Faith: A Matter of Life and Death.* Ramsey, NJ: Singular Press, 1990.

————. *On Being a Theologian of the Cross: Reflections on Luther's Heidelberg Disputation, 1518.* Grand Rapids: Eerdmans, 1997.

————. *Theology is for Proclamation.* Minneapolis: Fortress Press, 1990.

Gallagher, Nora. *The Sacred Meal.* Nashville: Thomas Nelson, 2009.

Gibbs, Jeffery. *Concordia Commentary: Matthew 1:1—11:1* St. Louis: Concordia, 2006.

Gilley, Gary. *This Little Church Went to Market. Is the Modern Church Reaching Out or Selling Out.* England: Evangelical Press, 2005.

————. *This Little Church Stayed home: A Faithful Church in Deceptive Times.* England: Evangelical Press, 2006.

Green, Michael. *Evangelism in the Early Church.* Grand Rapids: Eerdmans, revised edition. 2003.

Grenz, Stanely J. *A Primer on Postmodernism.* Grand Rapids: Eerdmans, 1996.

Guinness, Os. *Dining With the Devil: The Megachurch Movement Flirts with Modernity.* Grand Rapids: Baker, 1993.

————. *Time for Truth. Living Free in a World of Lies, Hype & Spin.* Grand Rapids: Baker, 2000.

Hauerwas, Stanley. and William H. Willimon. *Resident Aliens: A Provocative Christian Assessment of Culture and Ministry for People Who Know Something is Wrong.* Nashville: Abingdon, 1989.

————. *Matthew: Brazos Theological Commentary on the Bible.* Grand Rapids: Brazos Press, 2006.

Hirsch, Alan. *The Forgotten Ways: Reactivating the Missional Church.* Grand Rapids: Brazos Press, 2006.

Hunsberger, George R., and Craig Van Gelder eds. *The Church Between Gospel and Culture: The Emerging Mission in North America.* Grand Rapids: Eerdmans, 1996.

Hunter, Kent R. *Moving the Church into Action*. St. Louis: Concordia, 1989.

Huston, John. "Hibbs Examines 'Seinfeild,' other Shows about 'Nothing.'" *The Observer Online: The Independent Newspaper Supporting Notre Dame and St. Mary's*. vol. XXXIIII, no. 62, Dec.3, 1999.

Hybels, Bill and Mark Mittleberg. *Becoming a Contagious Christian*. Grand Rapids: Zondervan, 1994.

Jenson, Robert W. "How the World Lost Its Story." *First Things* (October 1993) 1–9 reprint.

Johnson, John F. "In This Church: A Brief Confessional Reflection." *Concordia Journal* 17:1 (January 1991): 43–48.

———. "Still A Place for Our Confessions?" *Concordia Journal* 32:4 (October 2006): 396–400.

Johnson, Luke Timothy. *The Creed: What Christians Believe and Why It Matters*. New York: Doubleday, 2003.

Just, Arthur A. Jr. *Heaven on Earth: The Gifts of Christ in the Divine Service*. St. Louis: Concordia, 2008.

Kelly, J.N.D. *Early Christian Creeds*. Singapore: Longman, 1972.

Kimball, Dan. *The Emerging Church: Vintage Christianity for New Generations*. Grand Rapids: Zondervan, 2003.

Kinnamon, Scot A., general ed. *Lutheranism 101*. St. Louis: Concordia, 2010.

Kirby, Alan. "The Death of Postmodernism and Beyond." *Philosophy Now: A Magazine of Ideas*, issue 58, 2006, online edition.

Klauber, Martin I. and Scott M. Manetsch eds. *The Great Commission: Evangelicals and the History of World Missions*. Nashville: B&H publishing, 2008.

Kleinig, John W., *Grace Upon Grace: Spirituality for Today*. St. Louis: Concordia, 2008.

———. "Oratio, Meditatio, Tentatio: What Makes a Theologian?" *Concordia Theological Quarterly*. 66:3 (July 2002): 255–68

———. "The Biblical View of Worship." *Concordia Theological Quarterly* 58:4 (October 1994): 245–54.

———. "Witting or Unwitting Ritualists." *Lutheran Theological Journal* 22:1 (1988): 13–22.

Klug, Eugene F. ed. *Complete Sermons of Martin Luther, Vol. 5*, Grand Rapids: Baker Books, 2000.

Kolb, Erwin J. "The Primary Church and the Mission of Its Detractors." *Concordia Theological Quarterly* 54:2–3 (April–July 1990): 117–30.

Kolb, Robert. "Confessing the Faith: Our Lutheran Way of Life." *Concordia Journal* 20:4 (October 1994): 356–67.

———. *Speaking the Gospel Today*. St. Louis: Concordia, 1995.

———. "That I May Be His Own: The Anthropology of Luther's Explanation of the Creed." *Concordia Journal* 21:1 (January 1995): 28–41.

———, and Charles P. Arand. *The Genius of Luther's Theology: A Wittenberg Way of Thinking for the Contemporary Church*. Grand Rapids: Baker Academic, 2008.

———, and Timothy Wengert, eds. *The Book of Concord: The Confessions of the Evangelical Church*. Minneapolis: Fortress Press, 2000.

Krispin, Gerald S. and Jon D. Viecker, eds. *And Every Tongue Confess: Essays in Honor of Norman Nagel on the Occasion of His Sixty-fifth Birthday*. Dearborn, MI: The Nagel Festschrift Committee, 1990.

Lathrop, Gordon W. & Timothy J. Wengert. *Christian Assembly: Marks of the Church a Pluralistic Age*. Minneapolis: Fortress Press, 2004.

LeBlanc, Douglas. *Tithing: Test Me in This*. Nashville: Thomas Nelson, 2010.

Linberg, Carter. "Church Growth and Confessional Integrity." *Concordia Theological Quarterly* 54:2–3 (April–July 1990): 131–54.

Lose, David J. *Confessing Jesus Christ: Preaching in a Postmodern World*. Grand Rapids: Eerdmans, 2003.

Luecke, David. *Evangelical Style and Lutheran Substance: Facing America's Mission Challenge*. St. Louis: Concordia 1988.

Lyotard, Jean-Françios. *The Postmodern Condition: A Report on Knowledge*. Translated by Geoff Bennington and Brian Massumi. Theory and History of Literature, Vol. 10. Minneapolis: University of Minnesota Press, 1984.

MacArthur, John. *The Truth War: Fighting for Certainty in an Age of Deception*. Nashville: Thomas Nelson, 2007.

Maschke, Timothy H. *Gathered Guests: A Guide to Worship in the Lutheran Church*, second edition. St. Louis: Concordia, 2009.

Maxfield, John A., ed. *Church and Ministry Today: Three confessional Lutheran Essays*. St. Louis: The Luther Academy, 2001.

McGavran, Donald. *Understanding Church Growth*. Third edition. Grand Rapids: Eerdmans, 1990.

McGrath, Alister. *I Believe: Exploring the Apostles' Creed*. Downers Grove: Intervarsity, 1997.

McLaren, Brian D. *A Generous Orthodoxy*. Grand Rapids: Zondervan, 2004

———. *Everything Must Change: Jesus Global Crisis, and a Revolution of Hope*. Nashville: Thomas Nelson, 2007.

———. *Finding Our Way Again: The Return of the Ancient Practices*. Nashville: Thomas Nelson, 2008.

Mayer, F.E., *The Religious Bodies of America*. St. Louis: Concordia, 1961.

Miller, Donald. *Blue Like Jazz: Nonreligious Thoughts on Christian Spirituality*. Nashville: Thomas Nelson, 2003.

Mittleberg, Mark. *Building a Contagious Church: Revolutionizing the Way We View and Do Evangelism*. Grand Rapids: Zondervan, 2000.

Morganthaler, Sally. "Worship as Evangelism: Sally Morganthaler Rethinks Her own Paradigm." *Rev!* (May/June 2007) 48–53.

Nagel, Norman. "Luther and the Priesthood of All Believers." *Concordia Theological Quarterly* 61:4 (October 1997), 277–98.

Niebuhr, H. Richard. *Christ and Culture*. San Francisco: Harper, 2001, 1951.

Noll, Mark A. *The Scandal of the Evangelical Mind*. Grand Rapids: Eerdmands 1994.

Nouwen, Henri J.M. *In the Name of Jesus*. New York: Crossroad, 1989.

Pelikan, Jaroslav. *Credo: Historical and Theological Guide to Creeds and Confessions of Faith in the Christian Tradition*. New Haven: Yale University Press, 2003.

———. *Acts: Brazos theological Commentary on the Bible*. Grand Rapids: Brazos Press, 2005.

Peter, David J. "A Framework for the Practice of Evangelism and Congregational Outreach." *Concordia Journal* 30:3 (July 2004): 203–16.

———. "Reaching Out Without Losing Balance: Maintaining a Theological Center of Gravity in Preaching." *Concordia Journal* 35:3 (Summer 2009): 251–78.

Peterson, Eugene H. *The Contemplative Pastor: Returning to the Art of Spiritual Direction.* Grand Rapids: Eerdmans, 1993.

―――.*Under the Predictable Plant: An Exploration in Vocational Holiness.* Grand Rapids: Eerdmans, 1992.

―――. *Working the Angles: The Shape of Pastoral Integrity.* Grand Rapids: Eerdmans, 1987.

Platt, David. *Radical: Taking your Faith Back from the American Dream.* Colorado Springs: Multnomah, 2010.

Pless, John. "Contemporary Spirituality and the Emerging Church," *Concordia Theological Quarterly* 71 no. 3/4 (July/ October, 2007): 347–63,

Powell, Jim. *Postmodernism for Beginners.* Danbury, CT: For Beginners, 1998.

Precht, Fred L. ed. *Lutheran Worship: History and Practice.* St. Louis: Concordia, 1993.

Pritchard, G. A. *Willow Creek Seeker Services: Evaluating a New Way of Doing Church.* Grand Rapids: Baker, 1996.

Putnam, David & Ed Stetzer. *Breaking the Missional Code: Your Church Can Become a Missionary In Your Community.* Nashville: Broadman & Holman, 2006.

Rainer, Thom S. *Breakout Churches: Discover How to Make the Leap.* Grand Rapids: Zondervan, 2005.

―――, and Eric Geiger. *Simple Church Returning to God's Process for Making Disciples.* Nashville: B &H Publishing, 2006.

Raschke, Carl. *GloboChrist: The Great Commission Takes a Postmodern Turn.* Church and Postmodern Culture Series. Grand Rapids: Baker, 2008.

Rollins, Peter. *The Orthodox Heretic and Other Impossible Tales.* Massachusetts: Paraclete Press, 2009.

Roxburgh, Alan J. and Boren, Scott M. *Introducing the Missional Church: What it is, Why it matters, How to Become One.* Grand Rapids: Baker, 2009.

Scaer, David. "The Relation of Matthew 28:16–20 to the Rest of the Gospel." *Concordia Theological Quarterly* 55:4 (October 1991): 245–66.

Schulz, Klaus Detlev. *Mission From the Cross: The Lutheran Theology of Mission.* St. Louis: Concordia, 2009.

Schumacher, William W. "Theology or Mission." *Concordia Journal* 30:3 (July 2004): 116–18.

Senkbeil, Harold L. *Dying to Live: The Power of Forgiveness.* St. Louis: Concordia, 1994.

―――. *Sanctification: Christ in Action.* Milwaukee: Northwestern, 1989.

―――. "Till the Trumpets Sound: Hold Fast and Hold Forth." *Logia: A Journal of Lutheran Theology* XV no. 2, Eastertide 2006, 17–28.

―――. "Generation X and the Care of the Soul", *Mysteria Dei: Essays in Honor of Kurt Marquart.* 2nd edition, Edited by Paul T. McCain and John R. Stephenson. Fort Wayne, IN: Concordia Theological Seminary Press, 2000, 287–304.

―――. *The Cure of Souls: Good for What Ails You.* Unpublished Paper.

Senske, Kurt. *The Calling: Living a Life of Significance,* St. Louis: Concordia, 2010.

Shenk, Wilbert R., ed. *Exploring Church Growth.* Grand Rapids: Eerdmans, 1983.

Slenczka, Reinhard, "Luther's Care of Souls for Our Times." *Concordia Theological Quarterly* 67:1 (January 2003): 33–64.

Smith, Christian. *Soul Searching: The Religious and Spiritual Lives of American Teenagers.* New York: Oxford University Press, 2005.

Smith, James K.A. *Introducing Radical Orthodoxy: Mapping a Post-secular Theology.* Grand Rapids: Baker, 2004.

———. *Who's Afraid of Postmodernism? Taking Derrida, Lyotard, and Foucault to Church.* Grand Rapids: Baker, 2006.

———. *Desiring the Kingdom: Worship, Worldview, and Cultural Formation.* Grand Rapids: Baker Academic, 2009.

Stetzer, Ed & David Putman. *Breaking the Missional Code.* Nashville, TN: Broadman and Holman, 2006.

Strobel, Lee. *Inside the Mind of Unchurched Harry and Mary: How to Reach Friends and Family who Avoid God and the Church.* Grand Rapids: Zondervan, 1993.

Sweet, Leonard. *Soul Tsunami: Sink or Swim in the New Millennium Culture.* Grand Rapids: Zondervan, 1999.

_____ *Post-Modern Pilgrims.* Nashville: Broadman & Holmman, 2000.

Tickle, Phyllis. *The Great Emergence: How Christianity is Changing and Why.* Grand Rapids: Baker, 2008.

Towns, Elmer., C. Peter Wagner & Thom S. Rainer. *The Everychurch Guide Growth: How Any Plateaued Church Can Grow.* Nashville: Broadman & Holman, 1998.

Veith, Gene Edward Jr. *God at Work: Your Christian Vocation in All of Life.* Wheaton: Crossway, 2002.

———. *Postmodern Times: A Christian Guide to Contemporary Thought and Culture.* Wheaton: Crossway, 1994.

———. *The Spirituality of the Cross: The Way of the First Evangelicals.* Revised ed. St. Louis: Concordia, 2010.

Voelz, James W. *What Does This Mean? Principles of Interpretation in the Post-Modern World.* St. Louis: Concordia, 1997.

Waddel, James Alan. *A Simplified Guide to Worshipping as Lutherans.* Eugene, OR: Wipf & Stock, 2009.

Ward, Graham. *The Politics of Discipleship: Becoming Postmaterial Citizens.* Grand Rapids: Baker, 2009.

Walther, C.F.W. *Law and Gospel: How to Read and Apply the Bible—A Reader's Edition.* St. Louis: Concordia, 2010.

Wells, David F. *No place for Truth or Whatever happened o Evangelical Theology?* Grand Rapids: Eerdmans, 1993.

———. *God in the Wasteland.* Grand Rapids: Eerdmans, 1994.

——— . *Losing Our Virtue: Why the Church Must Recover its Moral Vision.* Grand Rapids: Eerdmans, 1998.

———. *Above All earthly Powers: Christ in a Postmodern World.* Eerdmans: Grand Rapids. 2005.

———. *The Courage to Be Protestant: Truth Lovers, Marketers, and Emergents in a Postmodern World.* Grand Rapids: Eerdmans. 2008.

Wenthe, Dean O. et al eds. *All Theology is Christology: Essays in Honor of David P. Scaer.* Fort Wayne: Concordia Theological Press, 2000.

Westphal, Merold. *Whose Community? Which Interpretation? Philosophical Hermeneutics for the Church.* Grand Rapids: Baker, 2009.

Willimon, William H. *Pastor: The Theology and Practice of Ordained Ministry.* Nashville: Abingdon Press, 2002.

Wingren, Gustaf. *Luther on Vocation.* Translated by Carl C. Rasmussen. Evansville, IN: Ballast Press, 1999.

Subject Index

Name Index

Scripture Index